D0322394

Very British Rebels?

Very British Rebels?

The Culture and Politics of Ulster Loyalism

James W. McAuley

Bloomsbury Academic
An imprint of Bloomsbury Publishing Inc

B L O O M S B U R Y
NEW YORK • LONDON • OXFORD • NEW DELHI • SYDNEY

Bloomsbury Academic

An imprint of Bloomsbury Publishing Inc

1385 Broadway	50 Bedford Square
New York	London
NY 10018	WC1B 3DP
USA	UK

www.bloomsbury.com

BLOOMSBURY and the Diana logo are trademarks of Bloomsbury Publishing Plc

First published 2016
Paperback edition first published 2017

© James W. McAuley, 2016

All rights reserved. No part of this publication may be reproduced or
transmitted in any form or by any means, electronic or mechanical, including
photocopying, recording, or any information storage or retrieval system,
without prior permission in writing from the publishers.

No responsibility for loss caused to any individual or organization acting on
or refraining from action as a result of the material in this publication
can be accepted by Bloomsbury or the author.

Library of Congress Cataloging-in-Publication Data
McAuley, James W.
Very British rebels? : the culture and politics of Ulster loyalism / James W. McAuley.
pages cm
Includes bibliographical references and index.
ISBN 978-1-4411-0903-3 (hardback : alk. paper) – ISBN 978-1-4411-2783-9 (pbk. : alk. paper)
1. Ulster (Northern Ireland and Ireland)–Social life and customs.
2. Ulster (Northern Ireland and Ireland)–Politics and government.
3. Group identity–Ulster (Northern Ireland and Ireland) 4. Unionism (Irish politics)
5. Paramilitary forces–Northern Ireland.
6. Northern Ireland–Politics and government. I. Title.
DA990.U46M118 2015
941.6–dc23
2015019301

ISBN: HB: 978-1-4411-0903-3
PB: 978-1-4411-2783-9
ePUB: 978-1-4411-0602-5
ePDF: 978-1-4411-9054-3

Typeset by Integra Software Services Pvt. Ltd.

For John Darby and Joe McCormack, from whom I learnt much.

Contents

Acknowledgements

As ever, I owe my thanks to Stephanie, Charlotte and Rowan for all their support and for putting up with my absences.

Most of all my sincere gratitude goes to Doctors Cameron Irving, Rob Stevenson and Tufail Patankar, alongside the nursing staff and ambulance service of West Yorkshire. Without their dedication and skill, this book would never have been finished.

Abbreviations

AIA	Anglo Irish Agreement
APNI	Alliance Party of Northern Ireland
DUP	Democratic Unionist Party
ICTU	Irish Congress of Trade Unions
IIP	Irish Independence Party
IRA	Irish Republican Army
NICRA	Northern Ireland Civil Rights Association
NILP	Northern Ireland Labour Party
NUPRG	New Ulster Political Research Group
PSNI	Police Service of Northern Ireland
PUP	Progressive Unionist Party
RHC	Red Hand Commando
RUC	Royal Ulster Constabulary
SDLP	Social Democratic and Labour Party
UDA	Ulster Defence Association
UDP	Ulster Democratic Party
UDR	Ulster Defence Regiment
ULA	Unionist Labour Association
UPRG	Ulster Political Research Group
USC	Ulster Special Constabulary
UUP	Ulster Unionist Party
UVF	Ulster Volunteer Force
UWC	Ulster Workers Council

Introduction

In seeking to unravel the complexities of Northern Ireland, few groups have proved such an enigma as those proclaiming Ulster loyalism as their principal creed and fundamental political motivation. For many observers, their pledge of loyalty to the British state is at best an unrequited love affair, while the paradox of those asserting to be its most devoted citizens directly challenging the statute, imperative and representatives of the same state remains all but incomprehensible. But conflicts between loyalists and the state are long-standing and have manifested throughout the history of Northern Ireland. Indeed, it is possible to argue that it was loyalist resistance and defiance that gave rise to the existence of Northern Ireland and contributed directly to the framing of its politics for the next fifty years. It remains central to its future political direction.

Loyalism has also regularly positioned itself in political opposition to both more mainstream Unionism and the government at Westminster (throughout this book I use Unionism/Unionist to refer to party politics and unionism/unionist when discussing the broader social movement). Nor has loyalist resistance always been restricted to the political sphere or public arena. It is often forgotten, for example, that the first member of the state forces killed in the most recent phase of violent conflict (most commonly, if somewhat euphemistically, referred to as the Troubles) was a Royal Ulster Constabulary (RUC) officer shot by loyalists during a riot in October 1969.

Much more recent tensions arising in the latter part of 2012 and the early months of 2013 saw Northern Irish society convulsed by a series of widespread demonstrations led onto the streets by loyalists remonstrating at the changed regulations permitting the flying of the Union flag at Belfast City Hall only on designated occasions rather than on a daily basis. The protest rendered parts of Northern Ireland at a standstill as demonstrators blocked major roads, clashed with police and caused widespread disruption to the everyday lives of many. By the early summer of 2013, loyalist street demonstrations over the issue had begun to abate, only to be almost immediately replaced by another very public row and further protests surrounding the annual 12th July parade by the Grand Orange Lodge of Ireland (the Orange Order).

This time much of the friction centred on the decision by the Parades Commission (the public body responsible for placing restrictions on any parades judged contentious) to ban an Orange Order march in north Belfast returning from the main procession to take a route that passed along an interface with the nationalist Ardoyne area. Loyalists reacted with unconcealed ire, and following another period of sustained street violence, aimed largely at the Police Service of Northern Ireland

Leabharlanna Poibli Chathair Bhaile Átha Cliath

Dublin City Public Libraries

(PSNI), the protests assumed a different form with the establishment of a loyalist 'civil rights' camp at Twaddell Avenue in north Belfast. Those in attendance set about overseeing what became the almost ritualistic daily attempt by Orange Order members and bandsmen to march the route only to be blocked by PSNI members.

The incumbents of the camp also set about highlighting what they saw as the continued attack on their Orange cultural heritage and a diminution of what many believed was still their right to march on their traditional routes. Moreover, many argued that the parade ban had been implemented largely because of violent protests from within the republican community (the march had been highly contested for some time, but the remonstrations had been particularly fierce in the previous two years) and the decision symbolized a peace process bias towards Irish nationalism and republicanism.

The prevalence of disorder and publically organized opposition to government-supported legislation around both the 'flags' and 'parades' disputes again brought to the fore what many see as the essential contradiction in the collective ethos of Ulster loyalism. The journalist Derek Brown previously highlighted this incongruity when he wrote this, following an earlier outbreak of loyalist inspired violence in the late 1990s:

> We call them loyalists, for there is as yet no more convenient word for those who are stoning, firebombing and even shooting at Crown forces in Northern Ireland. They say they are loyal to Queen and country, yet they are prepared to fight the British government and defy the will of the majority of British people to prove it.[1]

This conundrum, of how the political expression of those who claim to be the most loyal of citizens declares their primary adherence to the British Crown and to the imagined political community of Ulster, rather than to the government or political representatives of Westminster, has continued to bewilder and exasperate observers in equal measures.

Reflecting on this theme following another outbreak of loyalist street violence in Belfast, Theresa Villiers as Secretary of State for Northern Ireland pointed to the contradiction of British citizens using force to emphasize their 'Britishness' and loyalty, claiming: 'the idea that British identity and culture can be defended by people who wrap themselves in the union flag and attack police officers ... is grotesque'.[2] Her views found support from former Conservative prime minister, Sir John Major, who made clear his belief that those loyalists who claimed their British identity was being eroded were expressing a 'phantom fear'.[3] Such views reinforced that of other British politicians,

---

[1] D. Brown, 'Drumcree loyalists – but loyal to what exactly?', *The Guardian*, 5 July 2000.
[2] T. Villiers, 'Loyalists who attack police "grotesque"'. Available at: http://www.bbc.co.uk/news/uk-northern-ireland-24359712; accessed 11 October 2013.
[3] Sir J. Major, 'Loyalists identity fears "phantom"'. Available at: BBC News, http://www.bbc.co.uk/news/uk-northern-ireland-25357756; accessed 16 December 2013.

Leabharlanna Poiblí Chathair Bhaile Átha Cliath
Dublin City Public Libraries

who argue that unionism should recognize the security of the constitutional position enshrined in the Belfast Agreement, and: 'shed its fears [and] uncertainties of the past'.[4]

These assessments reflect other widely held views that regard loyalism as the manifestation of an almost entirely negative politics, emphasizing what is seen as the: 'ever-present paranoia'[5] of loyalists based on the notion: 'that a constitutional apocalypse is just around the corner',[6] the perceived hollowness of loyalist political thought and the inconsequentiality and inconsistency of its political actors. Often rejected as merely representing the most extreme or reactionary elements of unionism, more often than not the loyalist political leadership has been dismissed as ossified in ideas, stagnant in vision and regressive in political action. Within such perspectives Loyalism is seen as offering only 'strident voices of protests' and the deep-seated politics of 'siege mentality',[7] their views reducible to a violent and fanatical expression of unionism, located within the remit of 'hard bastards',[8] and others operating in an arena devoid of any coherent political ideology or strategy.

Media and public representations of loyalism largely continue to reproduce negative images of the ill-educated, inarticulate thug acting without political direction[9] and incapable of any positive civic engagement or constructive input in the public arena.[10] The persistence of such views causing one leading loyalist blogger to write:

The term 'Loyalist' appears to be one which is used by the media today in order to categorise and pigeon-hole those unionists who were/are prepared to 'misbehave'. For this reason Loyalists are stereotypically 'rough round the edge' unionists, but crucially they are unionists, usually working class unionists.[11]

Much contemporary journalism remains focused either on those within loyalism with seemingly sociopathic tendencies[12] or on those engaged in street protesters expressing an often visceral, irrational and sectarian worldview.

Such coverage does little to make loyalists challenge their perception that commentators 'are ever keen to lampoon them as stumbling, tattooed bigots'[13]; one journalist recently claiming the 'trouble with loyalists is that they have neither

---

4 P. Hain, 'Unionism needs to shed its fears', *News Letter*, 11 September 2006.
5 J. Darnton, 'Protestant and paranoid in Northern Ireland', *New York Times Magazine*, 15 January 1995.
6 F. Meredith, 'Loyalists feel sorry for themselves but the narrative of oppression doesn't hold up', *Irish Times*, 29 August 2013.
7 M. Pauley, 'Setbacks for unionism "self-inflicted"', *Belfast News Letter*, 22 June 1998.
8 K. Kray, 'Johnny Adair', in *Ultimate Hard Bastards* (London: John Blake, 2005), 9–26.
9 A. F. Parkinson, *Ulster Loyalism and the British Media* (Dublin: Four Courts Press, 1998).
10 G. Spencer, 'Constructing loyalism: politics, communications and peace in Northern Ireland', *Contemporary Politics*, 10, no. 1 (2004): 37–55.
11 jasonburkehistory 'What does it mean to be a loyalist'. Available at: http://www.jasonburkehistory.com/?cat=2; accessed 23 February 2014.
12 See, for example, M. Dillon, *God and the Gun: The Church and Irish Terrorism* (London: Orion, 1997); *The Trigger Men* (Edinburgh: Mainstream, 2003).
13 F. Meredith, 'How loyalism became a dirty word', *Irish Times*, 8 December 2012.

leaders nor a role'.[14] Hence, many self-proclaimed loyalists now argue that the label has by default become one of derision, shorthand for: 'signifying all that is alleged to be bad with unionism'.[15] In the view of one leading member of Progressive Unionist Party (PUP), loyalism 'has simply become a derogatory term', adding that 'if unionist representatives get into trouble with the law, suddenly they become "loyalists". If there is trouble at a unionist parade or demonstration, suddenly it changes and it becomes a loyalist parade or demonstration'.[16] The perspective is reinforced by the prominent Ulster Defence Association (UDA) member Jackie McDonald who elsewhere has argued that the term loyalist is nowadays rarely used without being followed by other idioms, such as 'thug, drug dealer, parade or violence'.[17]

Particularly during the late 1980s and 1990s, the dominant image of loyalist paramilitary leaders deeply surrounded their involvement in criminality, and often the highly public decadent lifestyles they led. The caricature was firmly established by leading journalists who set about giving leading loyalist paramilitarists labels such as the 'Paramafia'[18] or as 'Brigadiers of Bling'.[19] Since then the most consistent media portrayal of a loyalist remains that of a 'perma-tanned, tattooed, gold-necklaced, numerous ringed male, with a pit bull terrier and a tight t-shirt',[20] and the view lingers that contemporary paramilitarism remains self-interested and criminally motivated.

Such portrayals, however, do not even begin to encompass the loyalist paramilitary experience, let alone identify those who seek to express different visions of loyalism in the political or civic arenas. While loyalism has been unable to establish a dependable political project, or find any level of populist trust in its political representation, there are many examples of those from within loyalism displaying, and continue to demonstrate, considerable political ability and skill.[21] Throughout the most recent period, for example, some sections of loyalism, driven mainly by former paramilitary members, have engaged positively in processes of political and social change.[22] In some cases, the dominant caricature of loyalist paramilitarism is no doubt accurate, and while structured violence, machismo and turf wars are undoubtedly part of the story of loyalism, they are only part.

---

[14] F. O'Connor, 'Where to now for loyalism?', *Irish Times*, 29 July 2005.

[15] B. Mitchell, 'The Loyalist Commission offers hope for the future', *News Letter*, 7 March 2002.

[16] Interview with author, 11 November 2013.

[17] Cited in B. Rowan, 'Too many young loyalists don't care about the future as long as they can get drunk at weekends: UDA chief attacks band parade thuggery', *Belfast Telegraph*, 23 November 2011.

[18] J. McDowell, *Godfathers: Inside Northern Ireland's Drug Racket* (Dublin: Gill and Macmillan, 2008).

[19] A. Chrisafis, 'The death of Doris Day', *The Guardian*, 12 October 2005.

[20] J. Kyle, 'On faith and loyalism'. Available at: http://sluggerotoole.com/2012/01/23/john-kyle-on-faith-and-loyalism/; accessed 8 February 2012.

[21] Inter Action Belfast, *The Role of Ex-Combatants on Interfaces* (Belfast: Inter-Action Belfast, 2006).

[22] P. Shirlow, J. Tonge, J. W. McAuley, and C. McGlynn, *Abandoning Historical Conflict? Former Paramilitary Prisoners and Political Reconciliation in Northern Ireland* (Manchester: Manchester University Press, 2010).

Can loyalism really be defined merely as the politics of constitutional paranoia, its support dismissed simply as those expressing unionist extremism, or its expression confined to those articulating a worldview embedded in the ranks of paramilitarism or former combatants? While not seeking to deny the importance of paramilitarism in formulating parts of loyalist thought and deed, it represents only part of the expression of the identity of loyalism. Zygmund Bauman[23] proposes that in order for social identity to be strong, it must be seen as gratifying to those who uphold it. The strength of loyalist identity is palatable for all to see. So, what is it in Bauman's terms that makes a loyalist sense of identity rewarding and meaningful?

The answer is multifaceted and composite. Certainly, seeking to encapsulate loyalism within paramilitarism, or to reduce its character to that of the 'pit bull loyalist', does not begin to transmit the complexity or appeal of loyalist identity. Nor does it convey any appreciation of the depth of belonging generated by loyalism, or the political dynamics that have emerged from within loyalism, or other sections of working-class Protestantism over past decades. Works examining various aspects of loyalism from within both the academy[24] and journalism[25] have increased in volume in recent years. The majority of these writings have focused on paramilitarism and the actions of loyalist paramilitary members and organizations during the Troubles and in the post Belfast Agreement era.

While some have sought to examine loyalism in a broader context, there remains much to be done in providing a more nuanced interpretation of the formations, distinctions and shades of loyalist identity.[26] In particular, the main cultural formulations underpinning the social and political worldview of those who distinguish themselves and organize as loyalists must be identified and the political consequences of these be assessed.[27]

Underlying the widespread loyalist street protests of recent times, for example, was a deep sense of foreboding by those involved that the essence of their cultural identity is being hollowed out and diluted. In part, this draws on a much more widespread

---

[23] Z. Bauman, *Culture as Praxis. Theory, Culture and Society* (London: Sage, 1999), xxxi.

[24] See J. Bower Bell, *Back to the Future: The Protestants and a United Ireland* (Dublin: Poolbeg Press, 1996); S. Bruce, *The Edge of the Union: The Ulster Loyalist Political Vision* (Oxford: Oxford University Press, 1994); C. Crawford, *Inside the UDA: Volunteers and Violence* (London: Pluto Press, 2003); T. Novosel, *Northern Ireland's Lost Opportunity: The Frustrated Politics of Political Loyalism* (London: Pluto Press, 2013); P. Shirlow, *The End of Ulster Loyalism?* (Manchester: Manchester University Press, 2012); L. A. Smithey, *Unionists, Loyalists, and Conflict Transformation in Northern Ireland* (Oxford: Oxford University Press, 2011); I. S. Wood, *Crimes of Loyalty: A History of the UDA* (Edinburgh: Edinburgh University Press, 2006).

[25] See D. Boulton, *The UVF 1966–1973: An Anatomy of Loyalist Rebellion* (Dublin: Torc Books, 1973); J. Cusack and H. McDonald, *UVF* (Dublin: Poolbeg, 1997); H. McDonald and J. Cusack, *UDA: Inside the Heart of Loyalist Terror* (London: Penguin, 2004); S. McKay, *Northern Protestants an Unsettled People* (Belfast: Blackstaff Press, 2005).

[26] See, for example, material in J. W. McAuley and G. Spencer, eds. *Ulster Loyalism after the Good Friday Agreement* (Basingstoke: Palgrave Macmillan, 2011).

[27] I have begun to answer this in J. W. McAuley 'Constructing Contemporary Loyalism', in *Transforming the Peace Process in Northern Ireland: From Terrorism to Democratic Politics*, eds. A. Edwards and S. Bloomer (Dublin: Irish Academic Press, 2008), 15–27.

belief that loyalism (and much of unionism in general) has lost ground politically, socially and economically in the contemporary period. This is further underpinned by the parallel view that Irish republicanism has been much more successful at almost all levels in harnessing the peace process often at the expense of loyalism, whose voice is increasingly unheard and unrepresented.

In seeking to understand these views, and the span of responses to them, this book not only seeks to explain the changing political dynamics and social circumstances of loyalism, but also to distinguish loyalism as an everyday culture and ideology. In so doing, it examines the place of understandings of the past, community, collective memory, popular culture and identity within the broader loyalist sense of belonging and focuses not just on how political identification is formulated, but also how it is articulated and communicated. It will also expand on how loyalist politics is expressed both on and off the streets as a direct, although not always obvious, extraction of underlying social dynamics and conflicts and the differing political strains and tensions across loyalism and unionism.[28]

Being loyalist

Loyalism has often found itself in an uncertain and uneasy relationship with wider sections of the Protestant unionist population.[29] While often expressing distance from those participating in violence,[30] or communicating feelings of detachment from what are seen as overzealous views of loyalist actors, many unionists would nonetheless also recognize much of the substance of the core themes projected by loyalism.[31] There overlap between the views and politics of those calling themselves unionist and those who label themselves as loyalists is often considerable.

What difference does being a loyalist make? How does overt affiliation to loyalism, or being identified by others as a loyalist, matter in everyday life? There is, of course, a straightforward answer to these questions, namely that 'interactions of everyday life help people create a sense of place, themselves and others,'[32] and therefore, the identity of an Ulster loyalist becomes significant because of the context in which it exists. But to fully develop an answer to the question 'what difference does being a loyalist make?', we must consider in some detail the social context of power and the locations of political and social divisions that give loyalism its particular substance.

[28] C. Farrington, *Ulster Unionism and the Peace Process in Northern Ireland* (Basingstoke: Palgrave Macmillan, 2006).

[29] C. Farrington, 'Loyalists and Unionists: Explaining the Internal Dynamics of an Ethnic Group', in *Transforming the Peace Process in Northern Ireland: From Terrorism to Democratic Politics*, eds. A. Edwards and S. Bloomer (Dublin: Irish Academic Press, 2008), 28–43.

[30] B. C. Hayes and I. McAllister, 'Sowing dragon's teeth: public support for political violence and paramilitarism in Northern Ireland', *Political Studies*, 40 (2001): 910–922.

[31] J. Todd, 'Two traditions in unionist political culture', *Irish Political Studies*, no. 2 (1987): 1–26.

[32] H. C. Perkins and D. C. Thorns, *Place, Identity and Everyday Life in a Globalizing World* (Houndmills: Palgrave Macmillan, 2012), 13.

As Richard Jenkins[33] highlights, notions of the Self are always constituted within a broader social arena and through interactions with others. Individuals do not freely choose identity from a smorgasbord of social, cultural and political options; rather, identity is framed by and developed within highly specific social and political contexts.[34] Thus, people construe and comprehend their everyday lives at different levels: in the present, through contemporary political happenings and what they understand as their position in society at that point in time; through the relationships they sense they have with the past[35]; and often by way of a desire for an idealized, even romanticized future. The resulting political and social relations make communal identification vitally important.[36] People are far from inert or submissive in constructing their sense of identity, formulated and reinforced as it is through processes involving the continuous reformatting of biographical and group experiences to meet current psychological, political and social needs.[37] By drawing on collective histories and the common narratives[38] constructed around these communal interpretations of the past, people form affiliations and frame understandings, to interpret their social circumstances as these narratives become central element to communal identity.[39] These coalesce around distinct forms of belonging to create and reinforce a marked sense of identity.

Loyalism as a political identity exists because people self-define that identification through shared experiences, interests and concerns. Loyalist identity is also formed in part because others deem certain individuals or groups 'loyalist' because of their actions or values. Within loyalism, there are several interrelated aspects framing group identity, including broad political and social understandings and interpretations of the past, specific constructions of loyalism as an ethno-political marker, communal identifications and affiliations, that which is seen to encompass the Protestant/unionist/loyalist community and the various organizations that seek to represent loyalism in the political arena.

However, while loyalism may have multiple social and political strands and competing outlets for its political expression, it is bonded by a distinct common

[33] R. Jenkins, *Social Identity* (London: Routledge, 1996).
[34] J. A. Howard, 'Social psychology of identities', *Annual Review of Sociology*, 26 (2000): 367–393.
[35] P. Connerton, *How Societies Remember* (Cambridge: Cambridge University Press, 1989).
[36] D. G. Boyce, 'Weary Patriots: Ireland and the Making of Unionism', in *Defenders of the Union: A Survey of British and Irish Unionism since 1801*, eds. D. G. Boyce and A. O'Day, *Defenders of the Union* (London: Routledge, 2001), 15–38.
[37] See P. Ricoeur, *Time and Narrative*, translated by K. McGlaughlin and David Pellauer, (Chicago, IL: University of Chicago Press, 1984); *Memory, History, Forgetting*, translated by K. Blamey and D. Pellauer (Chicago, IL: University of Chicago Press, 2004).
[38] N. Hunt and S. McHale, 'Memory and meaning: individual and social aspects of memory narratives', *Journal of Loss and Trauma: International Perspectives on Stress and Coping*, 13, no. 1 (2008): 42–58.
[39] D. Bar-Tal, 'Collective Memory of Physical Violence: Its Contribution to the Culture of Violence', in *The Role of Memory in Ethnic Conflict*, eds. E. Cairns and M. D. Roe (Houndmills: Palgrave Macmillan, 2003), 77–93; 'Collective Memory of Physical Violence: Its Contribution to the Culture of Violence', in *Ethnicity Kills? The Politics of War, Peace and Ethnicity in SubSaharan Africa*, eds. B. Einar, M. Boas, and G. Saether (New York: St. Martin's Press, 2000), 77–93.

narrative and memory, which works to weave together and solidify a sense of collective identity, based on an interactive and shared definition around: 'the orientations of their action and the field of opportunities and constraints in which such action is to take place'.[40] As with other groups, an identifiable narrative (broadly those stories that give sequences, reason and coherence to selected events) provides loyalists with ways of organizing their political lives and the conceptual tools in the social processes of remembering (and forgetting), group identification and representation. All of these are brought together under the standard of the loyalist community.

Often this involves the transmission of ideas and beliefs in subtle, perhaps even unconscious ways, through conversations, storytelling, everyday and commonplace discourses, and popular culture and symbolism.[41] These are shared meaning and practices, through which people make sense of the world.[42] Such banal, everyday and sometimes seemingly trivial interactions, alongside commonplace representations and recurring narratives, are crucial in helping to organize political life.[43] Through narratives that relate directly to key specific events, particular senses of the Self[44] are reinforced.

Overview of the book

This book takes as a starting point the idea that loyalism marks a clear, legitimate and meaningful expression of a distinct social and political identity. That identity may be challenged and questioned, but it should also be recognized as intricate and compound. Certainly, it is beyond any simple expression of 'a sectarian pathology ... organized, armed and deployed to meet a British agenda',[45] or something simply akin to 'bigots in bowler hats'.[46] In recognizing the complex nature of loyalist identity, it is also important to acknowledge that beyond an identifiable socio-economic grouping, loyalism struggles to make itself relevant and accepted in contemporary society.[47]

---

[40] A. Melucci, *Challenging Codes: Collective Action in the Information Age* (Cambridge: Cambridge University Press, 1995), 70.

[41] D. Bryan and C. Stevenson, 'Flagging Peace: Struggles over Symbolic Landscape in the New Northern Ireland', in *Culture and Belonging in Divided Societies*, ed. M. H. Ross (Philadelphia, PA: University of Philadelphia Press, 2009), 68–84.

[42] C. Barker, *Making Sense of Cultural Studies: Central Problems and Critical Debates* (London: Sage, 2002).

[43] M. Billig, *Banal Nationalism* (London: Sage, 1995).

[44] F. Burton, *The Politics of Legitimacy: Struggles in a Belfast Community* (London: Routledge and Kegan Paul, 1978); R. White, 'Social and Role Identities and Political Violence: Identity as a Window on Violence in Northern Ireland' in *Social Identity, Intergroup Conflict, and Conflict Resolution*, eds. R. D. Ashmore, L. Jussim, and D. Wilder (New York: Oxford University Press, 2001), 159–183.

[45] L. Friel, 'Loyalist fascism exposes Brits', *An Phoblacht/Republican News*, 5 October 1999.

[46] D. G. Boyce, 'Bigots in Bowler Hats? Unionism Since the Downing Street Declaration 1993–1995', in *Political Violence in Northern Ireland – Conflict and Conflict Resolution*, ed. A. O'Day (Westport Connecticut: Praeger, 1997), 51–65.

[47] Intercomm and J. Byrne, *Flags and Protests: Exploring the Views, Perceptions and Experiences of People Directly and Indirectly Affected by the Flag Protests* (Belfast: Intercomm, 2013), 23.

Writings seeking to seriously explain broader loyalist culture, why loyalists hold the views they do, or detailing the component parts of loyalist ideology remain scarce. In engaging directly with these issues, this book seeks to explain how loyalism finds coherence and expression within a matrix of understandings and key reference points. Loyalists draw from diverse sources to construct their identity, included within this are diverse senses of Britishness, Protestantism; cultural, ethnic and civic identities; class; political expression and organization; and, loyalism as an everyday lived encounter.

These interact to become part of a distinct sense of loyalist identity and a distinct history reinforced in part by discrete foundation myths. References to such foundational ideas are of course central to the construction of many forms of identity, and importantly as Richard Kearney explains, such narratives carry 'the past into the present and the present into the past'.[48] Loyalism finds exclusive expression through notions of cultural separateness and a paradoxical willingness to engage in both political support for and opposition to the British state. This manifests through a variety of social, cultural and political forms that will be explored throughout this book.

The most common starting point for many loyalists is for them to regard themselves as part of a group with its primary political devotion to the British Crown and who give major emotional attachment to 'the people of Ulster'. Accordingly, the strength of cultural and political 'belonging' to Northern Ireland (or as it is commonly expressed to Ulster) is a central feature in the self-identity of loyalism. The potency of this often highly localized sense of fit, alongside the belief that loyalism offers the last line of defence for a culture that is continually threatened, begins to define the values and beliefs of contemporary loyalism. Moreover, the determination to preserve these core values means that loyalists often feel they must stand in opposition to any group, including if necessary the political representatives of mainstream unionism and the Westminster parliament, which is perceived to be in any way acting to weaken the Union or undermine Britishness.

The commitment to Northern Ireland as both an ideological location and a place of physical belonging is of immense significance within loyalism. It marks a continuity of thought and action dating back to at least the time of the Home Rule crises of the late nineteenth century (and as we shall see for some much further into the past). This point was clearly emphasized by the late Billy Mitchell who argued that the legitimacy of loyalist opposition today is drawn directly from the precedent set by the inclusion in the Covenant of 1912, which claimed that it was necessary to defend Ulster 'by all means necessary'.[49] As we shall see, the contemporary terrain over which resistance is deemed essential is widespread, embracing political, physical and cultural opposition to all those deemed to be the enemies of Ulster.

In considering structural, social and cultural aspects of loyalism, this book also seeks to challenge those narrow views that seek to locate the dynamics of loyalism almost entirely within paramilitarism. In so doing, it reveals the complexities of

[48] R. Kearney, *Postnationalist Ireland* (London: Routledge, 1997), 109.
[49] B. Mitchell, *Principles of Loyalism: An Internal Discussion Paper* (Belfast: no publisher, 2002), 40.

loyalism as a form of social identity and political expression beyond paramilitarism to other important routes for loyalist representation. To fully explain this while recognizing its distinctive ideological parameters and political expression, the book positions loyalism as part of a broader social movement and as a reaction to divergent social dynamics.

To clarify the significance of understanding loyalism in this way, the book identifies and draws upon a wide range of sources to trace religious, paramilitary, political and community influences within loyalism. Perhaps more importantly, it makes linkages between them to highlight the formation of contemporary loyalist identity and its political expression and outlet. This approach provides an important context and the framework for rethinking and reinterpreting loyalism from the inception of the Troubles to the present day.

It was in the late 1960s amid changing socio-economic and political circumstances, growing political cleavages and the social and physical fragmentation of long established working-class communities, often driven by government-led redevelopment schemes, that contemporary loyalism began to take shape. At the time, loyalism represented one riposte from sections of the Protestant working-class community to that hurriedly changing political situation. This response increasingly saw loyalists project themselves as a group apart. Such differentiation may be obvious in comparison with Irish nationalist and republican traditions, but many loyalists also increasingly came to recognize themselves as isolated from other sections of unionism, both in terms of their class experiences and because as loyalists they increasingly refused to recognize the validity of the established unionist political leadership.

This burgeoning sense of loyalism as an oppositional identity was reinforced by conflict. One outcome was that all those deemed outside of the boundaries of the group were excluded, reflecting the process experienced elsewhere in conflict societies, whereby 'often complex personal and social relationships are collapsed into a singular identity'.[50] Other consequences reflected the perceived need to enhance protection of the group through association with other like-minded individuals. Here, it is possible to introduce the notion of ontological security,[51] the starting point for which rests in emotional security and the psychological concept of the Self.[52] Amongst others, Anthony Giddens[53] has developed the notion to refer to the fundamental sense of safety in the world, within which a basic trust in other people is central in providing self-confidence of Self and collectives.[54] The self-confidence and security of Self is

[50] S. Cobb, 'Fostering Coexistence in Identity-Based Conflicts: Towards a Narrative Approach', in *Imagine Coexistence: Restoring Humanity after Violent Ethnic Conflict*, eds. A. Chayes and M. Minow (San Francisco, CA: Jossey-Bass, 2003), 298.

[51] C. Kinnvall, 'Globalization and religious nationalism: self, identity, and the search for ontological security', *Political Psychology*, 25, no. 5 (2004): 741–767.

[52] R. D. Laing, *The Divided Self* (Harmondsworth: Penguin Books, 1973).

[53] A. Giddens, *Consequences of Modernity* (Oxford: Blackwell, 1990).

[54] C. Kinnvall, *Globalization and Religious Nationalism in India* (Abingdon: Routledge, 2006).

located in the collective memory of the community[55] where bonds of trust offer 'protection against present and future threat and dangers'.[56]

Those who feel ontologically secure largely see the social world as non-threatening, compared with the ontologically insecure for which such worlds are endangered, politically and physically hazardous to the extent that the community can no longer offer protection and security. Feelings of insecurity are now deeply ingrained across large fractions of loyalism. This appears at several levels, manifest in expressions that loyalists have been deserted to stand alone, economically marginal and abandoned across the entire breath of the political and social arenas. For example, many loyalists now claim that the Protestant middle class has stepped away from any form of commitment to any common cause, largely to live increasingly high-quality lifestyles within which any overt attachment to traditional unionist ethno-political identity has lost any relevance or meaning.

Certainly, middle-class Protestants are less likely to vote than any other social category[57] and while some may retain links with loyalist communities established before upward social mobility, most remain disconnected from the social problems and political issues prevalent in these areas.[58] More broadly, many have also distanced entirely from political frame of reference which includes Northern Ireland as a distinct entity, to move that politics and towards integration with mainstream UK parties.[59] At best some may find affiliation with a developing sense of a Northern Irish identity, which they regard as a neutral category. All of these trends create conspicuous patterns of social, political and physical separation between those living in the loyalist heartlands of inner city Belfast and their co-religionists in the suburbs and towns surrounding Belfast.

Further, many believe that the Westminster parliament has little interest in understanding the loyalist political position for which there is even less empathy across the broader UK population. The resulting animosity once led Peter Hain, when Secretary of State for Northern Ireland, to conclude that in the contemporary period any political assurances from a British Ministers to loyalists were rarely accepted, and if anything had 'a tendency to be counter-productive'.[60]

Expressions of alienation from civil society and disconnection from the wider politic are now commonplace across sections of loyalism. Few beyond their immediate constituency seem to care for the plight of working-class loyalists, who have been

---

55 See B. J. Steele, *Ontological Security in International Relations* (Abington: Routledge, 2005); J. Mitzen, 'Ontological security in world politics: state identity and the security dilemma', *European Journal of International Politics*, 12 (2006): 341–370.

56 Giddens, *Consequences of Modernity*, 39.

57 L. Clarke, 'Middle class Protestants are least likely to vote: poll', *Belfast Telegraph*, 7 March 2012.

58 J. Brewer, 'Culture, Class and Protestantism in Urban Belfast'. Available at: http://www.discoversociety .org/culture-class-and-protestantism-in-urban-belfast-2/; accessed 17 March 2014.

59 See C. Coulter, *Contemporary Northern Irish Society: An Introduction* (London: Pluto 1999); 'Peering in from the window ledge of the Union: the Anglo-Irish Agreement and the attempt to bring British Conservatism to Northern Ireland', *Irish Studies Review*, 21, no. 4 (2013): 406–424.

60 *News Letter*, 11 September 2006.

relegated to what the late Billy Mitchell of the PUP often referred to as Northern Ireland's equivalent of 'poor white trash' in the United States. Nonetheless, despite direct political challenges, alongside dramatic economic decline and continuing change to social structure, loyalism endures as an identifiable body of thought and provides an important political dynamic within Northern Ireland's politics.

What follows, therefore, is an examination of some key political events, which have impacted on the senses of identity across loyalism. In so doing, it explains the construction and reconstruction of loyalist identity, and the major patterns of influence on that sense of identity brought about through a distinctive collective loyalist memory. It further examines how loyalism finds expression through senses of community, popular culture and by way of political representation. The book combines interviews and literature, alongside other material produced by loyalists themselves to identify insider perspectives on loyalism, its core narratives, sense of Self, the social configurations and political representations within loyalism, and the formation and use of loyalist collective memory. Importantly:

> Collective memory is not history, though it is sometimes made from similar material. It is a collective phenomenon but it only manifests itself in the actions and statements of individuals. It can take hold of historically and socially remote events but it often privileges the interests of the contemporary. It is as much a result of conscious manipulation as unconscious absorption and it is always mediated. And it can only be observed in roundabout ways, more through its effects than its characteristics.[61]

In seeking to understand the role of collective memory,[62] this book moves beyond many existing political and historical accounts to explore the broad political, social and cultural expressions of loyalism. In providing a comprehensive understanding of loyalism, it examines the major interwoven influences of community, narrative and identity; political organization; popular memory; and culture. Drawing on approaches from across social science, loyalist identity and politics are interrogated through socio-economic, religious, geographical, sociological, psychological and political forms of understanding.

Across all of these approaches, identity forms a core concept highlighting broadly held beliefs, values and narratives by which people locate a sense of belonging.[63] The onset of the Troubles may have widened and deepened many of the political antagonisms between groups, but it did not create them. Moreover, the incidents and events of inter-communal violence only added to pre-existing exclusionary memories, communal myths and sense of the Other. By actively drawing on presupposed shared

[61] W. Kansteiner, 'Finding meaning in memory: a methodological critique of collective memory studies', *History and Theory* 41 (2002): 179–197.

[62] N. Gedi and Y. Elam, 'Collective memory – what is it?', *History and Memory*, 8, no. 1 (1996): 30–50.

[63] D. McAdams, *The Stories We Live By: Personal Myths and the Making of the Self* (New York: Guildford, 1993).

memories,[64] loyalists locate themselves within an identifiable range of narratives and discourses. It is through the lens of these collective memories that particular actions are deemed legitimate and certain social relationship seen as valid.[65]

The loyalist narrative often parallels and sometimes overlaps with a broader unionist grand or meta-narrative,[66] but it offers a far from perfect fit. Unionism and loyalism differ in important ways and through the loyalist account it is possible to recognize a sense of community (both physical and imagined) that differentiates it from broader unionism. Sometimes the loyalist community is identified as directly aligning with the particular experiences of working-class unionism, sometimes it is understood as being bounded by local or regional geography and sometimes as having a much broader meaning, representing an identification with mutually understood points of social and political reference to form a broader imagined community of loyalism.

Shared points of reference and narrative allow loyalists to recognize, connect and associate with each other to establish and deepen a common identity. Loyalism constantly reproduces its own history through formal and informal social contact, everyday conversations and other forms of interaction such as meetings, correspondence, songs, community newsletters, prose, set piece speeches and forms of popular cultures. This is not a mono-causal or uniform construct. Despite what many of its critics and political opponents may claim, loyalism is a far from simple category to understand in sociological or political terms. Rather, it marks a complex weave of social forces and cultural expressions, drawing on extensive points of orientation, interpretations and reference points that work at an everyday level to bind together the social group. This manifests in an assortment of political groupings and outlets for the expression of identity, brought together under the heading of the loyalist community.

The construction of community marks the intersection of complex social processes, but it is possible to identify five core aspects and apply these to loyalism. First, loyalists define who they are by life experience. Second, community membership where people define whom they are through direct engagement with what is familiar, and reject that which is seen as different. Third, identity is defined through an understanding of where individuals and groups have been and where they are going. Fourth, multi-membership, where people reconcile and distil various forms of identity into one. Fifth, local vs. global relationships, where people define who they are by negotiating local ways of belonging in relation to broader experiences and discourses.

In exploring the various understandings and classifications of loyalism, this book necessarily and deliberately draws on an array of narratives, discourses and literature,

---

64 Connerton, *How Societies Remember*, 2–3.

65 See M. R. Somers, 'Narrativity, narrative identity, and social action: rethinking English working-class formation' *Social Science History*, 16, no. 4 (1992): 591–630; M. Somers and G. Gibson, 'Reclaiming the Epistemological "Other": Narrative and the Social Construction of Identity', in *Social Theory: The Politics of Identity*, ed. C. Calhoun (Oxford: Blackwell, 1994), 705–709.

66 N. Porter, *Rethinking Unionism: An Alternative Vision for Northern Ireland* (Belfast: Blackstaff, 1996).

but its particular emphasis rests on the construction of the notion of a loyalist community and with it the cultural and political memories of loyalism, determined through data collected from those who identify as loyalists. This material is used to explore experiences and convictions that have shaped loyalism in the modern period, including the collective interpretation of events actively selected from the past. Finally, through the concept of ontological security,[67] the book interrogates the notion of a 'siege mentality',[68] which at a populist level is seen to structure and drive loyalist political consciousness to rest at the core of a constantly negative and backward look formation of politics.

Structure of the book

Contemporary loyalism finds expression through a sense of common political purpose at the macro level and through what are often very localized senses of belonging and experiences, at the micro level. This finds form through commitment to a broad ideological position and through responses to experiences at a regional or even neighbourhood level. In turn, this brings us back to the significance of a loyalist sense of community, itself constructed by social actors mobilized through collective actions in attempts to find articulation for loyalist senses of identity and belonging.

This book focuses on several key locations for the communication and channelling of loyalist collective memory and identity, highlighting some of the core historical reference points used in composing the central loyalist narrative. In so doing, it draws on key themes from across sociology, political science, and social and political psychology to interrogate these core aspects of loyalism. In Chapters 1 and 2, we consider some of the main historical features of loyalist culture and the formation and establishment of the state of Northern Ireland. These chapters draw upon forms of identification that have found outlet through a variety of social groupings to establish loyalism as the heart of the state. Loyalist interpretations are located in communal perceptions of events and how these are continually reproduced through behaviour on a daily basis. This gives rise to ideas that we will encounter in various ways throughout much of the remainder of the book. In Chapter 3, we consider how loyalist identity is defined. Engagement with collective memory remains core in forming and sustaining identity often done by directly linking past and present in ways that reinforce identity, difference and common history.

The concept of community is central to loyalism, particularly intertwined with distinct ideas of place, a sense of belonging and form of class expression, seen to create a separate sense of identity. We explore this more fully in Chapter 4 and in particular the interface between physical and social boundaries. Chapter 5 considers

---

[67] S. Kay, 'Ontological security and peace-building in Northern Ireland', *Contemporary Security Policy*, 33, no. 2 (2012): 236–263.

[68] D. Bar-Tal and D. Antebi, 'Siege mentality in Israel', *International Journal of Intercultural Relations*, 16 (1992): 251–275.

the construction of loyalist memory and popular culture and its subsequent impact. Deliberation is made difficult by competing memories, and the role of commemoration is made particularly apparent in considering the loyalist paramilitary response in Chapter 6. Within loyalism, it is important to recognize how a sense of community is used not just to focus identity, but as a site for social organization and political action. In Chapter 7, we consider some of the consequences for loyalist politics, and how this has formed the basis for a cultural politics and for some the culture wars in which some loyalists now see themselves engaged. Finally, in Chapter 8, recognition is given to how this forms the basis for a politics forming around the contentious problems such as heritage and victimhood.

1

Ulster Loyalism, Identity and Belonging

A sense of belonging, experienced as an everyday awareness of identity, expression of ideological belief, common political desire and emotional attachment, is central to understanding contemporary loyalism. This involves family and friendship networks, alongside various religious and community associations as well as paramilitary organizations, fraternal organizations, formal political groupings, marching bands, pressure, protest and other social groupings. All of these groupings (and more) are framed by the loyalist sense of identity and bonded by a narrative endorsing and bolstering what is seen as the distinctive cultural and political history of loyalism.

Central to that narrative is the identification of several key locations for the construction of loyalist collective memory and identity. We highlight some of the central historical reference points used in the composition of loyalism, which present the reasons for conflict and its history to members[1] to provide a coherent narrative,[2] which consequentially carries great weight in the group's self-portrayal. The resulting account links collective memories in a highly accessible, if often rather simplified, account of political and social relations and the causes for conflict and its political consequences.

For some, the Northern Ireland polity is still best understood as an ethnic frontier society,[3] where the social categories of 'native' and 'planter' continue to resonate and convey meaning on a daily basis. Within an identifiable geographical and political terrain, competing national claims create 'chronic territorial force fields',[4] and the ensuing social and political tensions and divisions propel events of the past to the fore and make them subject to consistent reinterpretation and representation through the lens of the present. Indeed, Marianne Elliott has suggested that such processes form part of 'a deep sense of insecurity in Protestant psyche', whereby the fundamental

[1] E. Cairns and M. D. Roe, *The Role of Memory in Ethnic Conflict* (Houndmills: Palgrave Macmillan, 2002).
[2] P. Devine-Wright, 'A Theoretical Overview of Memory and Conflict', in *The Role of Memory in Ethnic Conflict*, eds. E. Cairns and M. Roe (Houndmills: Palgrave Macmillan, 2003), 9–33.
[3] D. Morrow. 'Escaping the Bind in Northern Ireland – Teaching and Learning in the Ethnic Frontier', in *Meeting of Cultures and Clash of Cultures: Adult Education in Multi-Cultural Societies*, eds. K. Yarn and S. Boggler (Jerusalem: Magnus Press, 1994), 77–91.
[4] F. Wright, *Northern Ireland: A Comparative Analysis* (Dublin: Gill and Macmillan, 1987).

divisions of planter and native are constantly revived, for example, to explain 'the attacks on Protestant property in successive IRA campaigns'.[5]

Thus, the reproduction, redefinition and reinterpretation of the past remain crucial. While the notion that social and political divisions in Ireland have deep historical roots, or that the major issues of contemporary Irish politics are framed by the past are far from novel,[6] this book is not directly concerned with 'history'. Rather, this book seeks to provide an analysis of Ulster loyalism through considering identified political ideas, leadership and events. Its focus is on how memories of the past become enclosed and reproduced within certain social groups, and how this often provides the framework for replication and reinforcement of common ideas, concerns and political perspectives. These processes are clearly witnessed in the contested and competing narratives of political history available at the everyday, populist and academic levels.[7]

Ireland has, of course, a long and divisive political history and has been subject to political and military intervention from England since the late twelfth century. Indigenous opposition was increasingly met with military force interspersed with phases involving the importation of people from England and Wales. For most, the origins of the modern conflict are located in the mutually antagonistic social relations and conflicting identities that arose on the Island following a series of Plantations (the confiscation of land and raw materials and the colonization of land with settlers by the English Crown), which began under the reign of James VI.[8] The strategic plantation of Ulster in the late Tudor and early Stuart monarchies in a bid to subdue the 'most remote and troublesome of the Irish provinces'[9] was a sizeable economic and political venture, involving the transportation of around 170,000 people, the vast majority of whom were Presbyterians from lowland Scotland.

Social, cultural and political divisions were amplified, and as Ed Moloney suggests, it was at this time the notion of 'conditional loyalty' was also implanted, through 'the idea that citizens and the state are bound together by a contract in which the citizens agree to support and defend the state only as long as the state defends and supports them'.[10] As we shall see, the concept of conditionality is one to which sections of loyalty have consistently returned. As a consequence, fundamental ethno-political and religious divisions were sharpened, making the history of the seventeenth century one of unadulterated hostility between settler and native.[11] The period from the 1640s saw the Scottish Presbyterian foothold established in the north-east of Ireland, consolidated by a further exodus from south-west Scotland, the stronghold

[5] M. Elliott, *When God Took Sides, Religion and Identity in Ireland – Unfinished History* (Oxford: Oxford University Press, 2009), 175.

[6] K. Stanbridge, 'Nationalism, international factors and the "Irish question" in the era of the First World War', *Nations and Nationalism*, 11, no. 1 (2005): 21–42.

[7] Smithey, *Unionists, Loyalists, and Conflict Transformation in Northern Ireland*.

[8] N. P. Canny, *Making Ireland British 1580–1650* (Oxford: Oxford University Press, 2001).

[9] M. Farrell, *Northern Ireland: The Orange State* (London: Pluto, 1976), 13.

[10] E. Moloney, *Voices from the Grave*, 324.

[11] P. Arthur, *Government and Politics of Northern Ireland* (Harlow: Longman), 2–3.

of Covenanting Presbyterianism, part of a tradition upon which unionists were to draw upon directly in the years to come.

This produced a 'significant body of Irish Protestants who were tied through religion and politics to English power,'[12] the bulk of planters following a reformed religion that was disdainful towards the indigenous faith. As competing interpretations and experiences of colonization and conflict deepened, assimilation became all but impossible as the ethnic and social estrangement of native from settler was further underpinned by other cleavages built around discordant cultural and religious dimensions.[13] Ireland's colonial experiences created long-lasting fundamental social, ethnic and political boundaries and a template for much of the subsequent conflict in Ireland.[14]

By the end of the seventeenth century, the Island had witnessed a further dramatic set of events that have become deeply located in the collective political memories of Ireland, as the Williamite war separated Irish society along with already established sectarian frontiers. As we shall encounter throughout the remainder of the book, for many Protestants these occurrences also formed the platform for a long history of celebration and commemoration of the King William's victory including activities such as the 'renaming of streets, painting the monarch on prominent buildings, and construction of monuments'.[15] Events such as the siege of Derry[16] and the series of skirmishes and battles, culminating in the conflict at the river Boyne gave rise to competing communal histories and collective memories to reflect and reinforce 'a prior history (and earlier remembrance) of colonization and resistance'.[17]

As a consequence, John Darby[18] suggests the next two centuries are best categorized as a period of continuing divergence when the consolidation of differences between the social groups and competing political loyalties was firmly established. In repost to continuing resistance towards English rule, which manifested in frequent risings, rebellions and generalized opposition, the Act of Union was introduced in 1801, abolishing the Irish parliament and allowing Westminster to take direct charge of Irish matters. The nineteenth century continued to witness the emergence of Irish nationalist social and political movements, some parliamentary based, others resting in militarism and expressions of physical force, but all intended to overthrow the Union.

---

[12] R. English, *Irish Freedom: The History of Nationalism in Ireland* (London: MacMillan, 2006), 59.

[13] J. Ruane and J. Todd, *The Dynamics of Conflict in Northern Ireland: Power, Conflict and Emancipation* (Cambridge: Cambridge University Press, 1996).

[14] See P. Clayton, *Enemies and Passing Friends* (London: Pluto, 1996); M. MacDonald, *Children of Wrath: Political Violence in Northern Ireland* (Cambridge: Polity, 1986).

[15] G. Beiner, 'Between trauma and triumphalism: the Easter rising, the Somme, and the crux of deep memory in modern Ireland', *Journal of British Studies*, 46 (2007): 271.

[16] The actual details of the siege are dealt with in some detail in Chapter 4.

[17] Beiner, *Between Trauma and Triumphalism*, 370.

[18] J. Darby, *Scorpions in a Bottle: Conflicting Cultures in Northern Ireland* (London: Minority Rights Publications, 1997).

Calls for Irish self-government culminated under the stewardship of Charles Stuart Parnell, founder of the Irish National League and first leader of the Irish Parliamentary Party (IPP). Parnell found the support of the British Liberal Prime Minister, William Gladstone, whose attempt to introduce Home Rule (as a form of semi-independent devolution of authority) was defeated in Westminster, albeit narrowly, in 1886. A second attempt to introduce Home Rule in 1893 won support in the Commons only to be defeated in the House of Lords, although Gladstone continued to promote Home Rule until the end of his public life in 1894.[19]

The gravest of disasters

Throughout the period, the vast bulk of Irish Protestantism remained united in its opposition to a Home Rule Parliament and remained solid in its political commitment to a future of Kingdom and Empire. Most believed that under a Dublin parliament, 'their religion, their way of life, and their economic interests would be endangered'.[20] In a culmination of much of the political activity from the 1880s onwards, the early twentieth century saw almost continual pressure build on the British government to grant Ireland independence. Home Rule introduced a political dynamic that fashioned the character of the Ulster problem and the dynamic of the politics surrounding it. Further, Liberal support for Home Rule 'had a seismic impact on British politics, reshaping the party system into two blocs, for and against Irish autonomy, in a struggle that would last until 1921'.[21]

Home Rule again came to the forefront of the political agenda in 1910, when following general election that resulted in a hung parliament, it became clear that the IPP would hold sway at Westminster. The IPP and the Liberal Party entered into a pact involving Asquith introducing a third Bill for Home Rule in return for Redmond's support in parliament. The Bill was supported through the Commons, and although there was widespread opposition in the Lords, the upper House could do no more than delay the implementation of the legislation.

Ulster Protestants began to make plans to organize against the possibility of Home Rule for Ireland. In an intensifying political atmosphere, sections of unionism openly threatened secession for the industrialized Northern part of the Island should plans proceed. Unionist resistance coalesced around their fear of dominance by a Catholic majority in all areas of political, social and cultural life,[22] the understanding that there

---

[19] T. W. Moody, 'Fenianism, Home Rule and the Land War', in *The Course of Irish History*, eds. T. W. Moody and F. X. Martin (Dublin: Mercier Press, 1994), 286–293.

[20] J. L. McCracken, 'Northern Ireland, 1921–66', *The Course of Irish History* (Dublin: Mercier Press, 1994), 313.

[21] J. Loughlin, 'Creating "a social and geographical fact": regional identity and the Ulster question 1880s–1920s', *Past and Present*, 195, no. 1 (2007): 159–196.

[22] J. Liechty, *Roots of Sectarianism in Ireland: Chronology and Reflections* (Belfast: Irish Inter-Church Meeting, 1993), 40.

were 'two nations' in Ireland, and the belief that absorption into a united Ireland would result in economic calamity for Ulster.[23] As Art Ó Broin explains:

> Ulster Protestants truly believed that Home Rule apart from being 'Rome Rule' meant an end to prosperity. They saw themselves as a future persecuted minority and took great comfort in the sense of being an embattled and gallant few, a return to the mentality that had so sustained their forefathers on the walls of Derry.[24]

In reporting a speech by Sir Edward Carson at a London banquet attended amongst others by the Duke of Somerset, Lord Londonderry and the Earls of Lancaster, Halsbury and Malmesbury, alongside some 30 MPs, the *Belfast News Letter* of 11 May 1912 gives some flavour of the mood across unionism. In his address, Carson declared that Home Rule was one issue upon which Unionism could not swayed, and that only by resistance could 'the gravest disaster' to the country be averted. Carson openly warned that any threat of coercion would transform Ulster into 'a hostile part' of the Empire[25] preparing the ground for an Ulster provisional government should Home Rule be enacted. One commentator summarizing the situation as follows:

> Edward Carson and the Ulster Unionists … [was] leading the opposition of Northern Ireland Protestants to Home Rule and bringing them to the edge of insurrection. Carson won the support of the British Conservative Party and set out on a whirlwind campaign throughout Ulster mobilising grass-roots Loyalists to the cause.[26]

Within Ulster, it was James Craig who set about galvanizing Carson's vision of organized resistance strategy by producing a written oath to be endorsed by opponents of Home Rule. Using the Scottish Covenant of 1638 as an archetypal, *Ulster's Solemn League and Covenant* was signed in a stage-managed event that took place on Saturday, 28 September 1912 (which subsequently became known as 'Ulster day'). At Belfast's City Hall, on an occasion that has become central to both loyalist collective memory and continually reproduced in popular culture, Carson was reported as the first person to sign the Covenant, followed by nearly half a million 218, 206 other men, while 228,991 women signed a separate *Ulster Women's Declaration,* and a further 19,612 people signed in several other cities across Britain.

While the Covenant is profoundly rooted in the loyalist collective memory, at the time it could be seen and even dismissed as little more than a highly choreographed publicity stunt, or what the *Irish News* referred to as a 'silly masquerade'.[27] Other

---

23   P. Ollerenshaw, 'Businessmen and the development of Ulster unionism, 1886–1921', *The Journal of Imperial and Commonwealth History*, 8, no. 1 (2000): 35–64.

24   A. Ó Broin, *Beyond the Black Pig's Dyke*, 133.

25   Reproduced in D. Armitage, 'Through the Archives', *News Letter*, 11 May 2009.

26   Moloney, *Voices from the Grave*, 329.

27   Ulster-Scots Community Network, *Understanding the Ulster Covenant* (Belfast: Ulster-Scots Agency, 2012).

events could not so easily be treated with such disdain. Unionists had also begun to organize militarily, threatening to use physical force opposition if there were any attempt to coerce them into a united Ireland. Military drilling took place amongst many Unionist Clubs and Orange Lodges, and the Ulster Volunteer Force (UVF) was mobilized as a private army of around 90,000 Volunteers aged between 17 and 65. By June 1913, Lieutenant General Sir George Richardson, who had been appointed as general officer commanding the UVF, set about establishing a regimental system or the group.

Again, it was Sir Edward Carson who set the overall tone, declaring in September 1913 to the massed ranks of Volunteers that their actions could not be considered criminal when 'committed in order to assert the freedom of the citizen'.[28] Although the UVF was somewhat lacking in experienced leadership and training,[29] the threat of armed loyalist resistance became more meaningful when in April 1914, the wooden rifles with which many had drilled were replaced with over 20,000 working German and Austrian weapons alongside several million rounds of ammunition. The munitions had been obtained following a smuggling operation masterminded by Fred Crawford, a British Army Officer and committed unionist.[30] The oath many had taken to resist Home Rule had taken a significant turn, as loyalists revealed the seriousness of their intent by presenting the reality of organized political and military opposition to Westminster. As the severity of political discord deepened, Irish nationalists formed their own armed Volunteers, while elements of the British Army made clear their refusal to stand against the UVF should they be ordered to do so. Ireland was seemingly set on an unswerving course towards civil war.

War and empire

It was, however, in a much wider arena that loyalist resolve and commitment to Crown and Empire was to be tested. The political situation in Ireland remained tense and unresolved, but international political events intervened directly as Britain declared war on Germany, forcing Irish politics onto the back boiler. At the outbreak of the First World War, with the Liberal government committed to ensuring that the third Irish Home Rule Bill was to become law, Irish nationalism's ultimate goal seemed to be within touching distance. With the onset of war, however, the legislation was suspended for the duration of the conflict. In part at least, this explains the support of many nationalists for the War, believing that Irish and Allied interests were now directly aligned in military victory in Europe, following which Home Rule would finally be fully implemented in Ireland.

[28] J. Biggs-Davison, *The Hand Is Red* (London: Johnson Publications, 1973), 84.
[29] T. Bowman, *Carson's Army: The Ulster Volunteer Force, 1910–22* (Manchester: Manchester University Press, 2007).
[30] See F. H. Crawford, *Guns for Ulster* (Books Ulster, 2014, first published 1947).

The Irish contribution to the war effort was not insignificant. Aside from those already recruited before the outbreak of war, around 200,000 Irishmen were enlisted into the British forces after the outbreak of War,[31] the majority serving in the 10th (Irish), the 16th (Irish) and the 36th (Ulster) Divisions. Many UVF members signed up directly to the Ulster Division. They were driven by the ultimate loyalist logic that although in the months before they had organized against the British government, apparently to the point of military resistance, they remained 'passionately loyal to the British Crown'.[32] As a result, large-scale enlistment from within the UVF was an almost inevitable outcome, seen by those joining as an overt expression of both their political identity,[33] their loyalty in preserving Empire[34] and in many cases even a sense of their masculinity.[35]

The first engagement by any Irish regiment in the First World War was in August 1915, when the 10th Division suffered severe losses following their landing at Gallipoli as part of the Mediterranean Expeditionary Force.[36] The other two divisions served on the Western Front, perhaps most notably at the Somme, where on the first two days of the July campaign the Ulster Division suffered appallingly heavy casualties losing 5,500 either killed, wounded or missing, out of a total of about 12,000 men.[37] By September 1916, the 16th Division was also engaged in the Somme campaign, where some eight months later, the 16th fought side by side with the 36th Division at the Battle of Wijtschate-Messines Ridge in June 1917.[38]

That the first day of the Somme campaign (1st July) coincided with the original date of the Battle of the Boyne in 1690 was to prove significant. The date already bore a 'very special significance', meaning that in Ulster Protestant political consciousness, the link between Boyne and Somme was quickly made. Indeed, one commentator has suggested that 'the sons of the victors' at the Boyne, 'after eight generations, fought this greater fight'.[39] As such, the day became, and remains, a major focus for the Orange and loyalist calendar. The horrendous casualties suffered by the 36th Division, many of whom were Orange Order and/or UVF members, ensured that commemoration of the blood sacrifice, overlaid the original significance of the date

---

[31] K. Jeffrey, 'Ireland and World War One'. Available at: http://www.bbc.co.uk/history/british/britainwwone/irelandwwone01.shtml; accessed 1 March 2012; K. Jeffery, *Ireland and the Great War* (Cambridge: Cambridge University Press, 2000).

[32] R. Grayson, *Belfast Boys: How Unionists and Nationalists Fought and Died Together in the First World War* (London: Continuum, 2010), 24.

[33] Bowman, *Carson's Army*.

[34] Clayton, *Enemies and Passing Friends*.

[35] See J. G. V. McGaughey, *Ulster's Men: Protestant Unionist Masculinities and Militarization in the North of Ireland, 1912–1923* (Kingston, ON: McGill–Queen's University Press, 2012); 'The language of sacrifice: masculinities in Northern Ireland and the consequences of the Great War', *Patterns of Prejudice*, 46, nos. 3–4 (2012): 299–317.

[36] B. Cooper, *The 10th (Irish) Division in Gallipoli* (Dublin: Irish Academic Press, 2003 [1918]).

[37] D. Murphy, *Irish Regiments in the World Wars* (Oxford: Osprey Publishing, 2007), 20.

[38] T. Burke, 'The 16th (Irish) and 36th (Ulster) Divisions at the Battle of Wijtschate-Messines Ridge, 7 June 1917: a battlefield tour guide' (Heuvelland, 2007).

[39] C. Falls, *The History of the 36th (Ulster) Division* (Aldershot: Gale and Polden, 1922, reproduced 1996).

to become located even more deeply in loyalist political consciousness and collective memory.[40] Indeed, as we shall see, for some the claimed ownership of such memories is central to the formulation of contemporary loyalism identity.

For other unionists, the events at the Somme were brought into even sharper relief by the seen contrast between events on the First World War battlefields and what was recognized as the betrayal of the armed rebellion instigated in Dublin during Easter week, 1916.[41] Around 1,800 members of the Irish Volunteers, alongside members of the Irish Citizen Army and *Cumann na mBan*, seized several major buildings in Dublin by force, proclaiming the formation of an Irish Republic.[42] They held out for a week before finally surrendering to the 16,000 British troops and heavy armaments that had been deployed to suppress them.[43] It was, however, events immediately in the aftermath of the rising that were to present the most profound long-term political impact.[44] In particular, the executions of fifteen rebel leaders drew revulsion from across wide sections of the Irish population,[45] unleashing a wave of support that found direct political expression in the general election of December 1918, when Sinn Féin brushed aside the IPP in a result that 'completely transformed the face of Irish politics'.[46]

It was this vastly changed political terrain that led to the establishment of an Irish parliament and precipitated a 'War of Independence' between British forces and the IRA. The Government of Ireland Act in 1920 split the Island into two administrative units with limited devolved powers. Each administration now had its own parliament: one in Belfast to control what is now Northern Ireland and another in Dublin, governing what is now the Republic of Ireland. These were to be supported by the Council of Ireland to deal with issues of common interest, but with the ultimate responsibility resting with London. Such arrangements were acceptable to most Ulster unionists, who implemented the Act, but not to many Irish nationalists.

The 1920 Act led to bitter disagreement between those who were prepared to accept and those who rejected partition, and whether or not to support the formation of an independent Irish State within the British Empire.[47] All political attempts to reconcile pro- and anti-Treaty forces failed, and bloody conflict broke out in late June 1922. The new State was 'born into civil war',[48] and the conflict between Republicans and Free State forces raged until 1923, when those willing to agree to partition and the resulting political arrangements gained dominance. With the full accord of Westminster and Dublin administrations, the Irish Free State was established, later declaring itself a Republic on Easter Monday 1949.

---

[40] D. Officer and G. Walker, 'Protestant Ulster: ethno-history, memory and contemporary prospects', *National Identities*, 2, no. 3 (2000): 298–301.

[41] P. De Rosa, *Rebels: The Irish Rising of 1916* (New York: Fawcett Columbine, 1990).

[42] S. McMahon, *A Short History of Ireland* (Cork: Mercier Press, 1996), 168–172.

[43] C. Townshend, *Easter 1916: The Irish Rebellion* (Hammondsworth: Penguin, 2006).

[44] See material in R. O'Donnell. ed. *The Impact of the 1916 Rising: Among the Nations* (Dublin: Irish Academic Press, 2008).

[45] F. McGarry, *The Rising: Ireland Easter 1916* (Oxford: Oxford University Press, 2010).

[46] F. S. L. Lyons, *Ireland since the Famine* (London: Fontana, 1973), 399.

[47] B. Kissane, *The Politics of the Irish Civil War* (Oxford: Oxford University Press, 2005).

[48] Arthur, *Government and Politics of Northern Ireland*, 18.

Creating the Unionist State

From at least the end of the First World War, it had become clear to key fractions of the Ulster Protestant community that 'the attempt to defeat Home Rule for all of Ireland was not feasible, and the most that could be hoped for was the creation of a separate Unionist homeland in the north-east'.[49] With this realization the political parameters for unionism on changed dramatically[50] as many unionists accepted that to maintain political control over as much of Ireland as they possibly could, they would need to concede not just three of its provinces, but also three of Ulster's counties. Moreover, large sections of unionism were quick to take advantage of the deepening populist notions that the 'blood sacrifice' for Britain offered during the First World War should be repaid by supporting demands that the predominantly Protestant counties of northeast Ulster remain part of the UK.[51]

The establishment of Northern Ireland reflected the transformation of Irish unionism to Northern Irish unionism, but it also marked the failure of both British and Irish state nation building.[52] That at the opening of the new devolved parliament, King George V lauded Ulster's 'patriotic devotion to the Empire which you proved so gallantly in the Great War',[53] should not disguise the fact that sizeable sections of Irish unionism viewed partition as a failure. Craig in a letter to Lloyd George outlined 'the sacrifices…made in agreeing to self-government and in consenting to the establishment of a Parliament', further explaining that it was 'much against our wish but in the interests of peace'.[54]

Although largely written out of the subsequent loyalist narrative, or at least ignored by it, the prospect of partition was undoubtedly met with little enthusiasm amongst Protestant unionists, who were anything but categorical about the political division of the island. It was a reluctant Unionism that accepted what was seen the best arrangement they could hope for within the broader politics of the time.[55] Donald Akenson puts this perspective forcibly in stating:

> If there ever was a state that no one wanted, it was Northern Ireland: not the British, who had tried to rid themselves of all of Ireland during three attempts at passing 'home rule' measures; not the Irish nationalists, who wanted control over

---

[49] J. Loughlin, *Ulster Unionism and British National Identity since 1885* (London: Pinter, 1995), 160.

[50] T. Hennessey, *A History of Northern Ireland 1920–1996* (Dublin: Gill and Macmillan, 1997).

[51] J. Loughlin, 'Mobilising the Sacred Dead: Ulster Unionism, the Great War and the Politics of Remembrance', in *Ireland and the Great War: A War to Unite Us All?*, eds. A. Gregory and S. Paseta (Manchester: Manchester University Press, 2002), 136–145.

[52] G. Walker, *A History of the Ulster Unionist Party: Protest, Pragmatism and Pessimism* (Manchester: Manchester University Press, 2004).

[53] Cited in G. McIntosh, 'The Royal Visit to Belfast, June 1921', in *The Ulster Crisis, 1885–1921*, eds. D. G. Boyce and A. O'Day (Basingstoke: Macmillan, 2006), 262.

[54] Cited in J. Magee, *Northern Ireland: Crisis and Conflict* (London: Routledge and Keegan Paul, 1974), 11.

[55] P. Buckland, *Irish Unionism, 1885–1922* (London: Historical Association, 1973).

the entire island of Ireland; and least of all the Ulster Protestants, who wished to remain an integral part of the United Kingdom of Great Britain and Ireland. Unlike the southern nationalism of which Yeats sang, the northern state was not a terrible beauty, but a terrible embarrassment.[56]

No matter, however, how tentative sections of unionism were in accepting the new arrangements, partition was now a reality, and the existing divisions surrounding political, social and economic relations were quickly institutionalized across both jurisdictions on the Island. Although Article XII of the Anglo-Irish Treaty was deliberately vague on any future resolution of the border, proposals from the Boundary Commission of 1925 to shave off southern Armagh to the Free State and to transfer parts of eastern Donegal to Northern Ireland proved too controversial even to be given a public airing, let alone to be implemented. The border had become a legislative reality, under the formal administration of both states on the island.

Unionism responded by becoming increasingly exclusive and isolationist as it became clear that Northern Ireland's new border encompassed two mutually suspicious and oppositional communities, differentiated by religious affiliation, cultural heritage, national allegiance, core senses of belonging, expressions of identity and most essentially by their relationship to the new state. Moreover, it also was increasingly apparent that Northern Ireland was lacking in any commitment to creating a shared civil society that could reflect a more all-encompassing imagined community encircling all of Northern Ireland citizens. In recognizing this, John Darby[57] summarizes the overall situation as where one group believed that the land they occupied had been usurped, while the other thought the land they occupied was constantly under threat of rebellion.

For nationalists the new Northern state that could make no legitimate claim to be democratic, or to rightfully demand their allegiance. Indeed, for most Catholics, it represented little beyond the outcome of a British imperialist conspiracy to maintain control over as much of the Island as possible through an unnatural division of the existing territory. For them, the division of the Island was not just illegal, but the political separation of the Island against the majority will, and the creation of a state 'arbitrarily carved out of the state of Ulster',[58] was also unjust and immoral. The result was the creation of a society with an almost paranoid sense of its own security, divided along the lines of ethno-political identity, residence and employment[59] and characterized by sectarian politics. It was reinforced through discrimination against

---

[56] D. H. Akenson, *God's Peoples: Covenant and Land in South Africa, Israel and Ulster* (London: Cornell University Press, 1992), 183.
[57] Darby, *Scorpions in a Bottle*.
[58] L. De Paor, *Divided Ulster* (Hammondsworth: Penguin, 1970), xv.
[59] F. O'Connor, *In Search of a State: Catholics in Northern Ireland* (Belfast: Blackstaff, 1994).

Catholics in the domain of civil society and the threat of force by the 'Orange state' in the political arena.[60]

Following partition, unionists 'worked assiduously to firmly establish the institutions of government', while its 'propagandists enthusiastically endeavoured to invest [in] the constitutional entity of Northern Ireland'.[61] In so doing, however, the post-partition Unionist Government failed to address any thought of the need to develop some form of inclusive social and cultural identity based on the new territory, or to secure stable relationships within Northern Ireland itself. Rather, the overwhelming feature of unionist culture became the rejection, overtly or otherwise, of all things seen to be 'Irish', and a wariness of any within its boundaries deemed not to be fully committed to the state and Union. This application of 'Otherness' to all those deemed to be disloyal did little to assure the minority Catholic Nationalist population of their position in the new state. Underpinning all of this was the belief not just that Northern Ireland's Roman Catholics held different religious convictions and cultural values, but rather they could be seen as fifth columnists.

It was within this context that the discourses and narratives of loyalism were reformulated and reinforced. Moreover, the Unionist State chose to build its identity around a 'selective history', centered on largely sectarian events, which was not only irrelevant to the Nationalist population, but was more generally inadequate as a means of legitimization'.[62] The ideological gap between Dublin and Belfast quickly widened, as each set about constructing 'competing narratives of cultural identity'.[63] Both states set about building reciprocated exclusion, reinforced through the production of conflicting historiography and official memory[64] and often inflating perceived dissimilarities.[65] Moreover, in the decade following, partition 'the triangular relationship between North and South, between Dublin and London and between the two communities in the North appeared to grow more strained'.[66] For many Protestants and unionists, the South quickly became a distant and foreign place.

Meanwhile, the state of Northern Ireland, conceived and delivered as it was within the framework of loyalism, in direct opposition to the broader parliamentary will, and

---

[60] M. Farrell, *Northern Ireland: The Orange State; Arming the Protestants: The Formation of the Ulster Special Constabulary and the Royal Ulster Constabulary, 1920–1927* (London: Pluto Press, 1983).

[61] Loughlin, 'Creating "a social and geographical fact"', 194.

[62] B. Graham, 'No place of the mind: contested Protestant representations of Ulster', *Ecumene*, 1, no. 3 (1994): 267.

[63] N. C. Johnson, *Ireland, the Great War and the Geography of Remembrance* (Cambridge: Cambridge University Press, 2003), 2; B. Graham and Y. Whelan, 'The legacies of the dead: commemorating the troubles in Northern Ireland', *Environment and Planning, Society and Space*, 25, no. 3 (2007): 476–495.

[64] M. Kennedy, *Division and Consensus: The Politics of Cross-Border Relations in Ireland, 1925–1969* (Dublin: Institute of Public Administration, 2000).

[65] D. Kennedy, *The Widening Gulf: Northern Attitudes to the Independent Irish State, 1919–1949* (Belfast: Blackstaff, 1988).

[66] C. Kennedy-Pipe, *The Origins of the Present Troubles in Northern Ireland* (London: Longman, 1997).

through a response to the perceived needs and desires of Ulster Protestants ahead of the majority of those on the Island, was also taking form. While few unionists may have actively welcomed partition, many did see it as some form of formal recognition of the differences between two peoples on the Island. In the words of Donald Akenson, the conflict with Irish Catholic nationalism:

> reinforced a particular sense of identity among the Protestant population of Ulster, the cultural and political leaders of whom were preponderantly Presbyterian in religious heritage and Ulster-Scots in ethnicity. The state that ... emerged in the north of Ireland ... Northern Ireland ... was founded morally on the terms of the Ulster Covenant, and pragmatically on the promise that it would be a Protestant state for a Protestant people.[67]

---

[67] Akenson, *God's Peoples*, 150.

2

Establishing Loyalism and the Unionist State

The Northern Ireland state was established amid widespread communal bloodshed, much of which centred in Belfast. Although far from the first outbreak of sectarian conflict in the history of the city, the fighting of the 1920s was particularly intense, brutal and had a clear sectarian hue. Politically motivated killings became everyday events, and the use of retaliatory tit-for-tat violence and indiscriminate attacks resulted in nearly 500 deaths in Belfast in the two years following July 1920.[1] Marc Mulholland summarizes the violence of the period as follows:

> Overall, the violence in Ulster following partition, a bloody front in the Anglo-Irish War, was almost as much against Protestants as Catholics; 157 Protestants died in the two years up to July 1922, and 37 members of the security forces, compared to 257 Catholics.

After the agreed Treaty between the British government and the Sinn Féin leadership was signed in 1922, however, the violence became:

> more one-sided; Catholics were battered into submission. More people died in Belfast during three months of violence in 1922 than in the whole two years following the formation of the state. A substantial majority of the 232 victims were Catholic, and 11,000 were made jobless and 23,000 homeless. Over 4,500 Catholic-owned shops and businesses were burned, looted, or wrecked.[2]

In response to the violence and civil disruption, Westminster had set up the formal structures of a Northern Ireland administration (even though the legislation had not passed fully through parliament or received Royal Assent). Following elections in May 1921, the new government, with Craig as Prime Minister, introduced draconian legislation, including the Civil Authorities (Special Powers) Act in April 1922, followed by a whole series of initiatives, including proscription of the IRA, internment and curfew for those deemed enemies of the state.[3]

---

[1] N. Cunningham, 'The Social Geography of Violence during the Belfast Troubles, 1920–1922', CRESC Working Paper No. 122 (Manchester: University of Manchester, 2013).

[2] M. Mulholland, *Northern Ireland: A Very Short Introduction* (Oxford: Oxford University Press, 2002), 25.

[3] A. Jackson, *Ireland 1798–1998: War, Peace and Beyond* (Oxford: John Wiley, 2010), 334.

While unequivocal evidence of official involvement in the coordination of the violence by the new administration is limited, the unionist government was undoubtedly lethargic in its response, especially to violence emanating from loyalist groups. In particular, they exploited tensions by recruiting remnants of the UVF into the Ulster Special Constabulary (USC), an almost exclusively Protestant paramilitary reserve force, which was distrusted intensely by the nationalist population and criticized from day one as a divisive and sectarian force. Thus, from its formation, the ideological contours of the Northern Ireland state were determined in response to loyalist fears and its political framework set around the defence of the broad social, electoral and economic interests of unionism.

The shape of the resulting politics reflected a near obsession with ensuring security against enemies seen to be both without and within the state. This manifested at all levels of society. At Belfast's Harland and Wolff shipyard, for example, in the aftermath of a mass meeting in July 1920, Protestant workers expelled those who were deemed to be disloyal, mostly Catholics but also Trade Unionists and many who held broadly socialist or liberal outlooks.[4] There were further expulsions over the next two years.[5]

Across almost all areas of society, only overt and unquestioning allegiance to the new Northern state, both in thought and behaviour, was seen as appropriate. The dominance of unionist ideological values was given political form by the UUP, shored up by the Orange Order and fortified by the RUC, including its part time wings of the USC. Stephen Howe describes the intense pressures to conform, as resulting in almost unquestioning 'Loyalty to the crown, to Britishness, and to the Ulster Unionist Party'[6] (UUP). Anyone seen to raise even the smallest of doubts about the validity or nature of Northern Irish society, let alone directly challenge the dominant political and social values of the Unionist State, was marginalized, by the forcefulness of the conviction that existed and the new state's strength of belief in the need for Protestant unity.

The Unionist government, given substance by uninhibited control of the security forces, set about establishing difference, not only through control of state structures, but also by establishing a dominant narrative emphasizing the inherent Britishness of Northern Ireland. In part, this reinforced how clearly it differed from the South in terms of living standards, culture and economic life.[7] Incompatible narratives

[4] A. Morgan, *Labour and Partition: The Belfast Working Class 1905–23* (London: Pluto Press, 1991).
[5] J. P. Lynch, *An Unlikely Success Story: The Belfast Shipbuilding Industry 1880–1935* (Belfast: Belfast Society, 2010).
[6] S. Howe, 'Mad Dogs and Ulstermen: The Crisis of Loyalism (part one)', 2005a. Available at: http://www.opendemocracy.net/debates/article.jsp?id=6anddebateId=33andarticleId=2876; accessed 1 March 2012; 'Mad Dogs and Ulstermen: The Crisis of Loyalism (part two)', 2005b. Available at: http://www.opendemocracy.net/democracy-protest/loyalism_2885.jsp; accessed 1 March 2012.
[7] S. MacDougall, 'The Projection of Northern Ireland to Great Britain and Abroad, 1921–1939', in *The Northern Ireland Problem in British Politics*, eds. P. Catterall and S. MacDougall (Basingstoke: Macmillan, 1996), 29–46.

of Protestant/Unionist/Loyalist and the Catholic/Nationalist/republican political collectives were fortified through separate public commemorations,[8] cultural activities, popular media,[9] underpinned by an educational system transmitting competing historiographies and interpretations of the past.[10]

What is also readily evident is the level of prejudice and discrimination manifest in the workplace and at certain levels of local government. As John Whyte concluded, perhaps the 'most serious charge against the Northern Ireland government' therefore was not 'that it was directly responsible for widespread discrimination, but that it allowed discrimination on such a scale over a substantial segment of Northern Ireland'.[11] Marc Mulholland[12] suggests there were several underlying dynamics behind Unionists prejudice, including triumphalism, anti-Catholicism, social prejudice, populism, the overwhelming concern for security, and to need to maintain patterns of sectarian electoral geography that had been established.

The resulting construction of unionism largely reflected a worldview that Marianne Elliott[13] has described as intolerant of others, virulently anti-Catholic and at times reflecting a strange seventeenth-century antiquarianism. Further, following the settlement of the boundary in 1925 and the formal dissolving of the Council of Ireland in 1926, a breach developed in elite relations between the Dublin and Belfast administrations as each set about constructing 'competing narratives of cultural identity',[14] the exclusive nature of which for some became an obsession to the verge of fixation. As Caroline Kennedy-Pipe explains, throughout the 1930s, 'the triangular relationship between North and south, between Dublin and London and between the two communities in the North grew ever more strained and disparate'.[15]

Such dynamics helped determine much of the direction taken by the state and gave rise to the 'asymmetry of division of resources and access to political power between unionists and the Catholic minority'.[16] The organization and structure of the state apparatus reflected unionism's obsession with security and its determination to hold

[8] P. Devine-Wright, 'History and identity in Northern Ireland – an exploratory investigation of the role of historical commemorations in contexts of conflict', *Peace and Conflict: Journal of Peace Psychology*, 7, no. 4 (2001): 297–315.

[9] G. Dawson, *Making Peace with the Past?: Memory, Trauma and the Irish Troubles* (Manchester: Manchester University Press, 2007).

[10] See K. Barton and A. McCully, 'Teaching controversial issues … where controversial issues really matter', *Teaching History*, 127 (2007): 13–19; L. Terra, 'New histories for a new state: a study of history textbook content in Northern Ireland', *Journal of Curriculum Studies*, 46, no. 2 (2014): 225–248.

[11] J. Whyte, *Interpreting Northern Ireland* (Oxford: Clarendon Press, 1991), 35.

[12] Mulholland, *Northern Ireland: A Very Short Introduction.*

[13] Elliott, *When God Took Sides.*

[14] Johnson, *Ireland, the Great War and the Geography of Remembrance.*

[15] Kennedy-Pipe, *The Origins of the Present Troubles*, 25.

[16] J. W. McAuley, C. McGlynn, and J. Tonge, 'Conflict resolution in asymmetrical and symmetrical situations: Northern Ireland as a case study', *Dynamics of Asymmetrical Conflict*, 1, no. 1 (2008): 88–102.

political power, if needs be safeguarded by their control over its domestic security forces. As one loyalist leader was to put it many years later:

> For Protestants, politics was about supporting the State and the continuance of the Union with Gt. Britain. This allegiance and, consequently, those who purported to represent them in all spheres of life had carte blanche to do whatever they chose to do providing the flag was waved and the magical theme 'the Union' was invoked.[17]

The state took the overall shape and form it did because of the insecurity felt by the Unionist leadership, in face of what they perceived as a dual threat of 'a hostile Irish nationalist state to the south, and a large minority of Irish nationalists within Northern Ireland itself'.[18] The feasibility of 'a separate NI state in 1920/21 rested on the concentration of Protestant (and Unionist) industrial capital in the Belfast area'. The need to assure the Protestant population of this was paramount.[19] From the point of its creation, the Northern Irish state privileged Protestant unionist identity as a distinct category of social belonging over that of Catholic nationalism.

Moreover, distinguishing between those seen as loyal and those seen as potentially disloyal and the ranking of those categories directly influenced civil, political and security formations of the state and influenced the subsequent social relationships between the Catholic and Protestant population. As the subordinate social and political position of Catholics became institutionalized and normalized, the Catholic community 'turned in on itself' for support and: 'developed a parallel universe to the majority one',[20] as it set about creating a state within a state.

Meanwhile, the Unionist leadership 'allowed (and at times encouraged) discrimination against the supposedly disloyal within Northern Ireland, thereby furthering the process of northern nationalist disaffection which had occasioned such action in the first place'.[21] Unwilling to view the new state as a legitimate entity, or to fully integrate within it, this in turn influenced how most northern Catholics perceived and reconstructed their relationship with the state and their own sense of belonging. They defined their prime focus as opposition, thus reinforcing the northern Protestants view that they were subject to an 'endless repetition of repealed assaults'.[22]

---

[17] Community Relations Council, *Community Development in Protestant Areas* (Belfast: Community Relations Information Centre, 1992), 65.

[18] R. English, 'Coming to terms with the past: Northern Ireland: Richard English argues that historians have a practical and constructive role to play in today's Ulster', *History Today*, 54, no. 7 (July 2004): 6.

[19] L. O'Dowd, B. Rolson, and M. Tomlinson, *Northern Ireland: Between Civil Rights and Civil War* (London: CSE Books, 1980), 30.

[20] Elliott, *When God Took Sides*.

[21] English, Coming to terms with the past, 18.

[22] T. Brown, 'The whole Protestant community: the making of a historical myth', *A Field Day Pamphlet*, 7 (1985): 8.

Structuring the Unionist State, 1921–1972

The new Northern state faced manifold problems, not least of which were the contested claims around its authority and the validity of its very existence. Little wonder, Bryan Follis[23] described Northern Ireland in its formative years as a state under siege, facing internal turmoil around its political legitimacy, outbreaks of communal sectarian violence and increasingly turbulent political relationships with the governments of both Westminster and Dublin. All this made for a highly conflicting set of social and political relations and created a civic arena dominated by the border and the reinforcement of oppositional social and political identities.[24]

Not only were political and social relationships within the new state increasingly divergent, its economic base was also extremely perilous, uncertainty compounded by an unemployment rate that stood at 23 per cent in 1922. While the psychological core of Belfast's industrial society, the Harland and Wolff shipyard seemed in reasonable financial shape, it became apparent after the death of the company's leading partner, Lord William James Pirrie in June 1924 that even that company stood on the edge of bankruptcy. Indeed, the annual demand for shipping fell throughout the 1920s and 1930s, to the point where between December 1931 and May 1934, Harland and Wolff did not launch a single ship.

The new Northern Ireland state had no tax-raising powers and suffered badly from the capitalist downturns of the 1920s and 1930s, primarily because of an over reliance on a narrow economic base located in small farms, textiles, engineering and shipbuilding. Unemployment figures began to rise relentlessly, the levels of which 'bad enough in the Twenties, worsened at the beginning of the Thirties, and with it the frustration of the unemployed workers with unionist politicians'.[25] Around half of the 100,000 unemployed lived in Belfast alone, approaching 30 per cent of the total working population,[26] while employment in the shipyard fell by 87 per cent.[27] The general living conditions for the working class were appalling, and for many of the unemployed they were horrendous.[28] State support, if it could be obtained, only lasted for thirteen weeks, after which there was little option for the unemployed but to apply to the Poor Law Guardians for Outdoor Relief (ODR).

In response, many of the unemployed and those on ODR engaged in large-scale protests and organized demonstrations, which came to a head in October 1932, when in seeking to bring an end to task work, payments in cash at trade union rates, and an increase in relief payments, they organized the boycotting of ODR work and took

---

[23] B. A. Follis, *A State under Seige: The Establishment of Northern Ireland, 1920–1925* (Oxford: Oxford University Press, 1995).

[24] R. Rose, *Governing without Consensus: An Irish Perspective* (Boston, MA: Beacon Press, 1991).

[25] P. Devlin, *Yes We Have No Bananas*, 16.

[26] B. White, 'The day Catholic and Protestant workers marched – and fought – side by side against the common enemy of poverty and destitution', *Belfast Telegraph* (8 October 1982): 10–11.

[27] R. Munck, 'Class and religion in Belfast – a historical perspective', *Journal of Contemporary History*, 20, no. 2 (1985): 249.

[28] R. Munck and B. Rolston. 'Oral history and social conflict', *Oral History Review*, 13 (1985): 1–21.

to the streets in numbers to attend mass meetings and demonstrations. The protests escalated, many participated in a rent strike and street disorder broke out across several districts in Belfast, where Protestant and Catholic strikers fought alongside each other in hand-to-hand battles with the police. With a curfew in place, hundreds of strikers in jail and its leaders seriously contemplating calling a general strike, the police responded to the escalating tensions and street violence with gunfire, killing two demonstrators, one Protestant and the other Catholic, during a riot on the Falls Road.

For the embryonic unionist government, the strike was immediately cast as a conspiracy to undermine the state, Lord Craigavon describing the strikers as 'hirelings of Dublin, Glasgow and Moscow', seeking to secure a 'Republic for all Ireland'. The motivations of those engaged in strike action ranged considerably. For some of those involved, it marked 'a glorious two weeks in the history of working class struggle'.[29] For others, events were driven almost entirely by economic need, rather than political ideology, and the resulting collective action was strictly non-political and non-sectarian social movement.

Whatever the main reason for participation, any sense of working-class unity created was short lived. By the mid-1930s, relationships between the two communities had deteriorated to the point where 1935 saw the worst sectarian riots since the formation of the state.[30] The celebrations surrounding the silver jubilee of George V dissolved into extensive communal violence, resulting in eleven killed and over five hundred injured. The twelfth of July demonstration was attacked in central Belfast, precipitating widespread street violence resulting in the killing of eight Protestants and five Catholics, and around 2,000 Catholics being driven from their homes.[31] As the city once again fragmented along readily recognized sectarian fault lines, the then Belfast Coroner set the blame: 'fairly and squarely on the unchristian utterances of the government politicians in the … campaign to divide and rule'.[32] Despite their record, however, the unionist government remained in a seemingly unchallengeable position of power at Stormont throughout the decade.

It was the outbreak of the Second World War that introduced some vibrancy into the economy. Manufacturing industries that had struggled to emerge from the depression of the 1920s and 1930s were revitalized, as Belfast became one of the vital cockpits of allied military manufacture and output for the war effort. In the absence of conscription, increased demand for workers and volunteers for the armed forces did expose further social problems, however, including the ill health and poverty of many ordinary families. Not that the brutal living conditions was to give rise to a class aware politics or political organization in the same ways as it did elsewhere. Although living

---

[29] White, 'The day Catholic and Protestant workers marched – and fought – side by side', 10.
[30] See A. C. Hepburn, 'The Belfast riots of 1935', *Social History*, 15 (1990): 76; R. Munck, 'Class conflict and sectarianism in Belfast: from its origins to the 1930s', *Contemporary Crises*, 9 (1985): 252.
[31] Ó Broin, *Beyond the Black Pig's Dyke*, 133.
[32] Cited in J. Kelly, *Bonfires on the Hillside: An Eyewitness Account of Political Upheaval in Northern Ireland* (Belfast: Fountain Press, 1995).

in some of the worst social conditions in Europe and subject to a unionist leadership: 'which repaid its working-class supporters with total indifference… class war in Northern Ireland continued to be lateral rather than vertical'.[33]

For many Protestants, 'the class enemy was not the bosses but the feckless, lazy, clerically manipulated, and intermittently dangerous Fenians'.[34] The relationship that developed between the Unionist leadership and the majority of working-class Protestants was essentially paternalistic.[35] Following the formation of the state, if class tensions did bubble to the surface within the Protestant community, those involved were most often brought back to the fold by the intervention of organizations such as the Unionist Labour Association (ULA), which under the direct tutelage of the Unionist Party sought to successfully curtail the influence of the trade union movement, generally functioning to induce support from Protestant workers for the wider unionist political agenda.[36] All this was underpinned by a dominant discourse that emerged to convince large sections of working-class Protestants that they 'had an interest in the preservation of the state of affairs, [and were] marginally better off… if only in the sense that they "belonged" to the ruling class'.[37]

The sense of unionist cohesion was consistently reinforced through a redefinition of a hegemonic political and cultural order that appropriated and obscured all other basis for a legitimate politics beyond the constitutional. Unionist hegemony was constructed through processes, which, although not necessarily prescribing the specific content of ideas, did set 'the *limits* within which ideas and conflicts move and are resolved'.[38] Thus, although many ordinary Protestants were also economically and materially marginalized, often they were 'convinced that – even the poorest – were in some sense "better" than Catholic fellow citizens',[39] and that any challenge to the socio-economic structure of Northern Ireland would set in motion a series of social forces that would result in the demise of the state itself.

Unionist authority was in large part maintained by convincing Protestants of the dangers of the enemy within, and that all Catholics could be seen as potentially disloyal to the state.[40] Moreover, through access to common cultural and political resources, many of which directly reflected the values of the state, Protestants were persuaded

[33] Howe, 'Mad Dogs and Ulstermen'.

[34] S. McMahon, *A Short History of Ireland* (Cork: Mercier Press, 1996), 68.

[35] B. Probert, *Beyond Orange and Green: The Political Economy of the Northern Ireland Crisis* (London: Academy Press, 1978), 48–56.

[36] C. Reid, 'Protestant challenges to the "Protestant State": Ulster Unionism and independent Unionism in Northern Ireland, 1921-1939', *Twentieth Century British History*, 19, no. 4 (2008): 419–445.

[37] G. Da Fazio, 'Civil rights mobilization and repression in Northern Ireland: a comparison with the U.S. Deep South', *Sixties: A Journal of History, Politics and Culture*, 2, no. 2 (2009): 171.

[38] J. Clarke, S. Hall, T. Jefferson, and B. Roberts, 'Subcultures, Cultures and Class: A Theoretical Overview', in *Resistance through Rituals: Youth Subcultures in Post-War Britain*, eds. S. Hall and T. Jefferson (London: Hutchinson, 1976), 39, emphasis in original.

[39] Da Fazio, 'Civil rights mobilization and repression in Northern Ireland': 171.

[40] M. L. R. Smith, *Fighting for Ireland? The Military Strategy of the Irish Republican Movement* (London: Routledge, 1997), 118.

they 'had a sense of belonging to the state that poor Catholics lacked'.[41] This was given outlet through the structures of the Orange Order, and the UUP, which acted in unison for the next sixty years. Together, they reinforced to large sections of the Protestant working class that their economic and social conditions were of secondary weight compared to the security of the state, which was seen as constantly under threat (both from without and within).

The adherence of working-class Protestants and the existence state were seen as deeply interwoven, with the security of both seen to rest on support for the greater cause of unionism, which the leadership set about establishing in different ways. Throughout the economic turmoil of the 1930s, for example, the Unionist leadership engaged in a series of public set piece rituals and performances, including the opening of the Stormont parliament building and in 1933 the unveiling of a statue honouring Edward Carson.[42] In part at least, these were designed to reinforce and deepen unionist unity by emphasizing the desirability of social homogeneity and the need for political unity amongst Protestants. Other proceedings included the celebration of the George V silver jubilee, the funeral of Carson in 1935, and the coronation visit in 1937 of George VI and Queen Elizabeth.

Crucially, McIntosh argues that it was though such events that 'unionist certitudes were affirmed', and especially in 'a period in which unionism was trying to rally its faithful in a show of strength; their state rituals made a high-profile point that unionist collectivity was not only possible, but was a reality'.[43] Such a perspective was actively nurtured and encouraged by the unionist political leadership and was underpinned by the strength of the unionist foundation myth of the state.[44] The Unionist governments attempt to rapidly establish autonomy was aided by disinterest and detachment expressed by the Westminster administration. As Sean Farren and Robert Mulvihill point out:

> Relationships between Unionist administrations and the British Government throughout this period tended to be distant, exactly as the Unionist Party preferred, and the British themselves were happy to allow ... [meanwhile] North-South relationships had become even more distant as both parts of Ireland grew steadily apart in the years following the country's partition.[45]

The overriding Protestant unionist, and ultimately loyalist personality of the state, was directly revealed in the mechanisms of the Stormont parliament, the 'factory of grievances',[46] within which unionist attention continued to focus on the perceived treachery of their opponents rather than in the attempt to rectify social and economic

---

[41] G. I. Higgins and J. Brewer, *Anti-Catholicism in Northern Ireland, 1600–1998: The Mote and the Beam* (Houndmills: Macmillan, 1998), 52.

[42] G. McIntosh, *The Force of Culture: Unionist Identities in Twentieth-Century Ireland* (Cork: Cork University Press, 1999).

[43] McIntosh, *The Force of Culture*, 36–37.

[44] A. Jackson, 'Unionist Myths 1912–1985', *Past and Present*, 136 (1992): 164–185.

[45] S. Farren and R. F. Mulvihill, *Paths to a Settlement* (London: Colin Smythe, 2000), 17–18.

[46] P. Buckland, *The Factory of Grievances: Devolved Government in Northern Ireland 1921–39* (Dublin: Gill and Macmillan, 1979).

problems (of which there were many). Parliamentary politics became increasingly torpid and stagnant. Moreover, it has been suggested that unionists only held regular elections because they recognized the need 'to keep Westminster from interfering with their running of Northern Ireland', and the appearance of a working constitutional opposition meant 'that wider support would be created externally for its existence as a state'.[47]

The divisive and contested nature of politics was, however, still readily exposed at election time, when calls for unionist unity (alongside opposing calls for nationalist accord) found their loudest articulation. In 1921, the first election to a Northern Ireland parliament held under proportional representation was conducted as a virtual referendum on the right of the state to exist. The unionist-orientated *Belfast Newsletter*[48] identified the election as a headcount of 'who is for Empire and who for a Republic?', while the nationalist leaning towards *Irish News*[49] branded it as a chance 'to rescue north-east Ulster'. Whatever the character of the poll, the UUP quickly established electoral dominance with 67 per cent of the overall vote, and a majority of votes in all constituencies except Fermanagh-Tyrone.

Nationalists remained explicitly opposed to partition but also internally divided, largely on whether to boycott the new parliament or fight for their cause from within it. Although the Nationalist Party emerged as the main opposition in the 1925 election (with ten of the eleven candidates standing elected), it fought only a limited number of seats reflecting a support base that was overwhelmingly rural and Catholic. Nonetheless, support for the Nationalist Party, alongside support for several Labour candidates and Independent unionists was enough to raise political concerns amongst the UUP, even although with 55 per cent of first preference votes they clearly held a comfortable majority.[50]

The Unionist Government responded by abolishing the proportional representation system of voting. Although as a result the Ulster Unionist vote dropped slightly, to just over 50 per cent, the 1929 election (the first in which all men and women over the age of 21 could vote) saw unionists win an extra five seats, bringing their total to thirty-seven. The overall model that emerged saw an increasing number of seats go uncontested, especially where it was clear that either the unionist or nationalist bloc was in a clear ascendency. In the four decades following the mid-1920s, the minimal competition around ideological space was directly reflected in the ossified nature of completion for seats in electoral politics.

While specific, sometimes highly localized, issues arose with each poll, in broad terms the period saw the establishment of a rigid set of voting patterns within which Unionist dominance was not and could never be seriously challenged. Robert Osborne[51] reveals that between 1925 and 1965, in 111 rural constituency

---

[47] Devlin, *Yes We Have No Bananas*, 43.

[48] *Belfast Newsletter*, 26 April 1921.

[49] *Irish News*, 11 May 1921.

[50] See Farrell, *Arming the Protestants*, 242; Munck, 'Class and religion in Belfast': 156–157.

[51] R. D. Osborne 'Voting Behaviour in Northern Ireland 1921–1977', in *Integration and Divison: Geographical Perspectives on the Northern Ireland Problem*, eds. F. W. Boal and J. N. H. Douglas (London: Academic Press, 1982), 145.

elections held, fewer than one-third (31.5 per cent) involved direct competition between Unionists and nationalists. Within Belfast, where straight electoral contest was more commonplace, Unionists contesting all but two (Falls and Central) of the sixteen constituencies, which after 1945 were conceded, not to Irish nationalism, but to Anti-Partition Labour candidates. In other parts of Belfast where Unionists held seats, the level of support for the UUP varied considerably from election to election. In the Woodvale constituency in north Belfast, this ranged from 33.1 to 54.7 per cent, while in Willowfield in the east of the City, it differed from 35.5 to 87.5 per cent.[52]

Labour did represent something of an electoral challenge to Unionism with five candidates elected across Belfast, and in June 1945, amid the social democratic turn across the UK, their support was driven in part at least by the general wave of dissatisfaction with the existing social conditions laid bare by those returning from the war. Both the electoral growth of Labour and the social gains they brought about, however, proved short lived. The seats were lost in the Westminster election the following month, and thereafter, Northern Ireland's ideologically conservative Unionist government set about stalling and diluting the introduction of welfare state reform prevalent in the rest of the UK.

In truth, the fortunes of the Labour movement had begun to wane following much internal conflict surrounding its position on partition.[53] The movement split in 1949, when the Northern Ireland Labour Party (NILP) formally backed the separation of the two states, leading to widespread desertion by many Catholic supporters who turned to anti-Partition Labour groupings or to find an outlet for their politics. Nonetheless, the significance of the NILP should not be too understated.[54] It was through the Party, for example, that 'important sections of the Protestant proletariat [came] under the influence of relatively secular labourism',[55] and in 1958, the NILP became the official opposition after winning four of the fifty-two seats in the Stormont parliament, representing around 16 per cent of the popular vote.

The Party retained all four seats in the 1962 election increasing its share of the vote, but support wilted in the November 1965 poll, and the Party ended up with just two seats, meaning that in February 1965, the Nationalist Party agreed to become the official opposition. Part of the reason for the reason for the demise of the NILP was the changing broader political circumstances. As politics became more contested and society more discordant, there were growing concerns amongst Protestant workers that the Party could no longer represent their best interests. For example, Frank Wright in

[52] *Ibid.*, 147.

[53] A. Edwards, *A History of the Northern Ireland Labour Party: Democratic Socialism and Sectarianism* (Manchester: Manchester University Press, 2009).

[54] A. Edwards, 'The Northern Ireland Labour Party and Protestant Working Class Identity', in *Irish Protestant Identities*, eds. M. Busteed, F. Neal, and J. Tonge (Manchester: Manchester University Press, 2008), 347–359.

[55] P. Bew, P. Gibbon, and H. Patterson, *Northern Ireland, 1921–1996: Political Forces and Social Classes* (London: Serif, 1995), 221.

tracing the decline of the NILP and the emergence of Ian Paisley's Protestant Unionist Party in the Woodvale constituency notes:

> The major difference was that whereas in the former case the tacit assumption was that the interests of Protestant and Catholic workers were the same with regard to unemployment; in the latter case the Protestant unionist manifesto dwelt upon the preferential treatment which it was alleged that the Catholic working class on the Falls were receiving.[56]

The concerns that section of the Protestant community could not have been eased, when in September 1966, the NILP, alongside the Northern Committee of the Irish Congress of Trades Unions (ICTU), issued a joint statement supporting the call of the civil rights movement for 'one man, one vote' and an end to discrimination. While, however, many NILP members supported and were no doubt involved the civil rights campaign, the Party did not give it any formal backing. The failure to endorse the civil rights movement precipitated a split in the Labour movement, many of the more active and radical members joining Peoples Democracy[57] a group based in and around Queen's University, which further agitated for the repeal of special powers legislation, and the end to discriminatory employment practices.[58]

Conclusions

Loyalist senses of history are bonded by a distinct sense of cultural identity highlighting key historical reference points, which are used in loyalist narrative and present the reasons for conflict. From its formation, the ideological contours of the Northern Ireland state were structured in response to loyalist fears and their reading of history. But by the mid-1960s, the dominant discourse of Unionist unity, which had been established with the State itself, was being challenged by Protestant workers on the one hand, and a growing Catholic middle class on the other. In Northern Ireland, political and social relationships have always been divergent and competing, but few could have predicted what was to come in terms of loyalist reaction.

---

[56] F. Wright, 'Protestant ideology and politics in Ulster', *European Journal of Sociology*, 14, no. 1 (1973): 262.

[57] P. Arthur and K. Jeffery, *Northern Ireland since 1968* (Oxford: Blackwell, 1996), 6.

[58] S. W. Beach, 'Social movement radicalization: the case of the people's democracy in Northern Ireland', *The Sociological Quarterly*, 18, no. 3 (1997): 305–318.

3

Modernization, Loyalist Reaction and Identity

By the 1960s, the need for wider debate and engagement, perhaps even a change of political direction, had become apparent to some sections of unionism,[1] and the decade 'witnessed the promise of great improvement in political relations in Ireland, north and south'.[2] The election in 1963 of Terence O'Neill to succeed Lord Brookeborough, ahead of his leading competitor Brian Faulkner, seemed to indicate the reinforcement of a liberal turn within the Unionist Party. On coming to office, O'Neill seemed to usher in a new era of politics, especially when he pronounced that 'Unionism armed with justice will be a stronger cause than Unionism armed merely with strength'.[3] He seemed to introduce a period of political change and present some level of economic, social and political innovation, initiating a programme of reform to 'modernize' Northern Ireland, while trying to normalize some of the more stark sectarian differences in an attempt to draw Catholic support to the state.

Although Henry Patterson[4] suggests O'Neill's leadership was rather longer on rhetoric than it was in commitment, it is important to highlight the colossal challenges he faced as Prime Minister. In party terms, he still needed to win back both the ideological space and votes that Unionism had lost to the NILP. Everyday sectarian tensions remained tangible, not just in the major urban centres of Belfast and Londonderry, but also across many rural areas and especially in those border regions where the brief, if futile, campaign waged by the IRA between 1956 and 1962 had left a discernible legacy of fear and distrust amongst many Protestants[5] of threat republicans remained intense.

More broadly, the sectarian structure of Northern Irish society formulated at the state's inception remained more or less intact and continued to directly impose on everyday life. As a result, O'Neill found support for his reform agenda of regional development, economic regeneration and social modernization, particularly difficult to find in the rural border areas east of the Bann, such as Fermanagh, Tyrone and

---

[1] P. Bew, *Ireland: The Politics of Enmity 1789–2006* (Oxford: Oxford University Press, 2007), 488.
[2] B. M. Walker, *A Political History of the Two Irelands: From Partition to Peace* (Houndmills: Palgrave Macmillan, 2012), 107.
[3] Cited in Magee, *Northern Ireland: Crisis and Conflict*, 115.
[4] H. Patterson, *Ireland since 1939: The Persistence of Conflict* (London: Penguin, 2007), 191.
[5] H. Patterson, *Ireland's Violent Frontier: The Border and Anglo-Irish Relations during the Troubles* (Basingstoke: Palgrave Macmillan, 2013).

Londonderry. Indeed, every attempt at transformation, whether symbolic or real, was met with trepidation, apprehension and resistance from one section of unionism or another.

In June 1963, for example, the decision to lower the Union flag at Belfast City Hall to half-mast as a mark of respect for the death of Pope John XXIII raised incredulity from some unionists. When in January 1965 O'Neill met his opposite number, the Irish *Taoiseach* Séan Lemass, as part of a campaign to improve relationships between the two States (as well as to mollify growing concerns from Westminster) it was met with enmity from sections of unionism. That is not to suggest that O'Neill and his followers were without support, the *News Letter* editorial of the time arguing that 'No danger to the unionist cause would be involved' and that during the meeting 'Captain O'Neill would show the strength of his position'.[6]

For others within the Protestant unionist community, however, O'Neill was displaying the very opposite qualities. For them, the existing norms of their society were being openly questioned, if not directly undermined by their own leadership. Moreover, O'Neill had arranged the meeting with Lemass without giving any prior notice to many leading colleagues in the party. This in a society where almost every decision (and in many cases non-decisions) made in the civic arena carry deep political undertones and draw on collective memories of the past, which are seen the reinforce a legacy of division.

O'Neill faced other problems in seeking to rally support to his political and social agenda. Described as 'vain, aloof and disinclined to take his less sophisticated colleagues into his confidence or seek their advice',[7] he certainly was no man of the people. Moreover, many within the unionist leadership had an issue with somewhat idiosyncratic personal style alongside his tendency towards a presidential approach to leadership. Although not unaware of his internal opposition (O'Neill had sought to by-pass some of the mounting internal hostility by carrying out a cabinet reshuffle in July 1964, when most of the existing members were on holiday), he further alienated many within his party by centralizing power, drawing heavily on 'a small coterie of trusted civil servants'[8] rather than consulting the wider cabinet. In reviewing the fiftieth anniversary of O'Neill's tenure, former Unionist Member of Parliament (MP) John Taylor commented on O'Neill's perceived aloofness and suggested that he was always seen 'more to be English rather than Ulster and that was a great disadvantage for the Ulster Unionist party'.[9]

A major part of the modernizing strategy of O'Neill drew heavily on ideas devised by planners that sought to attract new industry to the region east of the river Bann, where the development of the physical infrastructure and introduction of up-to-the-minute transport links were seen as desirable and viable prospects. Whether or not,

---

[6] *News Letter*, 20 November 1964.
[7] J. Loughlin, *The Ulster Question since 1945* (Basingstoke: Palgrave Macmillan, 2004), 37.
[8] *Ibid.*
[9] Cited in G. Gordon, 'Captain Terence O'Neill: Visionary or failure?', BBC News Northern Ireland. Available at: http://www.bbc.co.uk/news/uk-northern-ireland-21875466; accessed 7 June 2013.

this was the preferred effect, in the sum-zero game that characterized Northern Irish politics then, and often since, many Irish nationalists perceived this as another direct snub from the state in an attempt to starve the predominantly Catholic region west of the Bann of jobs and resources at the expense of the chiefly Protestant east. While the Unionist government's thrust towards economic modernization did find some success, universal support proved elusive, and as David Cairns and Shaun Richards explain:

> ...a fraction of the leading group within the Unionist alliance attempted to mobilize ideologically for economic development and to recast the form of its hegemony, only to find that the subjects (including many of its functionaries) who themselves had been produced by that ideology, employed its formulations to criticize and reject proposals for development which would lend comfort to the enemy at the gate.[10]

Challenging the Unionist State

The view of many Catholics that they were being directly discriminated against was hardly alleviated by the pronouncement that Northern Ireland's new city was to be named 'Craigavon' after its first Prime Minister.[11] Such concerns were compounded following the publishing of the Lockwood Report on 10 February 1965, and the decision to locate a new university in the predominantly 'Protestant' town of Coleraine, rather than in the largely 'Catholic' city of Londonderry, where Magee College had long been established as a centre of learning. Locating the university in a largely Protestant town was seen as yet another deed of pure bias and a further attempt to reinforce the strength of the Belfast/Coleraine/Portadown economic triangle. Rather than providing any communal feeling of achievement regarding the expansion of higher education, the location of the new institution became yet one more entry into an expanding catalogue of grievances felt by the Catholic Nationalist communities.

By the time the gates of the campus of the New University of Ulster opened in Coleraine in October 1968, political tensions had escalated considerably. The marginalized place of Catholics in Northern Irish society was brought to the fore of the public domain by the foundation of the Northern Ireland Civil Rights Association (NICRA). Its original steering group included radical republicans, representatives from the NILP and the trade union movement, who set about channelled opposition to the systematic discrimination in the public arena. In particular, they focused on

---

[10] D. Cairns and S. Richards, ' "Pissing in the Gale of history": contemporary protestant culture and the "Ancient Curse" ', *Ideas and Production: A Journal in the History of Ideas*, no. 8 (1988): 24.

[11] M. J. McCleery, 'The creation of the "New City" of Craigavon: a case study of politics, planning and modernisation in Northern Ireland in the early 1960s', *Irish Political Studies* 27, no. 1 (2012): 89–110.

the areas of housing allocation, the gerrymandering of local elections, the Special Powers Act and role of the RUC.

The civil rights movement emerged against a backdrop where unemployment stood at over twice the UK average (with some areas west of the Bann experiencing sixfold unemployment). Following the model set in the United States, the NICRA increasingly took their grievances unto the streets, not to demand an end to partition, or a dismantling of the Northern Irish state, but rather that Catholics be afforded the same rights as other citizens across the UK. Indeed, as one commentator put it, in its quest of the demands for 'civil rights and social justice', the movement could be seen as demonstrably British in its approach.[12] The NICRA articulated its position through five basic demands to reform the state: one person one vote, end to gerrymandering, laws against discrimination, repeal of the Special Powers Act and an end to the B-Specials.[13]

The transformation programme initiated by O'Neill sought to tackle head-on those weaknesses he feared might undermine the state, addressing Northern Ireland's fragile economy; the political challenge set to Unionist hegemony, particularly by the NILP; the need for Northern Ireland's Catholics to be made to feel full citizens of the state; and the need to round-off the harder edges of sectarian culture.[14] In the end, however, his five-point plan seeking to directly address the core demands of the NICRA as part of a broader programme of reform that was to prove to be too little and too late.[15]

The strategy set in place by O'Neill to ensure the continued existence of the Northern Irish state, by reconstructing unionism into a more contemporary and softer form, quickly unravelled as civic society crumbled amid sweeping sectarian conflict. As Raphael Samuel puts it, the 'sectarian divide' took 'the place of civil order'.[16] With the genie out of the bottle, the situation moved apace; within four years of the first official meeting of the prime ministers of the two states, Northern Ireland was spiralling towards unbridled communal violence and the most serious political predicament since its foundation. The worsening situation was marked by a visit by the British Home Secretary, Jim Callaghan and the deployment of troops on the streets (who in the short term at least were fêted by Catholics in Derry and Belfast) in an attempt to quell spiralling sectarian violence.

Whether it was based on a misunderstanding of his strategy, a belief that he was politically inept, or that his tactics were either undermining the Unionist State, or

---

[12] Arthur, *Government and Politics of Northern Ireland*, 108.

[13] B. Purdie, *Politics in the Streets: The Origins of the Civil Rights Movement in Northern Ireland* (Belfast: Blackstaff Press, 1990).

[14] See C. Hewitt, 'Discrimination in Northern Ireland: a rejoinder', *British Journal of Sociology*, 34, no. 3 (1983): 446–451; 'Catholic grievances and violence in Northern Ireland', *British Journal of Sociology* 36, no. 1 (1985): 102–105; D. O'Hearn. 'Catholic grievances, Catholic nationalism: a comment', *British Journal of Sociology*, 34, no. 3 (1983): 438–445; 'Again on discrimination in Northern Ireland: a reply to the rejoinder', *British Journal of Sociology*, 36, no. 1 (1985): 94–101.

[15] C. Hewitt. 'Catholic grievances, Catholic nationalism and violence in Northern Ireland during the Civil Rights Period: a reconsideration', *British Journal of Sociology*, 32, no. 3 (1981): 362–380.

[16] R. Samuel, 'Four Nations History', in *Island Stories: Unravelling Britain, Theatres of Memory, Volume II*, eds. A. Light, S. Alexander, and G. S. Jones (London: Verso, 1998), 21.

not going far enough to reform it, O'Neill, for differing reasons, found himself in confrontation with the Westminster government, key segments of the Unionist State, leading sections of the UUP, swathes of loyalism and broad fragments of Northern Ireland's Catholics and liberals. The increasingly hectic pace of events set in train a political dynamic that in less than two years was to see the suspension and eventual closure of the provincial parliament and direct political governance from Westminster. The tussle for civil rights had transformed into a struggle for the continued existence of the state, as Northern Irish society seemingly inched towards an outright civil war with the emergence of widespread political violence as an everyday event, the British Army on the streets and the emergence of organized armed groups intent on confrontation.

The loyalist response

The attempts by O'Neill 'to win over middle class Catholics to support the Union by engaging in symbolic acts of reconciliation such as visiting Catholic schools and extending condolences on the death of the Pope',[17] underpinned by the modest political and social reform he implemented, were to prove a bridge too far for some sections of unionism. Moreover, it precipitated a fervent loyalist response to what was seen as the growing appeasement of the Catholic and nationalist minority. Between March and April 1969, there were six bombings at key water and electricity installations across Northern Ireland. Initially blamed on an all but moribund IRA and radical elements of the civil rights movement, it was subsequently revealed that the explosives had been planted by loyalists as part of a strategy designed: 'undermine confidence in O'Neill's ability to maintain law and order', thus forcing him to resign.[18] A grouping calling itself the UVF had re-emerged in Irish history.

These actions were also an indication not just of increasing disillusionment with the O'Neill administration, but also of how directly some Protestants regarded the NICRA, and related groupings such as Peoples Democracy, as little more than a republican Trojan horse. While there was undoubtedly significant republican and communist input into the NICRA, the account given by Bob Purdie of the times is sceptical of any master plan concluding that 'the whole affair was a series of blunders', that there was no republican/communist conspiracy to sweep away Stormont and no unionist conspiracy to sweep the marchers and their politics off the streets.[19]

What was apparent, however, is that the relevance of the civil rights demands energized and politicized large sections of the nationalist population, particularly those west of the river Bann, and its membership and influence stretched far beyond the republican or Leftist movements. In seeking to respond directly to loyalist concerns, O'Neill isolated many moderates, both Catholic and Protestant, by claiming that the civil rights demonstrations were 'attempting to bypass and discredit the ordinary

---

[17] *News Letter*, 23 March 2013.
[18] J. Cusack and H. McDonald, *UVF* (Dublin: Poolbeg, 1997), 28.
[19] Purdie, *Politics in the Streets*, 146.

processes of democratic government'.[20] Meantime, the Trojan horse argument was openly being articulated by Bill Craig, the Stormont Minister of Home Affairs,[21] who claimed that the civil rights movement had a '...very large IRA content',[22] and their entire campaign was orchestrated around the aim of bringing down the state. As Craig increasingly questioned O'Neill's political judgement, the relationship between the two became more and more alienated. O'Neill finally lost patience, dismissing Craig in December 1968 after he had openly called for a unilateral declaration of independence for Northern Ireland,[23] but not before Craig's decision, in October, to ban a civil rights march in Derry.[24]

Reaction to the ban unleashed widespread resentment that had been festering amongst large sections of the Catholic minority and ignited widespread confrontation on the streets. The subsequent violence thrust the situation in Northern Ireland to the fore of national and international media coverage and brought to prominence a still reasonably obscure cleric, Ian Paisley. His views reflected a unique mix of his own brand of evangelicalism, personal interpretation of Biblical writings and understanding of the social and political position of the Catholic Church.[25] Paisley's politics showed little regard for the existing Unionist political leadership, and his ability to corral the growing loyalist concerns and widespread disquiet felt across the unionist community gave direction to his politics. It was this combination that set in place the foundation stones for the emergence of the Democratic Unionist Party (DUP) sometime later. Paisley had formed the Free Presbyterian Church and continued to express unbridled hostility to the development of ecumenical tendencies within Protestant churches in Ireland.[26] In the late 1960s, 'Paisleyism' found increasing political momentum and presence through a series of street demonstrations and public protests.[27]

After the emergence of the civil rights movement, the size and potency of loyalist populist political opposition quickly grew and continued to coalesce around Paisley whose interventions increasingly grew louder and more frequent.[28] Against a background of deepening turmoil on the streets, the political situation worsened. Paisley's oppositional politics took centre stage as for his supporters the 'disruptive experiments introduced by O'Neill and continued by his protégées... reached their

[20] M. Wallace, *Drums and Guns: Revolution in Ulster* (London: Geoffrey Chapman, 1970), 53.
[21] P. Taylor, *Loyalists* (London: Bloomsbury, 2000).
[22] HCNI Parliamentary debates, no. 74, (1969): 126–134.
[23] *The Guardian*, 'William Craig obituary: Stormont minister and founder of the Ulster Vanguard movement', 26 April 2011.
[24] *The Guardian*, 26 April 2011.
[25] R. L. Jordan, *The Second Coming of Paisley: Militant Fundamentalism and Ulster Politics* (New York: Syracuse University Press, 2013); F. E. Scott, 'The political preaching tradition in Ulster: Prelude to Paisley', *Western Speech Communication* 40, no. 4 (1976): 249–259.
[26] M. O'Callaghan and C. O'Donnell, 'The Northern Ireland Government, the "Paisleyite Movement" and Ulster Unionism in 1966', *Irish Political Studies*, 21, no. 2 (2006): 203–222.
[27] S. Bruce, *God Save Ulster: The Religion and Politics of Paisleyism* (Oxford: Oxford University Press, 1986).
[28] C. Smyth, *Ian Paisley: Voice of Protestant Ulster* (Edinburgh: Scottish Academic Press, 1987), 55.

logical conclusion of Party disintegration and public chaos'.[29] In direct response on Monday 9 December 1968, O'Neill made his now famous speech 'Ulster at the Crossroads', an appeal for continued support to help restructure and modernize Northern Ireland.

This became the cornerstone of the Unionist Party's manifesto for the election campaign of February 1969, which stated: 'this is no ordinary Election. Its outcome will decide the kind of country this will be'.[30] There was support within unionism for O'Neill's reform strategies, including in many of the editorial columns of the *Belfast Telegraph*, but large numbers of unionists were at best concerned with the proposed speed of social change, while others openly feared that what was occurring would destabilize Northern Ireland and act as a first step to breaking the Union.

While Ian Paisley's candidates amassed over 20,000 votes, none were elected, meaning that Pro-O'Neill unionism could assert victory.[31] The closeness of the result meant that any assertion of a mandate for reform was much less secure, and as a result, O'Neill resigned his premiership shortly afterwards, making clear his anger at those who opposed him from within:

> There are I know today some so-called Loyalists who talk of independence from Britain – who seem to want a kind of Protestant Sinn Féin .... These people are not merely extremists. They are lunatics who would set a course along a road which could only lead at the end into an All-Ireland Republic. They are not Loyalists, but Disloyalists: disloyal to Britain, disloyal to the Constitution, disloyal to the Crown, disloyal – if they are in public life – to the solemn oaths they have sworn to Her Majesty The Queen.[32]

As the politics of the period became ever more antagonistic and frenzied, the situation on the streets continued to worsen. There had been intermittent but largely confined clashes between NICRA marchers, the RUC and loyalists throughout 1969. On 12 August, however, the Apprentice Boys were given permission to hold their annual 'Relief of Derry' parade, part of the route of which fringed the overwhelmingly nationalist Bogside. Amid much verbal abuse and exchanges of missiles, circumstances spiralled for the worst, culminating in serious rioting between the RUC and large numbers of Bogside residents that precipitated several days of street violence, in what was to become rooted in nationalist collective memory as the 'battle of the Bogside'.[33]

[29] L. Gardner, *Resurgence of the Majority* (Belfast: Ulster Vanguard Publications, 1971), 40.
[30] Ulster Unionist Party, *Declaration of Principle and Statement of Policy for the General Election, Ulster at the Crossroads* (Belfast: UUP, 1969).
[31] S. Bruce, *Paisley: Religion and Politics in Northern Ireland* (Oxford: Oxford University Press, 2007).
[32] T. O'Neill, 'Television Broadcast by Captain Terence O'Neill, Prime Minister of Northern Ireland on BBC (Northern Ireland) and Ulster Television, Monday, December 9 (Ulster Office Press Notice, London, 1968), 2.
[33] T. P. Coogan, *The Troubles: Ireland's Ordeal 1966–1996 and the Search for Peace* (Boulder, CO: Roberts Rinehart Publishers, 1997); E. McCann, *War and an Irish Town* (London: Pluto Press, 1991).

In response to events, other nationalists organized protests led to further skirmishes with the RUC. As a consequence, public order began to deteriorate rapidly across several areas of Belfast with serious incidents of violence taking place across the city on the evenings of 14th and 15th August. In particular, in the west of the city, there were confrontations between large crowds that had gathered at opposite ends of the many streets running between the Shankill lower ends of the Falls Road, which quickly escalated into serious sectarian rioting. Amid widespread claims that members of the B Specials assisted Protestant rioters and counterclaims that what was being witnessed was an armed nationalist insurrection, a large number of pubs, shops, factories and private houses were destroyed.

Eventually, the violence was only quelled when British troops were sent unto the streets of Londonderry and Belfast to restore order. By the end of the week, however, eight people had been killed and over 750 injured. Moreover, more than 400 homes and businesses, the vast majority of which were Catholic owned, had been destroyed.[34] By the 19 August, the British Army had assumed formal responsibility for the RUC, including the B-Specials, the culmination of four days of rioting, which 'may not have shaken the world, but [which] certainly shook Northern Ireland to its very foundations and decisively altered the course of its political history'.[35]

One immediate corollary of the violence was the setting up of the Hunt Committee to examine the role and function of the RUC. Amongst its recommendations were that the RUC be made an unarmed force and the B-Specials disbanded entirely and replaced by a British Army part-time regiment, the Ulster Defence Regiment (UDR), which would contain a sizeable proportion of Catholics in its ranks. Unionists reacted with undisguised hostility. On the night following the publication of Hunt's recommendations (12 October), loyalists took to the streets in numbers to protest, and during subsequent violence that erupted in the Shankill area, a UVF member shot dead RUC officer Victor Arbuckle. The political and military backlash from loyalism was beginning to take form, as was the emerging struggle between militant Republicanism and the British state.

Unionism and loyalism

As one major newspaper review of the year 1969 suggested, this year will be regarded as 'one of the most critical of all the crisis years in Irish history'.[36] Despite the cascade of reform precipitated by the demands of the civil rights movement and the public commitment by both James Chichester Clark and Harold Wilson to continued restructuring, the violence showed little sign of abating. By 1972, Northern Ireland seemed to stand on the edge of outright civil war, and Unionists had lost control of the state following the suspension of the Stormont parliament.

[34] B. Walker. 'Northern Ireland troubles: battle of the Bogside', *Belfast Telegraph*, 11 August 2009.
[35] P. Buckland, *A History of Northern Ireland* (Dublin: Gill and Macmillan Ltd, 1989), 131.
[36] *The Times*, December 31, 1969.

From its formation, the Northern Ireland state had been governed by a Unionism, which broadly representing the interests of a distinct ethno-political grouping[37] and in particular an elite fraction within it. Moreover, the dominant state narrative from 1921 had overwhelmingly reflected the dominant ethno-political character of the Protestant Unionist State. While there had been dissenting voices, both from within and without, the hegemonic position of the UUP as the party of government was never seriously questioned.[38] For almost fifty years, the unionist leadership had consistently fashioned an exclusivist and triumphalist ideology that was reproduced across the public domain in many of their speeches and public utterances.[39] This consistently pointed to the possible enemy within, in what Edward Feeney suggests was a deliberate attempt to further sectarianize Northern Irish society.[40] All the perceived certainties for unionists were now seemingly crumbling, under direct challenge from Northern Ireland's citizens and for the first time the serious scrutiny of the Westminster government.

So how can we begin to understand the Loyalist response to the loss of state control and the fragmentation of unionist hegemony? There are of course several explanations, one of which rests with those who view loyalism simply as an extreme form of unionism and consequently as irrational, impossible to reform, and acting merely as dupes of the British state.[41] This understanding of loyalism as political extremism was reinforced in 1982, by Garret FitzGerald when he presented the major differences between unionism and loyalism as a dichotomy between moderates and extremists, defining loyalism as 'loyalty to Ulster not to the Union with Britain and it is mis-described as unionism which causes a lot of confusion for everybody'.[42]

But the key differences between unionists and loyalists do not simply rest on their location on some crude sliding scale of political action, or their willingness to engage in political violence, although that may be part. Rather, the difference rests in interpretation of events and broader worldview that for some justify engagement in various actions. Identification with loyalism rests not on some scale of moderation versus extremism, but rather is positioned at the intersection between religion, ethnicity, class and social place. Unionists and loyalists may, for example, remember and commemorate many of the same events but interpret the significance of those events in different ways, giving rise to different actions and behaviour.

There are also differences in political values of loyalism and unionism. One series of events illustrates this more fully. Throughout the summer of 1975, two of the great

[37] R. G. Crawford, *Loyal to King Billy: A Portrait of the Ulster Protestants* (Dublin: Gill and MacMillan, 1987).

[38] R. English and G. Walker, *Unionism in Modern Ireland* (Dublin: Gill and Macmillan, 1996).

[39] J. D. Cash, *Identity, Ideology and Conflict: The Structuration of Politics in Northern Ireland* (Cambridge: Cambridge University Press, 1996).

[40] E. V. Feeney, 'From Reform to Resistance: A History of the Civil Rights Movement in Northern Ireland' (Unpublished PhD thesis, University of Washington, Seattle, Washington, 1974).

[41] G. Horgan, 'The state of Loyalism', *Irish Marxist Review*, 2, no. 5 (2013): 46–52; S. Mitchell, 'The permanent crisis of 21st century Ulster Unionism', *Irish Marxist Review*, 3, no. 9 (2014): 27–42.

[42] G. FitzGerald, cited in F. Cochrane, *Unionist Politics and the Politics of Unionism since the Anglo-Irish Agreement* (Cork: Cork University Press, 1997), 39.

beasts of unionism, Paisley and Enoch Powell, clashed openly surrounding the meaning and future of loyalism. The controversy erupted when Powell, who at times simply could not fathom the form of 'ethno-nationalism' expressed by many loyalists,[43] and drawing on his strong belief that the UK was a unitary nation-state[44] defined his sense of loyalism as being: 'loyal to the Crown in Parliament. The Parliament of the United Kingdom'. He continued that to be a loyalist meant accepting the will of Parliament, which he described as 'the supreme and ultimately the sole expression of the unity of the realm itself'.[45]

In presenting this argument, Powell immediately drew the wrath of Paisley, who claimed in response that Ulster loyalists bore 'no allegiance to the Wilsons and Heaths of this world'. He went on to expand as follows: 'If the Crown in Parliament decided to put Ulster into a United Ireland, according to Mr. Powell we would have to obey if we were loyal. This is utter nonsense. We would be disloyal to Her Majesty if we did not resist such a surrender to our enemies'.[46] In Paisley's mind, the justification for his definition of loyalism was clear:

> I am loyal to the Principles of the great Protestant Reformation and refuse to barter my heritage for a mess of ecumenical pottage. I am loyal to the Queen and throne of Britain, being Protestant in terms of the Revolution statement. I am loyal to Ulster, the Ulster of our founding fathers.[47]

This understanding has at various times found favour across different sections of loyalism. In the 1970s, for example, David Burnside, then of Ulster Vanguard, argued that: 'Ulster's first loyalty was to the British Crown as a Protestant established monarchy, and not to the will of the British Parliament'.[48] At the time of suspension of the Stormont government, he expanded on this perspective as follows:

> In reaching a decision to overthrow Stormont Westminster omitted to consult the wishes of the Ulster people beforehand. Vanguard has subsequently demonstrated that the action Westminster was bent on taking would not have been supported in Ulster. The ease with which the principle of consent was cast aside in order to defy the majority is a measure of the strength of Westminster's attachment to principle. Westminster resorted to the jack-boot, disguise it how they may. Jack-boot government deserves only one response from free men – resistance.[49]

---

[43] G. Walker, *A History of the Ulster Unionist Party*, 3–8; 224–225.

[44] P. Corthorn, 'Enoch Powell, Ulster Unionism, and the British Nation', *The Journal of British Studies*, 51, no. 4 (2012): 967–997.

[45] D. Brown, 'Ulster row over Powell's definition of Loyalism', *The Guardian*, 8 July 1975, 6.

[46] *Ibid*.

[47] R. Rose, *Governing without Consensus: An Irish Perspective* (Boston, MA: Beacon Press, 1971), 227.

[48] Cited in Brown, 'Ulster row over Powell's definition of Loyalism', 6.

[49] Ulster Vanguard, *Ulster – A Nation* (Belfast: Ulster Vanguard, 1972).

Such views were strongly supported by the Ulster Vanguard leader Craig, who openly defied the London government,[50] claiming that resistance was fully justified as Westminster 'had defied our wishes as the majority of the people. The government was not loyal to the crown ... (t)he government compromised the crown.'[51] Indeed, Craig was eventually to push the logic of this position to its ultimate, calling for a unilateral declaration of independence from Britain. As unionist hegemony fragmented, it witnessed growing tensions not just within the previously dominant UUP, but also across the unionist bloc. Against a backdrop of the increasingly loud political rhetoric of the Paisley's mounting political opposition, the reappearance of paramilitarism on the streets, challenges surrounding the fitness of unionist government by Westminster and an intensifying international gaze, the contours of contemporary loyalism began to take shape.

Loyal rebels

It was the consistent challenges emanating from sections of loyalism towards the authority of Westminster that earned the contempt of Powell, regarded the position of many loyalists as representing a 'Protestant Sinn Féin'. However, rather than loyalism representing what both O'Neill and Powell saw as a lunatic element of unionism, the late David Ervine of the PUP suggested a different dynamic, arguing that it was during the period working-class Protestants were forced to redefine and rework loyalism following the ideological abandonment and political isolation of that section of society by the rest of unionism.[52] Hence, with the onset of the Troubles, many Protestants rapidly sought to put distance between what they regarded as 'respectable unionism' and its working-class followers, many of whom became marginalized as loyalists.[53]

Albeit from a very different perspective, this point is broadly supported by Samuel, when he suggests that following the breakdown of civil order loyalism emerged to represent a group which 'were as alienated from the government at Westminster, as hostile to British rule, and as murderous in their modes of intimidation, as their Republican and Catholic enemies.'[54] Samuel touches here upon the notion developed

---

[50] W. Craig, 'The Future of Northern Ireland', speech made at Ulster Vanguard's First Anniversary, Belfast, 1972. See also *The Guardian*, 'William Craig obituary: Stormont minister and founder of the Ulster Vanguard movement', 26 April 2011.

[51] *The Scotsman*, 1 May 2011.

[52] T. Hennessey, 'The Evolution of Ulster Protestant Identity in the Twentieth Century: Nations and Patriotism', in *Irish Protestant Identities*, eds. M. Busteed, F. Neal, and J. Tonge, 257–270.

[53] D. Ervine, 'Redefining Loyalism: A Political Perspective', in D. Ervine and J. W. McAuley, *Redefining Loyalism*, IBIS Working Paper No. 4 (University College Dublin: Institute of British Irish Studies, 2001).

[54] Samuel, 'Four Nations History', 21.

elsewhere suggesting that the relationship between Ulster loyalists the British state is best understood as essentially contractual.[55]

Recent history is filled with examples of political skirmishes, and sometimes open conflict, between loyalists and representatives of the UK state up to and including violent confrontation with its security forces. Perhaps the most forthright example can be found in the events surrounding the Ulster Workers Council (UWC) strike of May 1974. Unionist hackles had been raised by the Sunningdale proposals seeking to introduce both power-sharing and a wider 'Irish dimension', through a Council of Ireland to the governance of Northern Ireland. While 72 per cent of Catholics supported the Council of Ireland, only 26 per cent of Protestants did so, while a majority opposed the venture.[56]

The new political era began on 1 January 1974, but within seventy-two hours, the Ulster Unionist Council (UUC), the governing body of the UUP, had voting against the deal and for the resignation of the party leader (who supported the new arrangements). The Westminster election of February 1974 saw structured unionist opposition in the shape of the United Ulster Unionist Council. Anti-Sunningdale sections of the UUP (led by Harry West), the DUP and Ulster Vanguard secured 51 per cent of the vote, winning twelve out of the thirteen seats contested.

It was not, however, Unionist Party political opposition that was to bring down Northern Ireland's devolved government, but rather actions coordinated by the UWC, which had emerged from the Loyalist Association of Workers (LAW) whose power base rested in Belfast's heavy industry. At its formation, the UWC described itself as part of 'the long awaited loyalist backlash', claiming it was 'not only our call as Loyalists, but also our duty to resist ... any possible change contemplated to our Constitution'.[57] The UWC was backed by an extensive loyalist paramilitary network, involving most centrally the UDA and UVF, and with the full support of smaller loyalist paramilitary groupings such as the Orange Volunteers, the Ulster Special Constabulary Association, Red Hand Commando (RHC), Ulster Vanguard Service Corps and Down Orange Welfare. Together, they organized, intimidated, cajoled and generally propped up the strike, which began on the morning of 15 May 1974.

Loyalists had used industrial action as a political lever before, such as in 1971, when following the initial months of Provisional IRA bombing campaign, shipyard workers had marched from their workplace to central Belfast to demand the introduction of internment. The UWC, however, marked a sea change through the organization, and implementation of what was in effect was a general strike. Although initial support was limited, the action was given momentum as loyalist

---

[55] D. W. Miller, *Queen's Rebels: Ulster Loyalism in Historical Perspective* (Dublin: Gill and Macmillan, 1978); *Queen's Rebels: Ulster Loyalism in Historical Perspective*, reprinted with a new introduction by John Bew (Dublin: University College Dublin Press, 2007); S. Nelson, *Ulster's Uncertain Defenders: Loyalists and the Northern Ireland Conflict* (Belfast: Appletree Press, 1984).

[56] P. Dixon and E. O'Kane *Northern Ireland since 1969* (Harlow: Pearson Education, 2011).

[57] Loyalist Association of Workers, 'The Long Awaited Loyalist Backlash Starts on Thursday', *LAW Newsheet*, no date, 6: 1.

paramilitaries took to the streets for the first few days to 'persuade' people of the validity of what was going on. In what Paul Foot, certainly no apologist for Ulster loyalism, once described as 'the shortest, sharpest and most successful political strike in all history',[58] for fifteen days:

> a million British citizens, the Protestants of Northern Ireland, staged what amounted to a rebellion against the Crown and won…for the first time in over fifty years…a section of the realm became totally ungovernable. A self-elected provision government of Protestant power workers, well-armed private organisations and extreme politicians organized a strike which almost broke up the fabric of civilized life in Ulster.[59]

As the strike progressed, the UWC assumed many of the functions of a government: issuing travel permits and passes to those deemed 'essential workers' and giving permission for the distribution of food and other essentials. It was, however, the support of power workers and their ability to regulate the production of electricity that proved the most effective weapon in the UWC's arsenal. Crucially, the British army was incapable of undertaking the skilled power station jobs, while the UWC made clear that any widespread intervention would result in an all-out strike by power workers and a complete halt to electricity production. Moreover, despite the insistence of Faulkner unionists and the SDLP, many in the Army were loathed to become involved in any overt conflict with the UDA or the distinct possibility of opening up hostility on two fronts.

While paramilitary intimidation may have been core to kick-starting the protest, it was other factors that determined the outcome. The arguments, if not necessary the methods of the UWC resonated with large sections of the Protestant majority, who increasingly felt fearful for a future involving the Council of Ireland, which they saw as the first step on a slippery slope to a United Ireland. Although not all supported the role of the paramilitaries as enforcers or the tactics they used, there was a broad well of sympathy across the unionist community for the strikers' objectives into which loyalists could tap. This was illustrated by the *News Letter* editorial of 16 May stating that 'No reasonable person deliberately goes out of his way to embark on a destructive course unless all other options have been closed. And in Ulster the options have been closed.'[60]

The turning point in mobilizing populist support undoubtedly was not the actions of the strikers or the paramilitaries, but rather a national public broadcast made British prime minister, Harold Wilson. Emergency talks at Chequers, with party leaders Brian Faulkner (UUP), Gerry Fitt of the Social Democratic and Labour Party (SDLP) and Oliver Napier of the Alliance Party of Northern Ireland (APNI) were to no avail. In

---

[58] P. Foot, *Ireland: Why Britain Must Get Out* (London: Chatto and Windus, 1989), 43.
[59] R. Fisk, *The Point of No Return: The Strike Which Broke the British in Ulster* (London: Andre Deutsch, 1975), 27.
[60] *News Letter*, 16 May 1974.

his broadcast, Wilson openly denounced the strikers and other Ulster Protestant supporters of the strike in the starkest of terms, claiming, for example, that:

> British parents have seen their sons vilified and spat upon and murdered. British taxpayers have seen the taxes they have poured out, almost without regard to cost – over £300 million a year this year with the cost of the Army operation on top of that – going into Northern Ireland. They see property destroyed by evil violence and are asked to pick up the bill for rebuilding it. Yet people who benefit from all this now viciously defy Westminster, purporting to act as though they were an elected government; people who spend their lives sponging on Westminster and British democracy and then systematically assault democratic methods. Who do these people think they are?[61]

Although Wilson had apparently been persuaded to drop a reference to the actions undertaken by strikers as a direct 'rebellion against the Crown',[62] he reinstated the reference to spongers despite the advice of key advisors.[63] Loyalists were outraged, but even many moderate unionists were horrified by the tone and content of Wilson's speech, which only succeeded in drawing further Protestant unionist support to the UWC action.

That the paramilitary coalition eventually succeeded in forcing the resignation of Faulkner and other unionist ministers occasioning the collapse of the embryonic cross-community power-sharing executive agreed at Sunningdale in 1973[64] accentuates what Sarah Nelson highlights as the contradictory political characteristics of loyalism, namely, they 'are loyal to Britain yet ready to disobey her … they revere law and authority, then break the law'.[65] Such views were brought into relief by Billy Mitchell, the one-time UVF activist and later a prominent member of the PUP, who often expressed the view that the relationship between the loyalist community and Britain remained essentially indentured, and that loyalism was only constrained to 'honour its obligations and fulfil its duties to Parliament so long as Parliament acknowledges and upholds our right to equal citizenship within the United Kingdom'.[66]

Such covenantal views remain central to many loyalists in defining their sense of community and the horizontal bonds that bind it together. As this leading member of the UPRG explained: 'I think that to be a loyalist is to be loyal to the Crown, sort of thing.' He continued that to be a loyalist one needed to be 'loyal to the crown and loyal to the community'.[67] This must be set in its broader context. As Farren and Mulvihill

---

[61] H. Wilson, 'On UWC Strike', 25 May 1974. Available: http://www.totalpolitics.com/speeches/labour/labour-politics-general/34883/uwc-strike.thtml; accessed 1 March 2012.

[62] Foot, *Ireland: Why Britain Must Get Out*, 43.

[63] B. Pilmlott, *Harold Wilson* (London: Harold Wilson, 1992).

[64] S. McDaid, *Template for Peace: Northern Ireland, 1972–75* (Manchester: Manchester University Press, 2013).

[65] S. Nelson, *Ulster's Uncertain Defenders*, 9.

[66] B. Mitchell, *Principles of Loyalism: An Internal Discussion Paper* (Belfast: no publisher, 2002), 6.

[67] Interview with UPRG Executive member, 5 April 2005.

highlight, the entire history of unionism 'is replete with settler and convenantal themes of dependence', but for many unionists, recent political events have dramatically altered the 'historic settler-covenantal relationship', particularly following the signing of the Anglo Irish Agreement (AIA) and later the Good Friday Agreement. Following the outworking of these agreements, for many loyalists, the extent to which unionism could depend on the British state was seen to have 'diminished greatly'.[68]

Hence, for many loyalists, Mitchell's contractual perspective is an entirely logical position, namely, that if their right to British citizenship was not to be fully endorsed and validated, then loyalists despite openly and strongly pronouncing fidelity to the Crown reserved the rights to defend it, even if this meant confrontation with the British state. For some, this position justified loyalist violence and the formation and subsequent actions of loyalist paramilitaries. While loyalist paramilitarism did prove pivotal for some working-class Protestants as an outlet for political expression, it certainly does not mean that the paramilitaries have a claim to primacy in determining contemporary loyalist politics.

Put simply, not all working-class Protestants are loyalists, (although loyalism is predominantly working class in character), not all working-class Protestants joined, or even supported the loyalist paramilitaries, and most certainly many working-class Protestants do not vote for loyalist political parties, which have normally fared badly at the ballot box. Nor by any stretch does paramilitarism, in either its military or political form, represent the gamut of loyalist, let alone working-class Protestant thought or action. Therefore, we must consider three of the basic building blocs, which go to make up a loyalist identity. These are religion, social class, a sense of Britishness, nationalism and as a form of identity politics.

Loyalism and religion

It seems to many that Protestantism and loyalism are inexorably connected. Indeed, Jennifer Todd[69] suggests that given the size, number and role of politico-religious organizations within the Protestant community, religious loyalism can be seen to be the politically dominant form of loyalism.[70] That the two are inescapably coupled may appear all too evident in viewing the public iconography of the Orange Order, or images of Paisley in full flow at the pulpit, seamlessly synthesizing the religious and the political so that at times it was all but impossible to find any difference between them. Hence, for some, it is possible to characterize the conflict as an essentially sectarian one between two religious communities[71] contesting issues long since resolved in

[68] Farren and Mulvihill, *Paths to a Settlement*, 137.
[69] J. Todd, 'Loyalism and Secularisation', in *La Sécularisation en Irlande*, ed. P. Brennan (Caen: Presses Universitaires de Caen, 1998): 197.
[70] C. Mitchell, 'Behind the ethnic marker: religion and social identification in Northern Ireland', *Sociology of Religion*, 66, no. 1 (2005): 3–21.
[71] J. Fulton, *The Tragedy of Belief: Division, Politics and Religion in Ireland* (Oxford: Clarendon Press, 1991).

the rest of Europe.[72] For others, it is the influence of evangelicalism and religious fundamentalism[73] that plays a significant role in constructing loyalist ethno-political identity and in determining the politics of loyalism.[74]

The relationship between evangelical Protestantism and loyalism may not, however, be as straightforward as many suggest. As Phillip Orr points out, for example, 'despite their self-identification as Protestants, working-class loyalists often possess very limited connection to the church'.[75] While Patrick Mitchel[76] also demonstrates that while evangelicalism may be important to individuals in organizations such as the Orange Order and the DUP, such views do not sit at the core of either of these groups, both of which he characterizes as examples of religious nationalism. Gladys Ganiel and Paul Dixon[77] support the view that the more pragmatic approach to politics demonstrated by the DUP reflects a weakening commitment to religious fundamentalism by the Party, although it is still well represented in the party leadership and amongst activists.[78]

Claire Mitchell[79] makes the proposition that despite the apparent multiplicity and variance across the Protestant community, there are clear, shared processes of identification within it. In particular, relationships between religion, community and identity remain significant in the reproduction everyday life.[80] We can return to Jennifer Todd, who importantly has positioned loyalist ideology as a broad worldview that:

Provides one of the historically most comprehensive perspectives on the Northern Protestant world, opening out to a view of the 17th century plantation which other unionist ideologies prefer to elide. Moreover, the loyalist belief system – centered

[72] L. P. Barnes, 'Was the Northern Ireland conflict religious?', *Journal of Contemporary Religion*, 20, no. 1 (2005): 55–69; 'Religion, education and conflict in Northern Ireland', *Journal of Beliefs and Values*, 26, no. 2 (2005): 123–138; I. McAllister. 'The devil, miracles and the afterlife: the political sociology of religion in Northern Ireland', *The British Journal of Sociology*, 33, no. 3 (1982): 330–347.

[73] G. Ganiel, *Evangelicalism and Conflict in Northern Ireland* (Basingstoke: Palgrave MacMillan, 2008).

[74] S. Bruce, 'Fundamentalism and political violence: the case of Paisley and Ulster Evangelicals', *Religion*, no. 31 (2001): 387–405; C. Mitchell and J. R. Tilley. 'The moral minority: evangelical Protestants in Northern Ireland and their political behaviour', *Political Studies*, no. 52 (2004): 585–602.

[75] P. Orr, *New Loyalties: Christian Faith and the Protestant Working Class* (Belfast: Centre for Contemporary Christianity in Ireland, 2008), 27.

[76] P. Mitchel, *Evangelicalism and National Identity in Ulster 1921–1998* (Oxford: Oxford University Press, 2003).

[77] G. Ganiel and P. Dixon, 'Religion, pragmatic fundamentalism and the transformation of the Northern Ireland conflict', *Journal of Peace Research*, 45, no. 3 (2008): 419–436.

[78] J. Tonge, M. Braniff, T. Hennessy, J. W. McAuley, and S. Whiting, *The Democratic Unionist Party: From Protest to Power* (Oxford: Oxford University Press, 2014)

[79] C. Mitchell, *Religion, Identity and Politics in Northern Ireland: Boundaries of Belonging and Belief* (Aldershot: Ashgate, 2006); 'The push and pull between religion and ethnicity: the case of Loyalists in Northern Ireland', *Ethnopolitics: Formerly Global Review of Ethnopolitics*, 9, no. 1 (2006): 53–69.

[80] R. Wallis, S. Bruce, and D. Taylor, *"No Surrender!" Paisleyism and the Politics of Ethnic Identity in Northern Ireland* (Belfast: Department of Social Studies, Queen's University, 1986).

on the ethnic group of Northern Protestants – exists as a potential cultural background for many unionists who explicitly reject extreme religious loyalism but who find themselves forced back on an Ulster Protestant identity in moments of crisis.[81]

As John Brewer, David Mitchell and Gerard Leavey[82] suggest, many of the stereotypes prevalent during the Troubles were based on falsehoods, including the notion that loyalists were either 'irreligious thugs or evangelical madmen'. Rather, in reality, 'Combatant groups contained the array of religious commitment and unbelief found in the wider society'.[83]

Class structure of loyalism

In assessing and positioning contemporary loyalism, we should never loose sight of the salience of social class. While not all loyalists are from the same socio-economic background, class remains a key focus for political orientation from within loyalism, and a consistent point of cohesion within for that community. Class is central in generating a sense of identity that is 'fashioned from literal everyday experiences of social actors'.[84] While there are distinctions between unionism and loyalism surrounding the perceived nature of their relationship to the British state, it is class that continues to play a central role in defining loyalist identity.

While the story of contemporary loyalism is overtly defined by resistance to Irish republicanism, it is also cemented by its lack of trust of successive Westminster governments and its resentment of middle-class unionism, which after the beginning of the Troubles many loyalists believe abandoned them not just politically, but also to face the harsh realities of de-industrialization, community break-up and the responsibility of the struggle with the Provisional IRA. Moreover, for many, the class gap within unionism has continued to widen. This point is certainly recognized by John Kyle of the PUP who argues:

> By and large middle class Unionists simply do not understand Loyalists, they lack an appreciation of their everyday lives, their culture, their struggles, their deprivations, their fears and their aspirations. They are angered by the obduracy and stubbornness of Loyalists, dismissive of their concerns and scathingly critical of their actions. Their lives intersect infrequently.[85]

---

[81] Todd, 'Loyalism and secularisation', 197.
[82] J. Brewer, D. Mitchell, and G. Leavey, *Ex-Combatants, Religion and Peace in Northern Ireland* (Basingstoke: Palgrave Macmillan, 2013).
[83] Brewer, et al., *Ex-Combatants, Religion and Peace in Northern Ireland*, 44.
[84] C. Coulter, 'The character of unionism', *Irish Political Studies*, 9, no. 1 (1994): 1–24.
[85] J. Kyle, 'Talking with Loyalists … is anybody listening?'. Available at: http://blogs.qub.ac.uk/compromiseafterconflict/2013/11/02/talking-with-loyalists-is-anybody-listening/; accessed 17 March 2014.

Following the outbreak of the conflict, the subsequent public distancing of most mainstream unionist political representatives from those engaged in organized loyalist violence directly reflected the class cleavages within unionism. As this loyalist put it:

> unionists tried to define loyalism as only being working class people, they'd say they're working class, and that they wouldn't see themselves as having anything to do with us ones or anything like that. There's definitely a class politics, I see it.[86]

Another had this to say:

> ... there's a difference between unionism and loyalism. I mean the middle classes and the upper classes would use unionism. They think it's a class issue, that there's classes and they're in a better one – they're better than us. That we're just the dirt on their shoes, sort of thing, that we are definitely not the same as them sort of people and we are.[87]

Ulster loyalism: a very peculiar Britishness?

These differing understandings of loyalism manifested in diverse guises, finding outlet through a range of political organizations. Ulster loyalists are involved in the invention and reinvention of what it is to be a loyalist, including those of constructing national identity and national ideology. The most common expression of this is through an overt attachment to Britishness or the overt articulation of a British identity.[88] It is the strength of this sense of being British that explains why Ulster loyalism is often seen is as a forceful variant of British nationalism.[89] This sense of loyalism draws on a wide range of symbolism elicited from across the broad iconography of Britishness, both past and present, from both Britain itself and from across its former Empire. While recognizing that 'Britishness is a problematic type of nationalism',[90] an understanding of the specific form of Britishness,[91] history and memory to which loyalists attach is central to understanding their sense of identity and the politics emanating from this.

There is a reworking of those political memories that are seen as most prominent across the generations,[92] and current events are interpreted through everyday

---

[86] Interview with UPRG Executive member, 5 April 2005.

[87] Interview with UPRG Executive member, 6 April 2005.

[88] M. Crozier, ed. *Cultural Traditions in Northern Ireland: Varieties of Britishness* (Belfast: QUB, Institute of Irish Studies, 1990).

[89] J. McGarry and B. O'Leary, *Explaining Northern Ireland* (Oxford: Blackwell, 1995), 92–93.

[90] C. Farrington and G. Walker, 'Ideological content and institutional frameworks: Unionist identities in Northern Ireland and Scotland', *Irish Studies Review* 17, no. 2 (2009): 135.

[91] A. Heath, C. Rothon, and R. Andersen, 'Who Feels British' (Working Paper No. 5, University of Oxford: Department of Sociology, 2005).

[92] P. Devine-Wright, 'Identity, memory and the social status of groups in Northern Ireland: Relating processes of social remembering with beliefs about the structure of society', *Irish Journal of Psychology*, 22, no. 2 (2001): 1–21; 'A Theoretical Overview of Memory and Conflict'.

experiences and collective readings of the past. Elsewhere, Tom Hennessey[93] has usefully expanded on the changing emphasis in self-understandings in and between unionism and loyalism, throughout the course of the twentieth century. Immediately before the Troubles, many were content to express some form of Ulster British identity, similar to those in Scotland at the time that were able to fully conceive of a Scottish-British expression of identity.

Indeed, the classic study by Richard Rose clearly indicates how varied was the primary sense of national identification amongst Protestants at the outbreak of the Troubles, with 20 per cent seeing themselves as Irish, 39 per cent as British, 32 per cent as Ulster, 6 per cent sometimes British and sometimes Irish, 2 per cent Anglo-Irish and 1 per cent do not know. Moreover, as Colin Coulter points out, it was only following widespread political agitation by Irish nationalism that 'Irishness' and 'Britishness' were seen as essentially incompatible. Further, as:

> the demand for national autonomy gathered pace, unionists came increasingly to accept this particular reading. Throughout the (twentieth) century the unionist community has gradually demoted feelings of 'Irishness' in favour of a sense of Britishness.[94]

This point has been expanded upon by Hennessey,[95] who is forthright in his claim that it was the IRA campaign that cemented Ulster Protestant identity and gave coherence to their sense of Britishness. Further, Bruce[96] argues that while many of the social and political changes experienced by loyalists may well have occurred anyway, because of broader socio-economic changes which were underway globally, they instead perceive almost all of the social problems that have arisen as the direct result of IRA violence and a republican conspiracy.

In turn, such views reinforced loyalist self-identity and the heightened conflicting senses of the Self and of the Other, reinforcing social cleavages along these lines. The notion of belonging has remained central to loyalist identities, particularly in the context of what Bauman[97] points to as the building of the strongest collectives when they feel threatened by a recognized 'Other'.[98] One response was that loyalist identification with Britishness, which often took such an overt and unconcealed form, has been referred to as 'hyper loyalty'.[99] For Michael Ignatief, [100] this is best

---

[93] Hennessey, 'The Evolution of Ulster Protestant Identity', 257–270.

[94] C. Coulter, *Contemporary Northern Irish Society: An Introduction* (London: Pluto, 1999), 22.

[95] Hennessey, 'The Evolution of Ulster Protestant Identity', 261–267.

[96] S. Bruce, *The Red Hand: Protestant Paramilitaries in Northern Ireland* (Oxford: Oxford University Press, 1992); *The Edge of the Union*.

[97] Z. Bauman, *Culture as Praxis. Theory, Culture and Society* (London: Sage, 1999).

[98] M. Fitzduff and C. Gormley, 'Northern Ireland: changing perceptions of the "other"', *Development*, 43, no. 3 (2000): 62–65.

[99] A. Heath, C. Rothon, and R. Andersen, 'Who Feels British', Working Paper No. 5, (University of Oxford: Department of Sociology, 2005).

[100] R. Inglehart, *Modernization and Postmodernization: Cultural, Economic, and Political Change in 43 Societies* (Princeton, NJ: Princeton University Press, 1993).

understood as extreme British nationalism positioning loyalist Ulster as the utmost expression of Britishness within the UK.

Other commentators such as Pamela Clayton[101] have sought to locate loyalism directly in the context of post-colonial situation and its politics as the legacy of Northern Ireland as a settler society. This approach is developed by John Wilson Foster[102] and Liam O'Dowd,[103] who both draw on the conceptualization of settler – colonist relationships offered by Albert Memmi[104] to frame and define what they see as the distinct nature of loyalty found amongst of Ulster Protestants as akin to that in other colonial settler communities. In seeking to characterize the political response of loyalism, he recognizes the uncertainty of the loyalist position, citing Memmi's belief that the colonist 'is seized with worry and panic each time there is talk of changing the political status'.[105] Such views are reflected by Bob Rowthorn and Naomi Wayne, who propose that at the core of loyalism rests those social relationships created by Northern Ireland as a relic of Empire, within which the 'Protestant community, descendants of the original settlers to colonize Ireland more than three hundred years ago, still behaves as a settler community surrounded by hostile natives'.[106]

If loyalism is really to be accurately defined through the connection with a mainland core, however, it seemingly has resulted in an extremely unbalanced and uneasy relationship. Powell was constantly at pains to point out that the English state since 1919 has been determined to rid the United Kingdom of the province.[107] More broadly, it seems of little concern to many loyalist and unionists that when wider debates around Britishness have become prominent in public discourses, such as when Prime Ministers Brown and Cameron have openly deliberated concerning the nature of Britishness,[108] that these discussions have largely excluded Northern Ireland has as a reference point.[109]

---

[101] Clayton, *Enemies and Passing Friends*; 'Religion, Ethnicity and Colonialism as Explanations of the Northern Ireland Conflict', in *Rethinking Northern Ireland: culture, ideology and colonialism*, ed. D. Miller (London: Longman, 1998), 40–54.

[102] J. W. Foster, *Colonial Consequences: Essays in Irish Literature and Culture* (Dublin: Lilliput Press, 1991).

[103] L. O'Dowd. 'New Introduction', in *The Colonizer and the Colonized*, ed. A. Memmi (London: Earthscan, 1990), 29–66.

[104] A. Memmi, *Dependence: A Sketch for a Portrait of the Dependent*, translated by Philip A. Facey (Boston: Beacon Press, 1984); *The Colonizer and the Colonized*, introduction by Jean-Paul Sartre; afterword by Susan Gilson Miller, translated by Howard Greenfeld (Boston: Beacon Press, 1991); *Decolonization and the Decolonized*, translated by Robert Bononno (Minneapolis: University of Minnesota Press, 2006).

[105] Foster, *Colonial Consequences*, 266.

[106] B. Rowthorn and N. Wayne, *Northern Ireland: The Political Economy of Conflict* (Cambridge: Polity Press, 1988), 166.

[107] S. Heffer, *Like the Roman: The Life of Enoch Powell* (London: Weidenfeld and Nicolson, 1998).

[108] D. Cameron and D. Jones, *Cameron on Cameron: Conversations with Dylan Jones*, (London: Fourth Estate, 2008), 136–139.

[109] See material in M. D'ancona, ed. *Being British: The Search for the Values That Bind the Nation* (Edinburgh: Mainstream Publishing, 2009).

The non-reciprocal nature between unionism and parts of the British polity has been noted[110] and explored in some depth by Fergal Cochrane, who concludes that for the British, unionists were best thought of as 'adopted children rather than blood-kin'.[111] The feelings of insecurity expressed by many loyalists came to a head in the mid-1980s with their focus on the belief that the British government was no longer willing directly to defend their interests. They argue that this is because they had uncritically taken onboard the political analysis of the pan-nationalism (seen to be made up of the Irish government, the White House, the Irish American lobby and the republican movement). This was seen to become a central organizational principle of the peace process.[112] The insecurities felt by broad sections of Unionism and loyalism were neatly summarized in a *News Letter* editorial as follows:

> Unionism believes its traditions, culture and way of life are under threat from the pan-nationalist front, and what is perceived as a spineless, ungrateful, or even perfidious parent (Great Britain) across the Irish Sea.[113]

In response, many unionists feel the best rejoinder is to draw on deeply embedded collective memories of an idealized version of the Union. Even against a background of growing demands for Scottish independence, there is often little acknowledgement by large sections of loyalism (and unionism more widely) of just how far devolution has altered the institutional and democratic relationships between Westminster and the other constitutional hubs within the UK.[114] Other crucial trends involving the end of Empire, globalization,[115] migration or the emergence of a more culturally pluralist society remain in the background of the loyalist mind.

Nor apparently within unionism is there much appreciation of how the concept of Britishness is now a less homogeneous, intricate and multi-layered concept than it once was,[116] or just how contested the notion now is at the everyday level is across the UK.[117] As Bill Rolston suggests, loyalist allegiance is often to 'an imagined Britain rather than the reality of a society moving beyond the old assurances of empire, religious observance, and industry to a more liberal, multicultural and post-modern world'.[118] Moreover, loyalists (and most cultural unionists) are often seen to project a

---

[110] A. Brown, D. McCrone, and L. Paterson, *Politics and Society in Scotland* (Basingstoke: Palgrave Macmillan, 1996).

[111] Cochrane, *Unionist Politics and the Politics of Unionism since the Anglo-Irish Agreement*, 387.

[112] *Belfast Telegraph*, 11 June 2002.

[113] *News Letter*, 22 November 2001.

[114] V. Ware, *Who Cares about Britishness?: A Global View of the National Identity Debate* (London: Arcadia Books, 2007).

[115] M. Savage, G. Bagnall, and B. Longhurst, *Globalisation and Belonging* (London: Sage, 2005).

[116] Y. Alibhai-Brown, 'Muddled leaders and the future of the British National identity', *The Political Quarterly*, 71, no. 1 (2000): 26–30.

[117] A. Aughey, 'On Britishness', *Irish Studies in International Affairs*, no. 14 (2003): 45–56; 'The wager of devolution and the challenge to Britishness', *The Political Quarterly*, 78, no. 1 (2007): 136–148; 'Northern Ireland narratives of British democracy', *Policy Studies*, 33, no. 2 (2012): 145–158.

[118] B. Rolston, 'Dealing with the past: pro-state paramilitaries, truth and transition in Northern Ireland', *Human Rights Quarterly*, 28, no. 3 (2006): 659.

form of Britishness unrecognized and unrecognizable in other parts of the UK.[119] As John Barry argues, the relationship has often proved troublesome, and that unionist culture and collective identity:

> are problematic to the extent that their sense of 'Britishness' requires some recognition and acknowledgement of this from the British people and the British state. But since this recognition and affirmation is not forthcoming, this leaves the Ulster unionist identity unstable and unsure.[120]

This point was made by the former secretary of state for Northern Ireland, Peter Hain, who in addressing Ulster unionists argued that they should recognize the 'Union itself is evolving – it is not fossilized – and Northern Ireland cannot proceed as if it was hermetically sealed from that development'. Elsewhere, Hain has sought to articulate the difficulty the British state has in understanding loyalists, and in particular their refusal to recognize that 'the constitutional source of insecurity has been removed', and the unionists' position had 'never been less precarious in their entire history than it is now'.[121]

In so doing, Hain was drawing on the wider populist views of Northern Irish politics held by many, and consciously or not, highlighting a further paradox for unionism brought about by devolution. At a populist level, the conflict is seen as resolved and its status confirmed as a place apart. One consequence is that the more loyalists strive to display their particular sense of 'Britishness', the more it becomes apparent that the wider 'British public is… entirely uncomprehending of [loyalist] history, attitudes and culture'.[122] Further, for some, their current sense of loyalist identity draws on particular parts of collective memory seeking to locate a national past within a contemporary that is multi-ethnic. As a result, those seemingly symbolically closest to loyalism are found only in the most traditional sections of the Conservative Party and the British far-right extremism.

While in the contemporary period there is evidence of engagement by some from loyalist backgrounds in racist violence, this remains far from central to Loyalist ideology or political action. Evidence of racist violence undertaken by those who would term themselves as loyalists is readily available, but the substantiation of any structural involvement by Loyalist paramilitary groups is much less assured.[123] This is not to deny the significance of the social dynamics and politics of inclusion and exclusion in Northern Ireland, nor the possibility of particular social groups being racialized within that society. However, the notions that there is unison in the ideology and goals

---

[119] K. Meagher, 'Loyalism's one-sided love affair with the British state', *Labour Uncut*, 11 December 2012.

[120] J. Barry, 'National Identities, Historical Narratives and Patron States in Northern Ireland', in *Political Loyalty and the Nation-State*, eds. M. Waller and A. Linklater (London: Routledge, 2003), 190.

[121] *News Letter*, 11 September 2006.

[122] Bruce, *The Edge of the Union*.

[123] C. Steenkamp, *Violence and Post-War Reconstruction: Managing Insecurity in the Aftermath of Peace Accords* (London: I. B. Tauris, 2009).

of loyalism and the aims of British extreme Right, beyond a strong commitment to the Union, or that synergy exists because both groups because of overt displays of their strong affiliation to their sense of Britishness must be approached with some caution.

Loyalism as nationalism

Other social forces crosscut the dominant construct of Britishness amongst loyalism: most notably social class, together with varying forms of religious affiliation, regional attachment and sometimes gender. All have some impact on how British and loyalist identity are felt and expressed. What all these constructs of loyalism share in common, however, is a rejection of Irishness, and it is through this sense of belonging that loyalism seeks to create an inclusive sense of identity, which has led some to describe Northern Ireland a nation.

The concept of nationhood is constructed in complex ways around cultural and political collectivities[124] and defined through processes, which involve symbolism,[125] constructed traditions[126] and an attachment to agreed values and meanings.[127] Importantly, Michael Billig[128] has developed the concept of 'banal nationalism', while others have usefully introduced ideas concerning how nationalism is reproduced through the everyday,[129] the mundane and sometimes even the humdrum replication of its core cultural aspects.[130]

One consequence of these competing understandings has been that emblems have been used in differing ways by various fractions of unionism and loyalism to explain and support their political positions.[131] This in part involves a reappraisal by unionists of their own history and traditions, and the construction of a separate set of foundation myths, to produce a framework for understanding the past.[132] These are interconnected and made concurrent through a narrative that amongst much else addresses the Scots-Irish connection,[133] the settlement of the Protestant 'nation' in Ireland, the siege of Derry during the seventeenth century, blood sacrifice at the Somme, resistance to Home Rule and the signing of the Ulster Covenant, the formation of the Northern Irish state and the commitment made to the Allied cause during the Second World War. Others have used different foundation stories, such as those involving the Cruthin

---

[124] J. Breuilly, *Nationalism and the State* (Manchester: Manchester University Press, 1982).

[125] A. P. Cohen, *The Symbolic Construction of Community* (London: Routledge, 1985).

[126] E. Hobsbawm, 'Introduction', in *The Invention of Tradition*, eds. E. Hobsbawm and T. Ranger (Cambridge: CUP, 1984), 1–14.

[127] S. Reicher and N. Hopkins, *Self and Nation* (London: Sage, 2000).

[128] Billig, *Banal Nationalism*.

[129] T. Edensor, *National Identity, Popular Culture and Everyday Life* (Oxford: Berg, 2002).

[130] J. Hutchinson, 'Ethnicity and modern nations', *Ethnic and Racial Studies*, 23, no. 4 (2000): 651–659.

[131] N. Morag, 'The emerald isle: Ireland and the clash of Irish and Ulster-British nationalisms', *National Identities*, 10, no. 3 (2008): 263–280.

[132] B. Anderson, *Imagined Communities* (London: Verso, 1991).

[133] See K. Radford, 'Creating an Ulster Scots Revival', *Peace Review*, 13, no. 1 (2001): 51–57.

or Cuchulainn[134] as the justification underpinning the existence of a distinct people, the justification for an independent state and for some even as an attempt to invent a tradition for Protestant Ulster nation.[135]

Perhaps the leading proponent in promoting a core Ulster identity beyond any Gaelic essence is Ian Adamson,[136] who seeks to locate Ulster's distinctiveness in prehistory, arguing that rather than being the original inhabitants of Ireland, the Gaels merely displaced a pre-existing race, the Cruthin. Accordingly, they were driven north in face of Gaelic military advance and compelled to draw on pre-existing links to retreat, forced to undertake a mass migration to seek sanctuary in what is now Scotland. Crucially therefore, Adamson argues that because of this history, the plantation of Ulster in the sixteenth and seventeenth centuries marks a home coming rather than a colonization and that today's strong cultural links between the West of Scotland and Northern Ireland can be traced back to that point.

Elsewhere, inspired in part at least by Adamson's work, the UDA in the 1980s actively promoted the mythical hero Cuchuliann as a champion of Ulster defending its borders from invaders, presenting themselves in similar light for contemporary times. That the accuracy of Adamson's account is questioned, or that the Cuchulainn story originates in a set of ancient Irish mythical tales, is probably of less consequence than the attempted use to construct a different foundation myth. Central here is what Brian Graham calls an 'origin-legend'[137] and a narrative of reinforcing the separation of Ulster, in the contemporary form of the six county Northern Ireland, from both the remainder of the UK and the Republic of Ireland, and the belief that partition represents a natural division of the Island. Core too was the attempt to refute the Irish nationalist account, in the case of the UDA and Ulster Scots overtly so, by constructing counter-narratives[138] to challenge the primacy of the Gaelic 'ownership' of Ireland.[139]

While the historical tale and narrative differs, the social role of remembering is reinforced to claim a distinct sense of belonging, which has manifested in notions of Ulster's separateness from the rest of the Island. Thus, the commonplace use of the term Ulster by unionists and loyalists, or as in the case of Paisley the frequently use

---

[134] J. W. McAuley, 'Cuchulainn and an RPG-7: The Ideology and Politics of the UDA', in E. Hughes (ed.) *Culture and Politics in Northern Ireland* (Milton Keynes: Open University Press, 1991), 44–68.

[135] J. Anderson, 'Review of D. G. Pringle – One Island, Two Nations?: A political-geographical analysis of the national conflict in Ireland', *Annals of the Association of American Geographers*, 77, no. 3 (1987): 486–489.

[136] I. Adamson, *Cruthin: The Ancient Kindred* (Newtownards: Nosmada, 1974); *Identity of Ulster: The Land, the Language and the People* (Belfast: Pretani, 1982); *Ulster People: Ancient, Medieval and Modern* (Bangor: Pretani Press, 1991).

[137] B. Graham, ed. *In Search of Ireland: A Cultural Geography* (London: Routledge, 1997).

[138] See K. Stapleton and J. Wilson, 'A Discursive Approach to Cultural Identity: The Case of Ulster Scots', *Belfast Working Papers in Language and Linguistics* 16 (Belfast: University of Ulster, 2003): 57–71; 'Ulster Scots Identity and Culture: The Missing Voices', *Identities: Global Studies in Culture and Power* 11 (2004): 563–591.

[139] C. McCall, 'Political transformation and the reinvention of the Ulster-Scots identity and culture', *Identities* 9, no. 2 (2002): 197–218.

of the term the 'Ulster people', usually to mean the Protestant unionist community, as an equivalent to Northern Ireland, implies that it represents a recognized and uncontested division of territory. For some, the continued use of the term represents a latent form of 'embryonic nationalism; or, at the least, a state of mind out of which national, rather than merely regional, distinctiveness might, in certain circumstances emerge'.[140]

There is also a history of some loyalists treating their sense of identification with Britishness as a symbol of nation, rather than state. Such ideas were, of course, first aired during the Home Rule crisis, when the proposition that there were two distinct peoples in Ireland found favour with anti-Home Rulers including the British Conservative politician Bonar Law as a way of justifying partition. The notion of two nations on the Island resurfaced in a somewhat different form in the early 1960s when Marcus Heslinga[141] proposed that the extent and depth of clear cultural differences between a Catholic Irish nation and a Protestant Ulster nation justified partition. Following the outbreak of the conflict, the argument reappeared in a much more politicized form driven by the British and Irish Communist Organisation (BICO), which argued that the Island contained two distinct, if overlapping nations, both of which had rights which needed to be recognized in any future democratic settlement. Throughout the early 1970s, the BICO continued to develop this theoretical position arguing that the uneven expansion of capitalism across Ireland had given rise to the development of two nations in Ireland.[142]

Hence, for BICO, the Protestants of the north constitute a separate nation with the right to self-determination and partition of the Island was not only economically inevitable but actually represented the best interests of the Ulster working class.[143] Elsewhere, loyalism has occasionally lapsed directly into the pursuit of Ulster nationalism, (often as a fall back or position of last resort). One version of this manifested in the version of negotiated Independent Ulster outlined in plans by sections of the UDA[144] as a solution to the conflict. This rested upon what it claimed was the 'common Ulster identity' of the province's Catholic and Protestant peoples. A starker version is found in the 'doomsday plan' drawn up by the UDA in 1994 to repartition Northern Ireland in order to 'establish an ethnic Protestant Homeland' in the case of British withdrawal and in the calls made by Ulster Vanguard in the early 1970s for a Unilateral Declaration of Independence following the suspension

---

[140] J. C. Beckett, *The Making of Modern Ireland, 1603–1923* (London: Faber and Faber, 2011), 147.

[141] M. W. Heslinga, *The Irish Border as a Cultural Divide: A Contribution to the Study of Regionalism in the British Isles* (Assen: Van Gorcum, 1962, 1979, 2e).

[142] British and Irish Communist Organisation, *Ireland – Two Nations* (Belfast: Athol Press, 1971); *On the Democratic Validity of the Northern Ireland State* – Policy Statement No. 2 (Belfast: Athol Press), 171.

[143] British and Irish Communist Organisation, *The Home Rule Crisis* (Belfast: Athol Press, 1972); *The Economics of Partition* (Belfast: Athol Press, 1972); *The Birth of Ulster Unionism* (Belfast: Athol Press, 1984).

[144] New Ulster Political Research Group, *Beyond the Religious Divide* (Belfast: NUPRG, 1979); Ulster Political Research Group, *Common Sense* (Belfast: UPRG, 1984).

of the Stormont administration.[145] Much of this was on the basis that the demise of the Stormont parliament marked a broken contract with the Protestant people of Northern Ireland.[146]

From a different political stance, Tom Nairn supports the view of a disjuncture between Ulster unionism and nationalism, claiming that ensnared 'between past and future, Ulster Protestantism was unable to formulate the normal political response of threatened societies: nationalism',[147] although elsewhere he suggests that events surrounding the UWC strike saw the full-blown emergence of Ulster nationalism and 'made the Ulster nation'.[148] David W. Miller[149] has also articulated a coherent argument against Ulster nationalism proposing that Ulster loyalists do not possess all the characteristics necessary to claim full-blown nationhood, being neither a full part of the British nor Irish nation. The main allegiance of Ulster Protestants is as members of a community 'whose only instinctive allegiance is to each other'.[150]

For both Michael Gallagher[151] and David W. Miller, it is not the classification of Ulster Protestants as a distinct community or their claims to self-determination that mark the most crucial feature of Ulster loyalist identity. Rather, what is most important is the nature of the professed loyalty to Britain, which is always conditional on the continuance of the existing constitutional position. It is this that marks one of the key drivers within Ulster loyalist political culture. Although it is never fully developed elsewhere, the kernel of Miller's argument is mirrored in other works, such as those by Bruce, who argues that the most dramatic change in the recent period has been a changing emphasis in unionist identity, whereby now many consider themselves 'Ulster Protestants first and British second'.[152] In part, this reflects Miller's argument that loyalists constitute what he terms a pre-nationalist group, contending that what has emerged was a conflict between an Irish Catholic Nationalist 'nation' and an Irish Protestant Unionist 'community'.

Loyalism as identity politics

As can be see from the above, it is possible to recognize a variety of sources from which loyalism constructs its core senses of identity and belonging. The strength of

[145] G. Watson, ' "Meticulously crafted ambiguities": the confused political vision of Ulster Vanguard', *Irish Political Studies*, 28, no. 4 (2013): 536–562.

[146] Craig, 'The Future of Northern Ireland'.

[147] T. Nairn, *The Break-Up of Britain* (London: New Left Books, 1977), 236.

[148] Nairn, *The Break-Up of Britain*, 242.

[149] Miller, *Queen's Rebels*.

[150] M. Gallagher, 'How many nations are there in Ireland?', *Ethnic and Racial Studies*, 18, no. 4 (1995): 723.

[151] M. Gallagher, 'Do Ulster Unionists have a right to self-determination', *Irish Political Studies*, 5, (1990): 11–30.

[152] Bruce, *The Edge of the Union*, 1.

the bonds to British identity within loyalism was clearly highlighted by Billy Mitchell of the PUP when he explained that for him:

> The conflict in Northern Ireland is not about economics, religion or ethnicity. It is about identity and belonging. Those of us of Scottish and Anglican extraction, whose families have been a part of this island's history for more than 300 years, regard ourselves as the real British presence in Ireland.[153]

Here it is useful to return to Bauman, who provides the following insight into the construction of confident identities, by pointing out that few:

> thoughts are given to identity when 'belonging' comes naturally, when it does not need to be fought for, earned claimed and defended; when one 'belongs' just by going through the motions which seem obvious simply thanks to the absence of competitors.[154]

If we consider identity through this lens, we are continually drawn back to issues of ontological security and loyalism as an expression of politics constructed in part in relation to notions of threatened physical, political and ideological space. This provides points of common identification that bind loyalists together as a social group through shared reference points from which individuals construct their social world.

Importantly, as Henri Tajfel reminds us, peoples' knowledge that they belong to a specific social group 'together with [the] emotional and value significance...of group membership'[155] is central to their sense of social being and their place in society. Although it is sometimes understood in different ways by different disciplines, the concept of social identity has become central in providing a 'conceptual bridge between individual and group levels of analysis'.[156] Social groups do not exist just in themselves, but also in relation to other social groups.

Accordingly, social identity is constructed not just in terms of self-categorization, but also in relation to others. A positive social identity, based on the distinctiveness of the group, manifests through the promotion of the 'in-group', and the perceived value in membership of that group over all others.[157] In this sense, loyalist identity is constructed in part through continued polarization, not only from Irish nationalism and republicanism, but also from different fractions of unionism. Through these processes, people establish, develop and nurture an identity defining both senses of

---

[153] B. Mitchell, 'A Union of Diversity', *The Observer*, 18 June 2000.

[154] Z. Bauman, *Culture as Praxis. Theory, Culture and Society* (London: Sage, 1999), 47, emphasis in original.

[155] H. Tajfel, 'Social Categorization'. English manuscript of 'La catégorisation sociale', in S. Moscovici (ed.) *Introduction à la Psychologie Sociale*, 1 (Paris: Larousse, 1972): 292.

[156] M. Brewer, 'The many faces of social identity: implications for political psychology', *Political Psychology*, 22, no. 1 (2001): 115–125.

[157] H. Tajfel, *Differentiation between Social Groups: Studies in the Social Psychology of Intergroup Behaviour* (London: Academic Press, 1978).

Self and the relationships between Self, group and the construction of the Other,[158] which is often framed as dangerous, untrustworthy and illegitimate.

These understandings, of both belonging and exclusion, have profound meaning within loyalism. Hence, writing in the early 1970s, Martin Wallace explaining how these senses of difference find expression points not just to historical fears of Roman Catholicism, and/or of coming under an Irish parliament dominated by the Catholic Church, but also:

> an accompanying fear of betrayal; Ulster has its own word for traitor, 'Lundy', recalling a seventeenth-century governor of Londonderry who was prepared to yield the city to Catholic James II.[159]

The direct relevance of Lundy in the construction of the loyalist narrative will be discussed further in Chapter 3. Broadly, however, becoming an in-group member involves absorbing and adopting the ideology, culture and values of the group[160] and continued membership demands unquestioned loyalty and overt commitment (qualities that Lundy was seen not to possess) to those principles in order to continue to distinguish and a clear separation from the Other. Described in classic terms by Said,[161] these processes of inclusion and exclusion involve the definition of the Other, not just as different, but also as inferior, often seen as a dangerous enemy.

The perceived role of the dangerous Other plays a central part in coalescing loyalism identity, as the group must observe eternal vigilance and be ever wary of the traitor within. This identity is further compounded by the presence of sectarianized social relations and social space, one consequence of which is that those living within districts that tend towards either all Protestant or all Catholic exclusivity express higher levels of within-group cohesion and stronger levels of prejudice towards the other ethno-political groups than those living in mixed districts.[162]

Identity relies on the formation and maintenance of boundaries,[163] which confirms the understanding of 'us' and 'them', through the identification of those seen as alike and the marginalization of the Other. Here, Jenkins[164] usefully reminds us what is being discussed is not identity *per se* but rather processes of 'identification'. In divided

---

[158] J. Epstein, 'Remember to Forget: The Problem of Traumatic Cultural Memory', in *Shaping Losses: Cultural Memory and the Holocaust*, eds. J. Epstein and L. H. Lefkovitz (Chicago: University of Illinois Press, 2001), 186–204.

[159] M. Wallace, *Drums and Guns: Revolution in Ulster* (London: Geoffrey Chapman, 1970), 27.

[160] J. C. Turner, 'Social Categorization, Social Identity and Social Comparisons', in *Differentiation between Social Groups: Studies in the Social Psychology of Intergroup Relations*, ed. H. Tajfel (London: Academic Press, 1978), 61–76.

[161] E. Said, *Orientalism* (Hammondworth: Penguin, 1978).

[162] K. Schmid, M. Hewstone, J. Hughes, R. Jenkins, and E. Cairns, 'Residential Segregation and Intergroup Contact: Consequences for Intergroup Relations, Social Capital and Social Identity', in *Theorizing Identities and Social Action*, ed. M. Wetherell (Basingstoke: Palgrave Macmillan, 2009), 177–197.

[163] Z. Bauman, *Community* (London, Polity Press, 2001).

[164] R. Jenkins, *Social Identity* (London: Routledge, 1996).

societies such as Northern Ireland, where even in times of lessened conflict the level of social interaction between groups is limited, one of the dominant social relationships remains the sectarianized identification and rejection of the 'them' by the 'us'.[165]

In part at least, this draws on the collective memory of loyalism that provides a particular narrative of conflict, highlighting its origins reasons and course as forming the basis for identifying the Other. It is a narrative that emphasizes and in turn is strengthened by notions of us and them, whereby events are interpreted through a closed narrative offering only extremely limited interpretations of the past, and presenting the Other as the instigators of conflict and the cause of its prolongation. As such, this is typical of conflict discourses elsewhere in constructing a durable notion of a different and menacing Other.[166] The more intimidating or threatening the Other is seen, the greater the contrast is, and in the case of loyalists in Northern Ireland all republicans and nationalists (and therefore most Catholics) were quickly reinforced as a dangerous Other.

In placing these groups within this category, they were deemed as untrustworthy and disloyal and, therefore, excluded from the dominant political culture and social structure of the state.[167] Often, this construction was completed through a variety of negative stereotypes, applied to describe the oppositional community, and used to reinforce senses of inclusion and exclusion, seen to exist outside the social and moral boundaries of one's own community. More often than not in Northern Ireland this manifests as sectarian difference, and for some, the feeling of hostility aroused towards the Other is so intense as to legitimize a violent repost.[168] One part of such identity formation involves drawing on processes of stereotyping, through which people distinguish between Self and Other, defining themselves and their group in positive ways. For Tajfel,[169] such stereotypes serve three main functions: scapegoating the other, providing social justification for the actions of the in-group and emphasizing senses of social differentiation, which in Northern Ireland manifest most directly as sectarian differentiation.

During the Troubles, these differences were intensified and amplified through exposure to protracted violence, whether directly or indirectly experienced, and for some, the resulting negative characterization of the Other intensified to the point

---

[165] H. Tajfel and J. C. Turner, 'An Integrative Theory of Intergroup Conflict', in *The Social Psychology of Intergroup Relations*, eds. W. G. Austin and S. Worchel (Monterey, CA: Brooks/Cole, 1979): 33–47; 'The Social Identity Theory of Intergroup Behavior', in *Psychology of Intergroup Relations*, eds. S. Worchel and W. G. Austin (Chicago, IL: Nelson-Hall, 1986), 7–24.

[166] D. S. Bell, 'Mythscapes: memory, mythology, and national identity', *British Journal of Sociology*, 54, no. 1 (2003): 63–81; J. Edkins, *Trauma and the Memory of Politics* (Cambridge: Cambridge University Press, 2003).

[167] R. Kearney, *Postnationalist Ireland* (London: Routledge, 1997); R. White, 'Social and Role Identities and Political Violence: Identity as a Window on Violence in Northern Ireland', in *Social Identity, Intergroup Conflict, and Conflict Resolution*, eds. R. D. Ashmore, L. Jussim, and D. Wilder (Oxford: Oxford University Press, 2001), 159–183.

[168] H. Miall, O. Ramsbotham, and T. Woodhouse, *Contemporary Conflict Resolution: The Prevention, Management, and Transformation of Deadly Conflicts* (Cambridge: Polity Press, 2000).

[169] H. Tajfel, *Human Groups and Social Categories* (Cambridge: Cambridge University Press, 1981).

they were seen as undeserving of any normal level of social engagement or human sympathy.[170] With the continued intensification of the conflict, Northern Ireland increasingly witnessed the selective focus by one group on the political violence perpetrated by the other group. The strengthening and differentiated sense of group solidarities became ever more significant in conflict, highlighting 'the group cause … that which individual participants … are willing to fight for … [identifying] which group(s) we have an affinity with'.[171]

Drawing on existing patterns of collective remembering, awareness of violence by the opponent was heightened, while of the grounds for violence undertaken by one's own side was reinforced. Group beliefs about the causes of conflict, and the reasons for its duration were thus strengthened.[172] As a result, for loyalists, everything that their community is, the Other is not. Ultimately, such outlooks can come to justify hostile and often violent acts of one's own group against the rival group, underpinning what for some the highly sectarianized definitions of the Other that have become prevalent across Northern Ireland.

In part, it was these views that allowed for the continuation of the devastating cycle of violence, and tit-for-tat reprisals experienced throughout much of the Troubles. Such encounters were reinforced by beliefs about the inhuman and evil nature of the Other[173] and the use of negative stereotypes to delegitimize the perceived enemy.[174] John Cash has, for example, identified what he terms the dehumanizing position in Northern Ireland, splitting 'the political and social order into good and evil' and seeing 'political interaction as the conflict of these two forces',[175] while Daniel Bar-Tal suggests that in conflict, the intense negative categorization of the Other often means the adversarial group is denied their humanity, essentially seen as evil and inhuman.[176]

Loyalism emerged from, and remains governed and directed by, a dread of the Other. One result is the construction and enforcement of emotional, conceptual and sometimes physical boundaries between 'us' and 'them'. As the perceived level of threat intensifies, 'friends' and 'enemies' are clearly differentiated,[177] and those groups who see themselves as wronged regard the actions of the Other as unjust and unjustifiable. Bar-Tal elucidates this process, detailing that:

---

[170] D. Bar-Tal, *Intractable Conflicts: Socio-Psychological Foundations and Dynamics* (Cambridge: Cambridge University Press, 2013).

[171] S. M. Murshed, 'On the salience of identity in civilizational and sectarian conflict', *Peace Economics, Peace Science and Public Policy*, 16, no. 2 (2010): 1.

[172] J. A. Hunter, M. Stringer, and R. P. Watson, 'Intergroup violence and intergroup attributions', *British Journal of Social Psychology*, 30, no. 3 (1991): 261–266; 'Intergroup attribution and social identity', *The Journal of Social Psychology*, 132, no. 6 (1992): 795–796.

[173] N. Ferguson and E. Cairns, 'Political violence and moral maturity in Northern Ireland', *Political Psychology*, 17, no. 4 (1996): 713–725.

[174] See Bruce, *The Edge of the Union*, 39–47.

[175] J. D. Cash, 'The dilemmas of political transformation in Northern Ireland', *Pacifica Review: Peace, Security and Global Change*, 10, no. 3 (1998): 227–234.

[176] Bar-Tal, 'Collective Memory of Physical Violence: Its Contribution to the Culture of Violence', 80.

[177] J. E. Mack, 'The Psychodynamics of Victimization among National Groups in Conflict', in *The Psychodynamics of International Relationships*, eds. A. Julius and J. V. Montville (Lexington, MA: D.C. Heath, 1990), 124.

... societies develop beliefs about being victimized by the opponent. These beliefs focus on the losses, deaths, the harm, the evil and atrocities committed by the adversary while they delegate the responsibility for the violence solely to the 'other'.[178]

The whole period of overt conflict in Northern Ireland reinforced stereotypes of the out-group, emphasizing the view of the Other as capable of and engaged in appalling acts of violence, while confirming the status of one's own status as victim. In such circumstances, the life of a member of one's group is often seen as of higher worth than that of a member of the Other. Duncan Morrow reveals the frightening logic of this position as follows:

It is terribly striking in talking to people involved in the front line of conflict in Northern Ireland over the last forty years how often their involvement originates in violence or injustice done to them or their loved ones. Getting involved was an act of justice forced on people, communities and institutions by the actions of others. By far the majority of the people sometimes called 'perpetrators', including the state, believe that what they did was not violence, and certainly not crime, but a terrible necessary evil, a 'just war'.

Morrow concludes what he sees as the 'appalling and tragic implication' of this is:

that carnage has been generated through people who believed that their actions were a necessary aspect of justice. Too often, 'they' were responding to violence committed by 'us'. 'We' responded to injustice committed by 'them'.[179]

As a result between the late 1960s and the paramilitary ceasefires, unremitting political violence meant that social and political divisions were deepened and fortified, patterns of physical segregation and social disconnection reinforced and ideological differences heightened.[180] One manifestation of this was the reproduction of self-generated myths within each community, which set personal experiences within a collective identity.[181] In Northern Ireland, these identities are based in direct opposition to each other[182] and loyalists continue to identify strongly and directly with those with whom they see as having a common fate.

---

[178] Bar-Tal, *Ethnicity Kills*, 86.

[179] D. Morrow, 'Escaping the Bind in Northern Ireland – Teaching and Learning in the Ethnic Frontier', in *Meeting of Cultures and Clash of Cultures: Adult Education in Multi-Cultural Societies*, eds. K. Yarn and S. Boggler (Jerusalem: Magnus Press, 2007), 78.

[180] Darby, *Scorpions in a Bottle*, 71–94.

[181] B. Misztal, *Theories of Social Remembering* (Maidenhead: Open University Press, 2003); J. K. Olick, *The Politics of Regret – On Collective Memory and Historical Responsibility* (London: Routledge, 2007).

[182] M. Nic Craith, *Plural Identities – Singular Narratives: The Case of Northern Ireland* (Oxford: Berghahn, 2002).

This sense of belonging seeks to draw together all those with a similar sense of collectivity and self-awareness to fashion a community distinct to loyalism. People do of course conduct their everyday lives by referring to and acting upon more than one social role. Someone is never just a loyalist, but they are also a father, mother, lover, worker, unemployed, football team supporter and so on. But, while recognizing that people hold multiple identities, in Northern Ireland, everyday social life often defaults to and finds overt political expression through the collective, and through commitment to the collective and competing senses of national identity.

In building solidarity, both communities rely heavily on identifiable narratives and the intensity of collective memory to strengthen incorporation within ones own group and to create social and political distance from the other. Here, it is important to recognize that as Jeffrey Prager[183] points out, remembering is 'an active, interpretive process' through which we not only construct a sense of Self, but also how we relate to the broader social world.

Loyalism and Northern Irish identity

One demonstration of this is the expression of national identity In Northern Ireland, which by in large remains based on exclusive and divisive concepts. In the 2011 census, 40 per cent of those returning in Northern Ireland described their principal national identity as British, while 48 per cent included some sense of British in their national identity.[184] Loyalist bonding to Britishness finds outlets of expression through national symbols,[185] attachment to what are seen as core British values, achievements and attitudes, cultural habits, and to what are regarded as the core behaviour of British citizens.[186] While loyalists extricate from these identifiers to construct their major sense of identity, this does not mean, however, that there is a uniform understanding within loyalism of what identity is, or any agreed interpretation of what comprises Britishness.

The percentage claiming a Northern Irish identity has varied between slightly more than one-in-five[187] to around one-in-three,[188] with recent census and survey evidence

---

[183] J. Prager, *Presenting the Past: Sociology and the Psychoanalysis of Misremembering* (Cambridge, MA: Harvard University Press, 1998), 215.

[184] Northern Ireland 2011 Census. Available at: http://www.nisra.gov.uk/Census/2011_results_detailed_ characteristics.html; accessed 12 October 2013; *The Guardian* 'Census 2011: Northern Ireland', suggested 29 per cent held a Northern Irish identity, available at: http://www.theguardian.com/news/ datablog/2012/dec/11/2011-census-northern-ireland-religion-identity; accessed 18 September 2013.

[185] M. Geisler, *National Symbols, Fractured Identities: Contesting the National Narrative* (New York: Middlebury Press, 2005).

[186] Commission for Racial Equality, *The Decline of Britishness: A Research Study* (London: CRE, 2005).

[187] Northern Ireland Life and Times 2012 Survey. Available at: www.nilt.ac.uk; accessed 8 October 2013.

[188] *The Guardian*, 18 September 2013.

indicating that Protestants, especially younger ones, slightly more likely to identify as such than Catholics. Those actively promoting Northern Irishness often suggest that it offers a mutual sense of identity to both unionists and nationalists,[189] alongside those who define themselves as neither, and even that it may provide for the 'beating heart of a shared future'.[190]

This may well be a misreading. In highlighting findings within the Northern Ireland Life and Times Survey, Jennifer Todd[191] indicates clear distinctions within those affiliating to a 'Northern Irish' identity. As she correctly points, outmost Catholics emphasize the 'northern' dimension of their Irishness, while Protestants highlight how that identity still expresses a difference and form of British distinctiveness on the Island. As Aughey[192] puts it, even what is shared is shared differently. Certainly, the Northern Irish identity adopted by some loyalists is often understood as an oppositional position to Irishness, or as a fallback position, a counterbalance not just to Irish identity, but also to direct affiliation with British administrations that are regarded as duplicitous and untrustworthy.

National identity and loyalism

Within Northern Ireland, discussions about national identity, and politics in general, often seem to be reduced to little more than a sectarian headcount on the constitutional position. There is a multitude of research data that confirms the consistency of identity patterns in Northern Ireland.[193] In the census of 2001, for example, 46 per cent of Northern Ireland's population defined themselves as Protestant, and of these around three out of four categorized themselves as unionists. Equally importantly, however, was that less than 1 per cent of Protestants defined themselves as Irish, a trend emphasized by Pádraig Ó Riagáin,[194] who suggests that only 3 per cent of Protestants see their primary identity as Irish. His overall findings confirm existing patterns that a majority of Protestants continue first and foremost to identify themselves as British (70 per cent), while only 12 per cent of Catholics do so. On the other hand, a clear majority of Catholics (60 per cent) continue to identify themselves as 'Irish'.

These basic patterns were corroborated by the 2011 census, although this did offer for the first time the opportunity to express a somewhat more sophisticated definition

[189] J. Coakley, 'National identity in Northern Ireland: stability or change?', *Nations and Nationalism*, 13, no. 4 (2002): 573–597.

[190] J. McCallister, J. Unionism and a shared future', *News Letter*, 18 January 2013.

[191] J. Todd, 'Introduction: national identity in transition? Moving out of conflict in (Northern) Ireland', *Nations and Nationalism*, 13, no. 4 (2007): 565–571.

[192] A. Aughey, 'Northern Ireland narratives of British democracy', *Policy Studies*, 33, no. 2 (2012): 145–158.

[193] O. Muldoon, K. Trew, J. Todd, N. Rougier, and K. McLaughlin, 'Religious and national identity after the Belfast Good Friday Agreement', *Political Psychology*, 28, no. 1 (2007): 89–103.

[194] P. Ó Riagáin, 'Relationships between attitudes to Irish, social class, religion and national identity in the Republic of Ireland and Northern Ireland', *International Journal of Bilingual Education and Bilingualism*, 10, no. 4 (2008): 1–25.

of identity. Hence, the returns showed that 40 per cent of Northern Ireland residents claimed a 'British-only' national identity, with 25 per cent seeing themselves as 'Irish-only' and 21 per cent as Northern Irish-only. The overall results indicate that 48 per cent of respondents included British as a national identity, while 29 per cent included Northern Irish and 28 per cent Irish.

Despite this seeming flexibility, however, some 80 per cent of those who saw themselves as British only were raised as Protestant and 94 per cent of those who felt Irish-only were nurtured as Catholic.[195] Other key patterns of identification are also observable. Those claiming to be British-only strengthen with age, including half of those aged 65 or above. Protestants were almost as likely as Catholics to claim a Northern Irish identity but were less likely to regard themselves as exclusively Northern Irish. Moreover, some 25 per cent of people who were or had been raised as Catholics felt Northern Irish only, but this fell to 15 per cent of Protestants.[196]

The intensity of the attachment by large sections of Protestant community to the symbolism of Britishness remains readily evident, and this is especially true of sections of loyalism. As a result, in the lead up to the all-party talks in late 2013, chaired by the former US envoy to the region Richard Haass, which focused on flags, parades and the past, Gregory Campbell of the DUP warned that it would be impossible to achieve any form of concord if the proposals that emerged were seen 'as diluting our very essence of Britishness as Northern Ireland seeks to strengthen its position within the United Kingdom, not weaken it'.[197]

The strength of this affiliation within large sections of the Protestant community finds constant and consistent expression, with little to suggest that the attachment is weakening, or that support for the Union amongst Protestants in general is likely to diminish.[198] Although identification with Britishness amongst Northern Ireland's Protestants continues unabated, this does not mean that it finds uniform political, ideological or cultural expression. As Graham Spencer clearly explains, the absence of any real ideological consensus across unionism has direct political consequences, and:

> is a symptom of conflicting notions about unionist identity, which is further amplified when the prospect for political change becomes particularly likely. Antagonistic positions with regard to perceptions of the British state and where unionists stand in relation to that state merely serve to further destabilize the lack of political direction required and compound the factionalism which inhibits the emergence of progressive political initiatives.[199]

---

[195] *Belfast Telegraph*, 16 May 2013.

[196] *Belfast Telegraph*, 16 May 2013.

[197] *Londonderry Sentinel*, 23 December 2013.

[198] J. Brewer, 'Continuity and change in contemporary Ulster Protestantism', *The Sociological Review*, 52, no. 2 (2004): 265–283.

[199] G. Spencer, 'Constructing loyalism: politics, communications and peace in Northern Ireland', *Contemporary Politics*, 10, no. 1 (2004): 40.

Unionism, however, offers the broad historical and social framework and the entanglement of political, social and community identities, from which the collective ethno-political identity of loyalism is forged, reproduced and rearranged. In particular, this and previous chapters have highlighted the parameters for identifying what is seen as distinct within loyalism and the main points of historical reference. In particular, this is what is seen as delineating loyalism from other groups through the creation of distinct 'in-groups'[200] and through the identification of an 'out-group', comprising a dangerous and untrustworthy Other.[201]

This draws us to an interpretation of identity projected by Tajfel, defining social identity as 'that part of an individual's self-concept which derives from his knowledge of his membership of a social group (or groups), together with the value and emotional significance attached to that membership'.[202] One way to demarcate loyalism is by reference to particular and sometimes competing understandings of the past resting on communal views of the Self and the Other, and how this finds expression in the present through attachment to cultural or civic visions of loyalism.

Conclusions

Reactions to the outbreak of conflict in the late 1960s structured and gave direction to the response of loyalism for at least the next two decades. Underpinning much of this was a deep engagement with a sense of loyalist identity that was being challenged ideologically, politically and physically. Kay[203] demonstrates the resulting need for ontological security, the most visible response of which was the emergence of structural and organized violence through paramilitary groupings. The rapid need to reassess their core identity caused much flux and reconfiguration for many loyalists as social and political boundaries were redefined and reinforced.

The process of defining loyalist identity occurs through a dual assessment, of both what is seen to be similar and different. Engagement with collective memory remains core in forming and sustaining this identity. Much of this is done by directly linking past and present in ways that reinforce central loyalist senses of identity, difference and common history. While recalling key events of the past, this book offers little to advance the skill of the historian. It does not make any claim to do so; the focus throughout the book is not on the history of loyalism, but rather its collective memory and understandings of past events.

---

[200] R. De Cillia, M. Reisigl, and R. Wodak 'The discursive construction of national identities', *Discourse and Society*, 10, no. 2 (1999): 149–173.

[201] H. Tajfel and J. C. Turner, 'The Social Identity Theory of Intergroup Behavior', in *Psychology of Intergroup Relations*, eds. S. Worchel and W. G. Austin (Chicago, IL: Nelson-Hall, 1986), 7–24.

[202] H. Tajfel, *Differentiation between Social Groups: Studies in the Social Psychology of Intergroup Behaviour* (London: Academic Press, 1978), 630.

[203] S. Kay, 'Ontological security and peace-building in Northern Ireland', *Contemporary Security Policy*, 33, no. 2 (2012): 236–263.

Loyalist interpretations of the past are deeply located in communal perceptions and reproduced at both formal and informal levels through discourses, interactions and commemorations that are reproduced on a daily basis. Tradition is often invoked as part of a loyalist narrative to explain and account for such day-to-day encounters and to bond loyalists together, to rally political support or to position opposition to certain events. It works to explain broad economic, social and political circumstances and create collective solidarity of the group. These are ideas that we will encounter in various ways throughout much of the remainder of the book.

4

Inside a Loyalist Community

As Chapter 3 has indicated, loyalism is intertwined with distinct ideas of community, a particular sense of belonging and form of class expression within unionism. Loyalist discourse constantly calls for incorporation through a range of shared social norms and actions, which are seen to create a distinct sense of community, that recognizes Northern Ireland (or Ulster) as distinct, and which may, or may not, involve localized geographical boundaries. According to David McMillan and David Chavis,[1] there are four core elements in understanding community. Membership is experienced through: shared feelings of belonging and personal connection; through a sense that it makes a difference being part of a particular group; the belief that the physical and emotional needs of members are best met through the benefits that group membership brings; and, by way of shared feelings of connection, and commitment to the belief that members have a shared common history, sense of place, experience and identity. Ontological security finds expression through the narrative that stems from the Self, to a distinct community narrative and to the relationships the community has with other communities.

One starting point in seeking to understand loyalism therefore is to recognize it as a community expressing a rational sense of social belonging, displayed and articulated through the elements identified above. This gives rise to distinct forms of political, cultural and emotional attachment to both 'the people' and the physical entity of Northern Ireland and detachment from those seen as unable or unwilling to give support to that state. As Akhil Gupta and James Ferguson[2] identify, understood in this way community is 'a categorical identity that is premised on various forms of exclusion and construction of otherness'.

Loyalism as a form of political identification is located mainly within the Protestant working class, although by no means are all working-class Protestants are loyalists, or all those expressing loyalist views working class. Loyalism developed alongside other major cultural and political traditions within Protestant working-class communities, such as labourism and communalism, and at times, it has fought for supremacy within it. In reviewing Burke's[3] biographical work on singer Van

---

[1] D. W. McMillan and D. M. Chavis, 'Sense of community: a definition and theory', *Journal of Community Psychology*, 14 (1986): 6–23.
[2] A. Gupta and J. Ferguson, eds. *Culture, Power, Place: Explorations in Critical Anthropology* (Durham, NC: Duke University Press, 1997), 3.
[3] D. Burke, *A Sense of Wonder: Van Morrison's Ireland* (London: Jawbone Press, 2013).

Leabharlanna Poibli Chathair Bhaile Átha Cliath

Dublin City Public Libraries

Morrison, for example, Paul Bew suggests that the East Belfast in which Morrison grew up 'was distinctive politically in that it was represented by Labour in the Northern Irish Parliament, and leaned towards a progressive, secular – at least by Northern Irish standards – culture'.[4]

Sometimes the differing political expressions found within the working-class Protestant community overlapped and intertwined and sometimes they remained distinct in their organization and expression; sometimes labourism and communalism were more prominent, sometimes less so. At other times, loyalism appeared more central, but together these always formed the political building blocs of working-class Protestant life. It is important to recognize how community can be understood in different ways as linked to a recognized history, economy and demography, a localized geographical area[5] or as part of a broader imagined community.[6] The loyalist community is bound by a common sense of belonging and political expression developed through shared experiences and which finds expression through communal discourses that often precipitate collective social actions. This is an identity that has strengthened from the earliest days of the contemporary conflict onwards.

'Becoming' loyalist

Ulster loyalist identity, however, is not a pre-given, and an individual's self-concept as part of that social group 'together with the value and emotional significance attached to that membership'[7] must be nurtured and developed. To succeed in explaining everyday life and possibilities for the future loyalist identity, we must allow for the expression of feelings of social and emotional attachment and forms of political affinity. As Stuart Hall so clearly explains, cultural identity is always 'a matter of "becoming" as well as of "being". It belongs to the future as much as to the past'. Importantly, he further suggests that identities:

> are subject to the continuous 'play' of history, culture and power. Far from being grounded in a mere 'recovery' of the past, which is waiting to be found, and which, when found, will secure our sense of ourselves into eternity, identities are the names we give to the different ways we are positioned by, and position ourselves within, the narratives of the past.[8]

[4] Culture Northern Ireland, *A Sense of Wonder*. Available at: http://www.culturenorthernireland.org/reviews/music/sense-wonder; accessed 8 June 2014.
[5] R. Chaskin, 'Building community capacity: a definitional framework and case studies from a comprehensive community initiative', *Urban Affairs Review*, 36, no. 3 (2001): 291–323.
[6] H. Bauder, *Immigration Dialectic: Imagining Community, Economy and Nation* (Toronto, ON: University of Toronto Press, 2011).
[7] Tajfel, *Human Groups and Social Categories*.
[8] S. Hall, 'Cultural Identity and Diaspora', in *Identity: Community, Culture, Difference*, ed. J. Rutherford (London: Lawrence and Wishart, 1990), 225.

Leabharlanna Poiblí Chathair Bhaile Átha Cliath
Dublin City Public Libraries

But what are the social processes that make such identities matter? It is uncontested to point to how those from any generation experience similar historical and social circumstances, and may thus broadly express common preferences, and share common memories.[9] What is important here is to recognize how these collective memories cross generations or are passed on from one generation to the next.[10]

In most societies, it is usual for political identities to be reproduced and made resilient by the transmission of values and beliefs unto future generations.[11] In all cultures, social groups carry forward 'from generation to generation, that which they choose to pass on and, perhaps, that which they are not conscious of passing on'.[12] In Northern Ireland, such functions are fragmented,[13] and the transmission of values and beliefs largely reproduce collective memories that are distinctive to either Catholic/nationalist/republican, or the Protestant/unionist/loyalist communities. As a consequence, many of the major historical and political reference points are held in common, but the interpretation and understanding of these events are separated and disjointed, and any awareness and appreciation of the past competitive and often commemorated in contested ways.

Moreover, it is clear that in Northern Ireland the social reproduction and replication of collective political memory is bounded within mutually antagonistic political communities. For most political socialization and everyday encounters remain exclusive and oppositional, restricted to engagement with their own community's collective memories, partisan expressions of identity and political orientation.[14] These points of reference draw directly on collective memories of difference and divergence[15] that find expression in many ways, for example, through the transmission of community myths by way of murals and banners or the learning of traditional songs.

It was Morris Fraser[16] who suggested that in Northern Ireland political socialization starts in the cradle, while Ed Cairns[17] has gone further in proposing that such processes can begin even earlier, with the choice of a child's name prior to birth often being

---

[9] Misztal, *Theories of Social Remembering*.

[10] C. W. Blatz and M. Ross, 'Historical Memories', in *Memory in Mind and Culture*, eds. P. Boyer and J. V. Wertsch (Cambridge: Cambridge University Press, 2009).

[11] Inglehart, *Modernization and Postmodernization*, 1997; G. R. Murray and M. K. Mulvaney, 'Parenting styles, socialization, and the transmission of political ideology and partisanship', *Politics and Policy*, 40, no. 6 (2012): 1106–1130; R. Siemienska, 'Intergenerational differences in political values and attitudes in stable and new democracies', *International Journal of Comparative Sociology*, 43, nos. 3–5 (2002): 368–390.

[12] J. Rodriguez and T. Fortier, *Cultural Memory: Resistance, Faith and Identity* (Austin, TX: University of Texas Press, 2007), 7.

[13] F. Burton, *The Politics of Legitimacy*.

[14] E. Cairns, *Caught in Crossfire: Children and the Northern Ireland Conflict* (Belfast: Appletree Press, 1987).

[15] J. W. Pennebaker and B. L. Banasik, 'On the Creation and Maintenance of Collective Memories: History as Social Psychology', in *Collective Memory of Political Events: Social Psychological Perspectives*, eds. J. W. Pennebaker, D. Paez, and B. Rimel (Mahwah, NJ: Lawrence Erlbaum, 1997), 3–19.

[16] M. Fraser, *Children in Conflict* (London: Seeker and Warburg, 1974).

[17] E. Cairns, *Caught in Crossfire; Children and Political Violence* (Oxford: Blackwell, 1996).

regarded as a key marker of identity. Certainly, for many by the time children are old enough to enter the formal schooling system, their pattern of political socialization is frighteningly predictable. The consequences are profound, not least because in Northern Ireland the strength of group solidarity may be directly correlated with levels of prejudice towards those outside the group. Again following Halbwachs,[18] it is possible to argue that 'individual memories always crystallize in a social framework'[19] and that memory involves the rebuilding of an individual's past within society.[20]

Within this system, collective memories, narratives and ideologies are powerfully reproduced. John Boyd[21] in his autobiographical account of growing up in one Protestant community, for example, recounts his introduction into a social world filled with banal sectarianism, through which each community's unawareness of the others values and worldview was reinforced and which was central in determining perceptions of the Other. He later recognized that the dominant narrative often bore little overlap with 'reality', admitting that neither he nor any of his immediate peers had ever seen a Catholic.

He goes on to point out, however, that somehow this did not seem to matter, because more important to them was that 'there was a big fight going on and we Protestants wanted to be on the winning side'.[22] In describing his experiences of growing up in Belfast in pre-Troubles Belfast of the late 1950s, Robert Harbinson[23] talks of his profound ignorance of anything seen as part of what he terms, 'the Catholic world'. Such patterns of social division were reinforced and re-emphasized by the conflict. As the poet Gerald Dawe recalls, in the late 1960s, many of his peer group which 'were politically interested had a liberal-minded, left-wing, social-democratic view of things'. However, Dawe further explains: 'then the Troubles broke, and that became a life then for people for a quarter of a century'.[24]

A later wave of loyalist writings have also developed in the form of a series of (auto) biographies (some ghost written), largely deriving from individuals who became involved in paramilitary ranks, and who often rose to positions of prominence.[25] One common theme emerging from across these works is the strength of the socialization in a particular worldview, reinforced by strong self-perpetuating narratives of identity,

---

[18] See material in L. A. Coser, ed. *Maurice Halbwachs on Collective Memory* (Chicago: University of Chicago Press, 1992).

[19] A. Becker, 'Memory gaps, Maurice Halbwachs, memory and the Great War', *Journal of European Studies*, 35 (2005): 102–113.

[20] P. Jedlowski, 'Memory and sociology: themes and issues', *Time and Society*, 10, no. 1 (2001): 29–44.

[21] J. Boyd, *Out of My Class* (Belfast: Blackstaff, 1985); see also *The Middle of My Journey* (Belfast: Blackstaff, 1990).

[22] Boyd, *Out of My Class*, 176.

[23] R. Harbinson, *No Surrender: An Ulster Childhood* (Belfast: Blackstaff Press, 1960), 131–132.

[24] *Mayo News*, 29 May 2012.

[25] See, for example, J. Adair, with G. McKendry, *Mad Dog* (London: John Blake, 2007); C. Anderson, *The Billy Boy: The Life and Death of LVF leader Billy Wright* (Edinburgh: Mainstream Publishing, 2002); R. Garland, *Gusty Spence* (Belfast: Blackstaff Press, 2001); H. Sinnerton, *David Ervine: Uncharted Waters* (Dingle: Brandon, 2002); M. Stone, *None Shall Divide Us* (London: John Blake, 2004).

drawing directly on collective memories,[26] collective forgetting[27] and sometimes even a politically induced amnesia. Ideas, historical points of reference and political values continue to be passed across the generations, through discourses making reference to recognizable 'traditions' and 'stories'.[28] Such stories, discourses and political memories are corralled within a particular ethno-political worldview and a recognizable set of discourses and narratives through which loyalists make their social and political worlds understandable.[29]

The identification of loyalism as a coherent social grouping most often finds expression through the notion of community and a detailed understanding of those who are seen as belonging to, and those who are excluded from this loyalist community. While the concept of community is core to loyalist collective identities, it is important to recognize this has been shaped through a number of influences: by demographic features; by shared experiences of recognition and non-recognition; through common economic location and shared cultural values; through a process of hailing and narrative construction; and through a deep sense of togetherness and emotional attachment. In Belfast, the segregation of the communities led to the formation of solidarities within them,[30] the concentrating of solid stereotyping and the creation and reinforcement of the Other.

Community and connections

Cultural distinction and political separateness are seen therefore as core features of loyalist identity. In particular, social identity theory[31] has been usefully applied to Northern Ireland[32] to explore how identity is fashioned through the experiences growing up in a divided and discordant society. For loyalists, distinct senses of social and cultural difference provide the legitimacy for their sense of belonging and crucially frame the boundaries of what they regard as the loyalist community.

---

[26] D. Middleton and D. Edwards, eds. *Collective Remembering* (London: Sage, 1990).

[27] B. Schwartz, 'The social context of commemoration: a study in collective memory', *Social Forces*, 61 (1982): 375–402.

[28] S. Hopkins, 'History with a divided and complicated heart? The uses of political memoir, biography and autobiography in contemporary Northern Ireland', *The Global Review of Ethnopolitics*, 1, no. 2 (2001): 74–81; 'A Weapon in the Struggle? Loyalist Paramilitarism and the Politics of Auto/ Biography in Contemporary Northern Ireland', in *Irish Protestant Identities*, eds. M. Busteed, F. Neal, and J. Tonge (Manchester: Manchester University Press, 2008), 319–333; *The Politics of Memoir in Northern Ireland* (Liverpool: Liverpool University Press, 2013).

[29] A. Finlayson, 'Loyalist political identity after the peace', *Capital and Class*, 23 (1999): 47–75.

[30] F. W. Boal, 'Belfast: walls within', *Political Geography*, 21 (2000): 687–694.

[31] Tajfel, *Differentiation between Social Groups*; 'Individuals and groups in social psychology', *British Journal of Clinical Psychology*, 18, no. 2 (1979): 180–190; *Human Groups and Social Categories*; 'Social psychology of intergroup relations', *Annual Review of Psychology*, 33 (1982): 1–39; Tajfel and Turner, 'An Integrative Theory of Intergroup Conflict'; 'The Social Identity Theory of Intergroup Behavior'.

[32] E. Cairns, R. Wilson, T. Gallagher, and K. Trew, 'Psychology's contribution to understanding conflict in Northern Ireland', *Peace and Conflict: Journal of Peace Psychology*, 1, no. 2 (1995): 131–147.

But there are challenges arising from defining community,[33] which is often blurred by everyday 'commonsense' usages of the term, and its increasingly nebulous use in the public arena by politicians, policy makers and the media or as part of a broader imagined community.[34] Overall, Joseph Gusfield[35] provides a useful starting point in trying to cut through the plethora of definitions by suggesting that essentially community can be understood in two main ways. The first, as being bound by territory and the second, as bonded by relationships and interactions (with or without reference to location). Both geographically and socially bounded communities invoke strong feelings of belonging and find different articulation through the symbolic, discursive and the representational. These can include relationships arising from a shared locality and feelings of belonging, generating through much wider connections than those bound by geography.

As a result, community is often at the core of the 'complex matrix of social organization and individual identity that characterizes modern life'.[36] Perhaps most importantly, as Caroline Howarth points out, communities 'impinge into people's lives: they orient the social construction of knowledge; they ground the negotiation of common identities; they marginalize and stigmatize certain social groups; and, they provide the tools for empowerment and social inclusion'.[37] The broadest conceptualization of community encompassing loyalism is the 'Protestant community', which of course includes members with different political allegiances, religious denominations, those who populate different social worlds and are subject to highly divergent social experiences and those who have different access to political power.

To more fully understand the structure of the loyalist community, it is useful to draw on the work of Gerry Mooney and Sarah Neal[38] who suggest that it is possible to identify four connected approaches to understanding community: space and face-to-face interaction; identity formations and imagined connections; as a boundary that exists to include some and exclude others; and as a site for political regulation. By approaching community in this way, it is possible to identify what gives particular meaning to the loyalist formations of social and cultural identity.

So what is the loyalist community?

As we can see from the above mostly, communities can be conceptualized from within three main perspectives: broadly those who see community as spatially based; those

---

[33] C. Bell and H. Newby, *Community Studies* (London: Unwin, 1971).

[34] T. Cantle, *Community Cohesion: A Report of the Independent Review Team* (London: Home Office, 2001); R. D. Putnam, *Bowling Alone: The Collapse and Revival of American Community* (New York: Simon and Schuster, 2000).

[35] J. R. Gusfield, *The Community: A Critical Response* (New York: Harper Colophon, 1975).

[36] A. Little, *The Politics of Community: Theory and Practice* (Edinburgh: Edinburgh University Press, 2002), 7.

[37] C. Howarth, 'Towards a social psychology of community: a social representations perspective', *Journal for the Theory of Social Behaviour*, 31, no. 2 (2001): 223.

[38] G. Mooney and S. Neal, 'Community: Themes and Debates', in *Community: Welfare, Crime and Society*, eds. G. Mooney and S. Neal (Maidenhead: Open University Press, 2009), 1–34.

who understand community as built upon a network of aligned social relationships; and those who focus on imagined connections.

So what can be recognized as the building blocs of the Loyalist community? First, the loyalist community can be seen as a group that has shared identities, interests and concerns. Second, but of at least equal importance is a strong sense of identity based around what they are not. Third, loyalists can be understood as a grouping that is identified and defined by others in the wider society. Fourth, the loyalist community can be understood as a grouping expressing themselves in terms of social and political boundaries such as culture, language, religious bonds, economic, class and political interest. Finally, the notion of a loyalist community finds expression and association at the personal level, resting on memories, shared cultural narratives, communal experiences and feelings of safety and security.

It is important to identify the necessary context for constructing loyalist identity, the role of community within that identity and the place of a self-contained social system, which provides a coherence of meaning within loyalism. For Anthony Cohen,[39] our understanding of community rests in the strength of attachment to its symbolism, while others[40] regard it more as an identity-based concept. However defined, identification with community invokes powerful feelings of attachment that link across identity, location and social relationships and often act to give rise to direct social and political expressions. As we shall, although many loyalist communities often remain geographically demarcated, they are also socially, politically and economically bonded, invoking intense expressions of belonging for those who identify with these communities. This will be examined by considering one such long-standing loyalist community, that of inner east Belfast, often known locally as Ballymacarrett. In so doing, the rest of this chapter will further explore notions of the loyalist community based on both imagined and physical understandings of what it is that gives it coherence.

Locating East Belfast

At the beginning of the nineteenth century, Belfast was a small town of some 20,000 people. The rural hinterland on the east bank of the Lagan remained geographically distinct and was linked to the rest of Belfast only by the 'long bridge'. From around 1830, however, Belfast experienced a rapid expansion in its population (to around 50,000), and the period saw the rows of artisans' houses that had developed in the west of the city spread rapidly over the Lagan to the east. The expansion of the city continued, driven by high levels of migration from rural districts brought about by the Famine. The infrastructure of the city changed dramatically, and as a result, what was

---

[39] Cohen, *The Symbolic Construction of Community*.
[40] F. Polletta and J. M. Jasper, 'Collective identity and social movements', *Annual Review of Sociology*, 27 (2001): 283–305.

a minor port became a major point of trade as linen manufacturing and shipbuilding grew to world prominence.

Belfast remained, however, desperately void of natural raw materials, and the need for widespread imports put growing pressure on the city's port facilities. In order to accommodate the rapidly expanding demand for port capacity, shipbuilding was transferred to the east side of the river, which had now been joined to Belfast by two new bridges. However, very few Catholic migrants to Belfast ventured across the river. Instead, typically of many migrant groups, most drew on established patterns of support to cluster around specific mills and other workplaces. They largely settled in other parts of the city having arriving into Belfast from its western and southern approaches by way of the established transit through the Lurgan and Lisburn corridors.

As Belfast continued to grow, competition for scarce resources increased, as did sectarian differences, precipitating a series of riots that 'reproduced patterns of conflict that had been common in the Ulster countryside for generations.'[41] In part, this ensured the development of a distinct urban geography, established through economic migration, sectarian division and local patterns of settlement,[42] whereby the Protestant and Catholic working class became segregated between distinct communities.[43] These configurations largely explain why inner East Belfast has traditionally had such a small Catholic population. Those who did settle remained encamped immediately on its eastern bank in a small enclave known as Short Strand.

By the time Belfast expanded its boundary in 1896, a clear sectarian layout to the city was visible, and the political ideologies of Unionism and nationalism were becoming increasingly consequential to everyday life. During frequent periods of political tension, sectarian rioting established itself as a feature of nineteenth-century Belfast life,[44] reinforcing the patterns of sectarian demarcation and division. The political character of Belfast altered dramatically in the latter part of the nineteenth and early part of the twentieth centuries as relations between Catholic and Protestant workers worsened.[45] The city emerged transformed as the capital of Irish Unionism, obscuring its previous status place as the source of a United Irish movement.[46] John Bew[47] suggests that this burgeoning civic unionism was rooted in the growth of Belfast and was driven by association with the British state and British constitution, so much so that it became immersed in the imagined community of the British nation after the Act of Union of 1801, which allowed for the roots of Ulster's opposition to Home Rule to be set down.

---

[41] M. Doyle, *Fighting Like the Devil for the Sake of God: Protestants, Catholics and the Origins of Violence in Victorian Belfast* (Manchester: Manchester University Press, 2009), 80.

[42] C. Hirst, *Religion, Politics, and Violence in Nineteenth-Century Belfast: The Pound and Sandy Row* (Dublin: Four Courts Press, 2002).

[43] F. W. Boal, 'Integration and division: sharing and segregating in Belfast', *Planning Practice and Research*, 11, no. 2 (1996): 151–158.

[44] Hirst, *Religion, Politics, and Violence in Nineteenth-Century Belfast.*

[45] Doyle, *Fighting Like the Devil for the Sake of God.*

[46] Loughlin, *Ulster Unionism and British National Identity since 1885.*

[47] J. Bew, *The Glory of Being Britons: Civic Unionism in Nineteenth-Century Belfast* (Dublin: Irish Academic Press, 2008).

A pattern was set. During times of relative calm, social physical demarcations were blurred, only to be reinforced during times of political tension and outbreaks of political violence. Niall Cunningham[48] has traced in detail the configuration of political killings during the period 1920–1922, identifying several epicentres of violence across Belfast, including in the east of the city, where a very high number of deaths were located in and around Short Strand. These patterns of separation were deeply embedded within and remained a consistent feature of Northern Irish society. It has subsequently been claimed that every resident of the province carries with them a complex and detailed political geography: they know which villages or streets are Protestant or Catholic, which are mixed, and which are safer than others to travel along.[49] While throughout the late 1950s and early 1960s, some of the physical lines of demarcation between Protestant and Catholic areas had weakened,[50] in a short period following the summer of 1969 these 'mixed' areas quickly evaporated.[51] Following a series of violent street confrontations, riots and attacks on private homes, sectarian residential patterns quickly re-emerged, as up to 15,000 families were made to flee their homes in the Greater Belfast area alone.[52]

This institutionalized an 'us and them mentality', manifesting in everyday behaviour through people avoiding town centres and/or following segregate routes to and from school and their workplace.[53] Increasingly, the growth in structural community violence saw the rapid loss of 'neutral space', with people creating social and physical distance from the Other, while as far as possible concentrating social life in their own areas where they felt some level of safety and security, reflecting patterns found in other conflict societies.[54] David Bleakley, former Minister of Community Relations in the Stormont government, describes the situation in the early 1970s accurately as one where many:

> town centres are deserted from about seven o'clock each evening…The Ulster 'local' has been hit badly by the troubles directly as well as indirectly…. Public houses are open to bomb attack simply because of the way they are associated with the neighbourhood in which they operate, or with the groups they serve….

[48] N. Cunningham, 'The doctrine of vicarious punishment: space, religion and the Belfast Troubles of 1920–22', *Journal of Historical Geography*, 40 (2013): 58.

[49] A. T. Q. Stewart, *The Narrow Ground: Aspects of Ulster 1609–1969* (London: Faber and Faber, 1977).

[50] *The Times*, 18 September, 1971.

[51] P. Doherty and M. A. Poole, 'Ethnic residential segregation in Belfast, 1971–1991', *Geographical Review*, 87, no. 4 (1997): 520–536.

[52] J. Darby, *Intimidation in Housing, A Research Paper* (Belfast: The Northern Ireland Community Relations Commission, 1974); *Intimidation and the Control of Conflict in Northern Ireland* (Dublin: Gill and Macmillan, 1986).

[53] R. Manktelow, 'The needs of victims of the troubles in Northern Ireland: the social work contribution', *Journal of Social Work*, 7, no. 1 (2007): 31–50.

[54] E. Staub, *The Roots of Evil: The Origins of Genocide and Other Group Violence* (Cambridge: Cambridge University Press, 1989); *The Psychology of Good and Evil: Why Children, Adults and Groups Help and Harm Others* (New York: Cambridge University Press, 2003).

To this account of diminishing outlets must also be added the closure of downtown hotels and theatres.[55]

Within these social relationships, the perception of threat became all pervasive, dominating many aspects of social life. The poet Gerald Dawe, himself a product of Orangefield Boys in East Belfast, recalls how life changed for him in the early 1970s:

> I used to walk girls home over to west Belfast and it never was a problem, but when The Troubles really started to dig in, that kind of freedom disappeared. I mean you'd take your life in your hands ... Belfast became a very dark and dangerous city. People didn't go out after 7 or 8 o'clock at night. It was pretty grim ... It wasn't the same city that I had known growing up.[56]

Across Belfast, many felt the need, or were physically compelled, to leave their homes to move to what they regarded as safer homogeneous areas. Most Protestants transferred to estates on the outskirts of the city or to other parts of the province.[57] While some have sought to emphasize positive aspects of coping that developed within communities, others described the loss of common bonds of class and communalism as the: 'two communities were polarized and preoccupied by their own safety – a feeling of enclave with ghettos like ghost towns at night'.[58]

Because of inherent sectarian geography of the city, however, Catholics who had been intimidated out of their homes often did not have much range of choice as to new surroundings. Many of those displaced in the north and south of the city fled to the already densely populated Catholic areas in west Belfast. In the east side of town, however, there were no other predominantly Catholic areas, and many Catholics displaced sought refuge in the already crowded Short Strand. As a result of increasing communal violence, the mixed area containing both Catholic and Protestant homes that existed around the fringes of Short Strand disappeared as sectarianized residential divisions became clear-cut.[59]

The Short Strand's status as a peripheral nationalist area, and the only such district on that side of the river lagan, was strengthened. The physical boundary between 'Catholic' Short Strand and 'Protestant' Ballymacarrett (now most commonly referred to as an interface) was institutionalized during the summer of 1970 when, following violent sectarian confrontations, the British army erected a series of barricades. The development of physically segregated areas between Protestants and Catholics directly reflected the extension of distinct cultures in the localized arena. Sectarian demarcation intensified as continued street violence saw the destruction of both private housing and public buildings such as pubs, halls and shops in the intermediate zone.

---

[55] D. Bleakley, *Peace in Ulster* (Oxford: A. R. Mowbray, 1972).
[56] *Mayo News*, 29 May 2012.
[57] Darby, *Intimidation and the Control of Conflict in Northern Ireland*, 59
[58] Manktelow,'The needs of victims of the troubles in Northern Ireland', 33.
[59] Ballymacarrett Research Group, *Lagan Enclave: A History of Conflict in the Short Strand, 1886–1997* (Belfast: Ballymacarrett Research Group, 1997).

This sectarianized physical space still dominates Belfast, so much so that in 2001 around half of all Belfast wards were either 90 per cent Protestant or 90 per cent Catholic. Such divisions continue to have social relevance, Madeline Leonard[60] has, for example, traced in detail just how strongly an awareness of sectarianized geography continues to influence young people's lives, in particular in determining their everyday movements in negotiating safe space particularly around interface areas.

In Protestant East Belfast, community identity had been built up over several generations and layered across residence, kinship and friendship networks, class identity, religious denomination and political affiliation and occupation.[61] For many years, these communities rested in densely populated and largely self-contained areas, with a localized social structure resting in geographical stability, cultural homogeneity and shared work experiences.[62] Such traditional social structures involved frequent contact with neighbours as part of the everyday experience, and alongside those social groupings formed around the workplace, it reinforced high levels of familiarity and prevailing norms and values.

The position within traditional working-class communities has no doubt been romanticized,[63] not least because alongside the strong senses of communal and craft identities were other everyday experiences such as domestic violence, family conflicts, significant levels of unemployment, deprivation, crippling poverty, social marginalization and other types of severe hardship and dependency.[64] People led highly gendered live patterns. Nevertheless, such communities did provide some form of supportive environment for the development of collective political identity through the expression of a plethora of shared beliefs, values, tradition and shared worldview, which were held as a common everyday knowledge possessed by the group.

Loyalism became one expression of these values and practices, but there were others, such as the strong Labour and Trades Union traditions emerging from the industrial workplace. The Protestant community in inner East Belfast was for decades employed in and around one main industry, shipbuilding, which at one point accounted for 7 per cent of the gross domestic product of the entire UK.[65] The experiences, resources and life chances of those in inner East Belfast were dominated by this local labour market and much social life prescribed by the work patterns that emerged from it.

[60] M. Leonard, 'Parochial geographies: growing up in divided Belfast', *Childhood*, 17 (2010): 329–342.
[61] R. Munck and B. Rolston, 'Oral history and social conflict', *Oral History Review*, 13 (1985): 1–21.
[62] In this sense, they resembled traditional working-class communities described in J. H. Goldthorpe, D. Lockwood, F. Bechhofer, and J. Platt, *The Affluent Worker: Political Attitudes and Behaviour* (Cambridge: Cambridge University Press, 1968). J. H. Goldthorpe and D. Lockwood 'Affluence and the British class structure', *Sociological Review*, 11, no. 2 (1968): 133–163; M. Savage, 'Working class identity in the 1960: revisiting the affluent workers study', *Sociology*, 39, no. 5 (2005): 929–946.
[63] A. Miles and M. Savage, *The Remaking of the British Working Class, 1840–1940* (London: Routledge, 1994), 14.
[64] J. Benson, *The Working Class in Britain, 1850–1939* (London: I. B. Tauris and Co. Ltd., 2003); G. Day, *Community and Everyday Life* (Oxford: Routledge, 2006).
[65] J. Muir, *Regeneration and Poverty in Northern Ireland: Evidence and Policy Review* (Sheffield Hallam University, Joseph Rowntree Foundation, 2014); N. I. Public Accounts Committee, Invest Northern Ireland: A Performance Review, report NIA 109 /11–15.

The cultures of community, workplace and political identity all affected how Protestant families viewed their participation in education. It was access to training through apprenticeships within recognized trades that acted as the main educational outlet within working-class Protestant communities.[66] For decades, the relatively easy reliance on finding work in industry as a means of advancing life chances led to the downplaying and relegation of the merits of further and higher education. But Northern Ireland suffered badly in the deindustrialization of the 1980s and 1990s.[67] In the two decades from 1973, for example, the sector declined from 67,000 to 18,000 people, the majority of job losses were in heavy industries like Harland and Wolff, Mackie's engineering works and Shorts Brothers. All of which had provided centrally to working-class Protestant employment.

Today, lack of educational success in Protestant working-class areas is a core social problem. Educationally four out of the five lowest achieving Wards in Northern Ireland are mainly Protestant, as are six out of the worst ten and twelve of the top twenty.[68] Catholics in the 16–44 age group are more likely to possess higher-level qualifications than Protestants, while the reverse occurs in the 45–74 age category. Young Protestants persistently underachieve at education resulting in many leaving school with no qualifications and with poor numeracy and literacy skills, which in turn determines work and life chances. Such problems are readily apparent in East Belfast.

In 2006, for example, of the 924 pupils living in the East Belfast wards who left school, 523 achieved the minimum government expectation after compulsory education of five GCSEs (A-C) and 370 achieved at least two A Levels (the minimum entry qualification for entry into higher education), representing 56 and 40 per cent, respectively. However, those coming from the predominantly Protestant working-class inner wards of Mount, Ballymacarrett and Woodstock failed to achieve the average for East Belfast. In these wards, for pupil educational achievement to match the overall ward average, improvements of 9 per cent at GCSE level and 23 per cent at A level would have been necessary.[69]

Strong senses of shared occupational experiences reflected the distinctive characteristics of a classical occupational community, with patterns of socialization based on the extended family and kinship networks alongside work-based friendships built up over many generations. Linked directly to broader processes of deindustrialization, such confined markets have altered dramatically, Northern Ireland has witnessed a vast reduction in the number of industrial skills based jobs, directly effecting opportunities for work, and the unemployment levels of Protestant workers,

[66] G. Mulvenna, 'The Protestant working class in Belfast: education and civic erosion – an alternative analysis', *Irish Studies Review*, 20, 4 (2012): 427–446.

[67] V. Borooah, 'Growth and Political Violence in Northern Ireland, 1920–96', in *The Political Dimension of Economic Growth*, eds. S. Borner and M. Paldam (London: Macmillan, 1998).

[68] Northern Ireland Statistics and Research Agency, 'Northern Ireland Multiple Deprivation Measure 2010' (Belfast: NISRA, 2010).

[69] East Belfast Partnership and the Department for Social Development, *East Belfast: Strategic Regeneration Framework* (Belfast: Paul Hogarth Company, 2008).

a point made in a report by Dawn Purvis, Peter Shirlow and Mark Langhammer[70] and later reinforced by the work of Paul Nolan.[71]

In June 2008, around 79,173 people lived in the East Belfast constituency for the Northern Ireland Assembly. The vast majority (84.6 per cent) of residents were Protestant, while just fewer than one in ten (9.9 per cent) were Catholic, most of whom are concentrated in the Short Strand district. Similar to many urban regions, East Belfast contains reasonably affluent wards in its outer ring, and several highly deprived wards at its inner core. Indeed, inner East Belfast contains some of the most socially depressed wards in the Belfast Urban Area and amongst the top 'Protestant' wards in terms of deprivation.[72]

Inner East Belfast has traditionally experienced a strong community identity comparable to other urban working-class Protestant communities such as the Shankill and Sandy Row,[73] and it was this that gave loyalist paramilitaries their authority, through claims to be defending their community. Recent decades, however, have seen the traditional sense of community in East Belfast dramatically challenged, mainly as a result of extensive economic decline and physical redevelopment involving dramatic reformulations in the infrastructure of the area. One upshot is that those who would traditionally have worked and grown up within the extended kinship networks of East Belfast have been forced to abandon the inner-city communities.

Many have moved to other parts of Northern Ireland or emigrated, either simply in search of a better life, in response to redevelopment, economic change or to escape from violence, threat (sometimes from loyalist paramilitaries) and the other everyday realities of the conflict. With some notable exceptions, the emigration patterns and experiences of Northern Irish Protestants remain under-researched,[74] but one certain result is that the population left behind is now much smaller, aging and economically marginalized, with a preponderance either benefit-dependent or on low income.

East Belfast: community myths and memories

Like any geographically and socially bounded community, inner East Belfast contains its own widely reproduced collective history, myths, communal narratives

[70] D. Purvis, P. Shirlow, and M. Langhammer, *A Call to Action?* (Belfast: Dawn Purvis MLA Office, 2012).

[71] P. Nolan, *Northern Ireland Peace Monitoring*, Number 3 (Belfast: Community Relations Council, 2014).

[72] Northern Ireland Statistics and Research Agency, 'Northern Ireland Multiple Deprivation Measure 2010'.

[73] Nelson, *Ulster's Uncertain Defenders*; R. Weiner, *The Rape and Plunder of the Shankill* (Belfast: Notaems Press, 1980).

[74] See P. R. Ireland, 'Irish Protestant migration and politics in the USA, Canada, and Australia: a debated legacy', *Irish Studies Review*, 20, no. 3 (2012): 263–281; J. D. Trew, 'Negotiating identity and belonging: migration narratives of protestants from Northern Ireland', *Immigrants & Minorities: Historical Studies in Ethnicity, Migration and Diaspora*, 25, no. 1 (2007): 22–48.

and shared remembering, which help in part to define these communities[75] and transmit political identity and values. Two sets of stories remain deeply impressed on the consciousness of many Protestants in the area: the first surround the Blitz in the Second World War and the second, events surrounding St. Matthews Catholic Church in the early summer of 1970.

The construction and narration of such stories is central to a process whereby social actors organize events that in part make up and in part link with, larger macro narratives, in this case the construction of an Ulster British identity. In doing so, of course, they draw on and reconstruct collective memories. It is not only that they interpret and give meanings to those memories, but it is also that the memories are themselves crammed with interpretations and overlaid with meanings. It is not simply that memory is fallacious (although of course it is), rather that memories are themselves fluid social products.[76]

Hence, here we will explore more fully how groups provide individuals with the frameworks within which to interpret wider events. I will concentrate on how memories are 'localised',[77] often through the construction of long-standing community narratives and shared stories, that are used to organize and build identities. These are passed on through the notion of tradition, heritage and communal understandings of politics and societal organization. One such community narrative surrounds the commitment shown to Britain and the allies during the Second World War. Fundamental to this is the bombing of Northern Ireland by the Luftwaffe in 1941.

German bombs on Belfast

When the Luftwaffe bombed Harland and Wolff on the night of 7 April 1941, it readily exposed the frailty of Belfast's air defence. Thirteen people died in the initial raids, but when the Germans returned in force on Easter Tuesday (15 April) 1941 and then again a week later, the bombing took a much heavier toll, resulting in 745 dead and more than 400 seriously injured. There was another raid on Belfast in early May; the primary strategic target was again Harland and Wolff shipyards, which at the time was producing up to three Royal Navy ships per week. However, much wider areas of East Belfast also bore the full force of the raids with firestorms devastating many residential areas (Public Records Office of Northern Ireland, D3038/3/12). There was widespread damage and to many public buildings, including many Churches, part of Belfast City Hall, the Ulster Hospital for Women and Children, Ballymacarrett public library, Strand Public Elementary School, one of Belfast's main Railway Stations and a Tram Depot. A smaller raid the following night reinforced the destruction in the

---

[75] J. K. Olick, 'Collective memory: the two cultures', *Sociological Theory*, 17, 3 (1999): 333–348; E. Zerubavel, 'Social memories: steps to a sociology of the past', *Qualitative Sociology*, 19, no. 3 (1996): 283–299.

[76] S. Lawler, *Identity: Sociological Perspectives* (Cambridge: Polity, 2008), 17.

[77] P. Connerton, *How Societies Remember*, 37.

east of the city. The Oval football ground, home to Glentoran, one of Ireland's leading football teams, was demolished, the pitch, terracing, stands and offices all completely destroyed (Public Records Office of Northern Ireland, FIN/30/AA/99, HA/32/1/764). It became symbolic of the devastation to life and property suffered in the east of the city, where several residential streets were all but levelled (Public Records Office of Northern Ireland, HA/32/1/764).

From a German perspective, the raids were remarkably successful, devastating the Harbour infrastructure and damaging the Shipyard so badly that it took six months to rebuild, severely delaying warship production (Public Records Office of Northern Ireland, D1896). Across the city, many residential areas also saw widespread destruction. In the four major raids that have become known as the 'Belfast Blitz', 955 people were killed, 2,436 people were injured and over 56,000 houses were damaged, 3,200 of which were demolished. It left Belfast as one of the worst affected cities in the UK, and it meant that outside of London, the city suffered the greatest loss of life in any single night raid during the Second World War.

If successfully constructed, social memory also helps build a narrative by which people understand the complex social world in which they live and function to enhance social cohesion amongst those buying into the dominant social narrative of the group. Loyalists read these raids in a certain way, namely:

> The people of Northern Ireland displayed their loyalty in Britain in two World wars, with great loss of life, through the sacrifice of its soldiers, sailors and airmen, and the 1,000 – plus citizens of Belfast who died in the German air raids of 1941.... Northern Ireland Protestants have nothing to feel embarrassed about as far as their membership of the United Kingdom is concerned. They are as British as the people of England, Scotland and Wales, and that is the way it will remain for the foreseeable future.[78]

Events of 27 and 28 June 1970

Another deeply localized set of memories surrounds the events that developed in Ballymacarrett on the evening of 27 June 1970. What happened remains highly contested. What is reasonably agreed, on what was described as 'East Belfast's worst night since air-raids',[79] is that following a day of unrest in West Belfast, during which three Protestants had been killed, darkness brought rioting, petrol bombing and intermittent gunfire. Much heavier gunfire broke out in the east of the city, and this developed into an extended 'gunbattle' between republicans in the Short Strand and loyalists in Ballymacarrett, which lasted throughout the night until dawn.

---

[78] *Orange Standard*, October 2006.
[79] *News Letter*, 28 June 1970.

At this point, however, any consensus evaporates. Either the events represented the fledgling Provisional IRA coming of age and launching a 'fiendish attack on the innocent population of the Lower Newtownards Road',[80] or what took place is best understood an isolated Catholic district fighting for 'survival' in defending the enclave from marauding loyalist hordes.[81] Either what took place was a valiant attempt by loyalists to defend residents from a cowardly premeditated plan attack by IRA snipers who had taken up prime position, or a case of valiant effort by a few republicans and Citizens' Defence Committee members in Short Strand to protect their community by drawing on what few resources were available to them.

The republican narrative is straightforward, involving 'a struggle for the very existence of a small nationalist, republican enclave which existed under the shadows of the giant cranes of the Belfast shipyard as a symbol of unionist power and domination'.[82] More directly, the events are seen as marking the coming of age of the Provisional IRA, under the leadership of its Belfast commander, Billy McKee, indicating a reinvigoration of the organization many working-class nationalists believed had failed them during the widespread street violence of August 1969. Indeed, republicans largely refer to events that night as 'The Battle of St Matthews', and with this, collective memory events are positioned as follows:

> … after the pogroms of 1969, the people of this Parish decided they wouldn't suffer the same fate as other vulnerable communities across the north had. With Loyalist marches taking place across the city throughout that day and attacks on areas in the north and west of the City predictably occurring, the people of this Parish (as they had done so many times before down through the generations) battered down the hatches [and] prepared themselves for the inevitable onslaught. The people, alongside the Irish Republican Army, took to the streets in defence of the community and to hold back the descending hordes of Loyalist attackers.[83]

The loyalist narrative is equally frank and uncomplicated, but in almost direct opposition to the above. From within this version, the narrative outlined above merely points to another example of 'the republican propaganda (spin) machine [which] 'throughout the conflict in Northern Ireland has been clever, sharp, focussed and has been very successful in getting their (the republican) message across'.[84]

For loyalists, what took place on Saturday 27 June 1970 was a series of planned and coordinated republican attacks across the city, which began early in the day in

---

[80] longkeshinsideout, 2013

[81] *An Phoblacht*, 30 July 2010.

[82] *Ibid.*

[83] *Coiste Chuimhneacháin Chath Naomh Máitiú*, '40th Anniversary Commemorative Events' (Belfast: Battle of St. Matthews Commemoration Committee, 2010).

[84] East Belfast Historical and Cultural Society, *Murder In Ballymacarrett – The Untold Story* (Belfast: EBHCS, 2006), 3.

West Belfast with confrontations between followers of the annual Orange Whiterock parade and nationalist youths, and culminating in three Protestants being shot dead in that part of the city. When Orangemen, bands and supporters returned to East Belfast, they too came under attack; first from stone-throwing youths, and sometime later from 'Republican gunmen ... [using] ... the grounds of St. Matthew's Chapel as their base'.[85] From the loyalist perspective therefore, the violence that occurred is set in the context of defence of their community against an unprovoked outbreak of Provisional IRA aggression, during which it was claimed that the IRA had fired 800 rounds.[86]

The consequences were both immediate and far-reaching. The following day, several hundred Catholic workers were expelled from the shipyard.[87] But there were wider outcomes. Liam Clarke suggests the events: 'gave two sets of paramilitaries the lift-off they needed, leaving the communities bitterly divided'.[88] For republicans, it was seen as key to the development of and recruitment to the Provisional IRA[89]; for loyalists, it confirmed their society was under direct threat, giving rise to claims that the local unit of the UVF was formed in direct response.[90]

Whatever the full details of events may be, and it is highly unlikely the circumstances will ever be agreed, what is of most consequence is that the incident has become a deeply significant historical reference point, a widely held 'community myth', part of the collective memory in the local district and beyond. Moreover, it is important to recognize that 'in a divided society, myths are a way of preserving old loyalties for a new generation and keeping old wounds fresh and unhealed'.[91] Certainly, for many loyalists, the story of the events dovetail neatly with the wider loyalist narrative surrounding the untrustworthy Other and the danger of the enemy within. This worldview is reflected in the words on the memorial stone erected on the Newtownards Road in commemoration of the events of 27 and 28 June 1970, which makes clear the perspective of those who placed it there. It reads:

> That night in a planned and unprovoked attack, the Provisional IRA introduced guns on to the streets of East Belfast from the sanctuary of St. Matthew's Chapel and surrounding area. They murdered James (Jimmy) McCurrie and Robert (Ginger) Neill also wounding 28 other men, women and children.

---

[85] *Ibid.*, 19.

[86] J. McCaffery, *The Irish Question: Two Centuries of Conflict* (Kentucky: University Press of Kentucky, 1995).

[87] CAIN [Conflict Archive on the Internet] 'A Chronology of the Conflict – 1970'. Available at: http://cain.ulst.ac.uk/othelem/chron/ch70.htm#Jun; accessed 10 February 2014.

[88] L. Clarke, 'It takes two sides to tear apart a myth', *Sunday Times*, 13 June 2010.

[89] R. W. White, *Provisional Irish Republicans: An Oral and Interpretive History* (Westport, CT: Greenwood Publishing Group, 1993).

[90] East Belfast Historical and Cultural Society, *Murder In Ballymacarrett*, 26.

[91] *Newsletter*, 22 June 2010.

Conclusions

Loyalist political consciousness is developed within a distinct framework within which social and political identifiers provide rationalization for social, political and physical separation, and ultimately for some people the justification for involvement in political violence against the Other.[92] Engaging in such political violence, and the subsequent experiences of victimhood, formed a crucial ingredient of the collective memory of both Protestants and Catholics influencing how each conceived both their own identity and that of the Other. These views were in turn often reinvigorated and reinforced by community myths and narratives of collective memory,[93] blame and injured party.

In particular, collective memories surrounding major events frequently provide the platform to for the legitimization of contemporary beliefs, attitudes and involvement in political action. As the conflict deepened, these formed the basis for contemporary orientations as each community sought to validate its position by reinforcing its own narrative, highlighting the worth of their own experiences and perspective, while minimizing those of the Other.

While this chapter has largely focused on the development of loyalist thought and organization within one identifiable geographical community, many of the processes of identity construction through reference to collective memory are universal. Finally, this chapter has identified community as a hub for identity formation, both as a point of economic and political resource and in its imagined sense as a key focus for loyalist identity. We will return to the importance of community for loyalist politics at several points in the remaining chapters.

[92] H. Hirsch, *Genocide and the Politics of Memory: Studying Death to Preserve Life* (Chapel Hill, NC: University of North Carolina Press, 1995).

[93] R. White, 'Social and Role Identities and Political Violence: Identity as a Window on Violence in Northern Ireland', in *Social Identity, Intergroup Conflict, and Conflict Resolution*, eds. R. D. Ashmore, L. Jussim, and D. Wilder (Oxford: Oxford University Press, 1991), 159–183.

5

Memory, Narratives and Popular Culture

At its outbreak, the Troubles witnessed diverging senses of community and oppositional collective identities that found an outlet in the inter-communal rioting that marked the conflict of the early 1970s. This gradually gave way to a lengthy if low intensity conflict involving the British state, republican paramilitaries (most prominently the Provisional IRA and Irish National Liberation Army) and loyalist groupings such as the UDA and the UVF. During the next three decades, overt acts of political violence became almost everyday events, including at least 35,000 shooting incidents and some 10,000 explosions. Between 1969 and 1997, the death toll from the conflict steadily mounted to total over three and a half thousand people.[1]

The impact on Northern Irish society and the legacy of such widespread social division and violence experienced throughout this period cannot be overstated. Such memories are long-standing and as Katy Hayward correctly reminds us, the transition from conflict requires not just a reduction of violence, but also the social and political space to 'debate peace'.[2] Any such deliberation in Northern Ireland is often compressed and made difficult by the strength of collective memories and oppositional readings of the past upon which different groupings draw. These are not used as a preservative for bygone events, but rather subject to contemporary interpretations.

This is further complicated in deeply divided societies where collective memory is grounded in a long history of ethno-political and sectarian difference, because as Connerton[3] notes 'experience of the present very largely depends on our knowledge of the past'. While communal separation is not absolute,[4] there certainly is no agreed collective memory of the past amongst members of the two dominant communities. Hence, often seemingly relatively uncontroversial matters are contested, because of the way in which they are viewed through the prism of what has gone before, and what are understood as the consequences for contemporary politics.

---

[1] See material in D. McKittrick, S. Kelters, B. Feeney, and C. Thornton, *Lost Lives: The Stories of the Men, Women and Children Who Died as a Result of the Northern Ireland Troubles* (Edinburgh: Mainstream Publishing, 1999).

[2] K. Hayward and C. O'Donnell, *Political Discourse and Conflict Resolution* (London: Routledge, 2010), 13.

[3] Connerton, *How Societies Remember*, 2–3.

[4] R. MacGinty, *International Peacebuilding and Local Resistance: Hybrid Forms of Peace* (Basingstoke: Palgrave Macmillan, 2011), 193.

Acts of remembrance, including commemorative displays and rituals, represent part of a fraught process of political competition. This has been writ large in the controversy surrounding plans for a publicly funded memorial on the site of the former Maze/Long Kesh Prison. Originally, a Second World War Royal Air Force base, it was used as a detention centre following the introduction of internment on 9 August 1971 and from then was in constant use until its closure in September 2000 as a place of imprisonment. Following the Gardiner Report in 1975, Special Category status was withdrawn and a new prison was built with a self-contained cellular structure.

The 'H Blocks' witnessed thousands of both loyalist and republican prisoners passing through its jurisdiction. Because of this, the Long Kesh/Maze prison holds a central position in the collective memory of both communities.[5] It is perhaps, however, closer to the core of the Republican narrative where a series of jail protests, the breakout of thirty-eight IRA prisoners in 1983, and in particular the hunger strikes of 1980/81, form crucial periods in the formation of that communities identity.

Advanced plans to build a peace centre at the site of the Long Kesh/Maze prison were halted when First Minister Peter Robinson withdrew DUP support. It took place amid mounting expressions of unionist fears that Sinn Féin would try to turn the project (and particularly the surviving prison hospital buildings where hunger strikers died) into what they termed 'an IRA shrine', thus dominating the Protestant Unionist view of the Troubles. As the Rev Mervyn Gibson, Grand Chaplain of the Orange Order, puts it, one of the core unionist concerns surrounding the Maze it that the story of the hunger strike will come to over-shadow the memory of the many other lives taken during the Troubles.[6] In this sense, the memorial risks becoming merely a 'ritualistic vehicles to remind communities of the depths to which the other side was prepared to sink'.[7]

That narrative of the past to which individuals and social groups subscribe and the version of history that is understood by those groups as being most legitimate always directly influence contemporary social and political developments. In turn, this often gives direction to political movements and organization in the present. Rebecca Graff-McRae puts this well when she says:

> For both Unionists and Republicans, the ghosts of the Troubles are symbolically tied to the Maze .... In both Unionist and Republican discourses, the preservation of a symbolic site is explicitly linked to the preservation of memory. For Republicans, the memory of the Troubles can be deployed in a positive transformative direction; for Unionists, such ghosts must be exorcized to prevent the past from continually troubling the present.[8]

---

[5] L. McAtackney, *An Archaeology of the Troubles: The Dark Heritage of Long Kesh/Maze Prison* (Oxford: Oxford University Press, 2014).

[6] 'Unionists, the Maze prison and Bobby Sands'. Available at: http://www.thedetail.tv/columns/steven-mccaffery/unionists-the-maze-prison-and-bobby-sands; accessed 14 September 2014.

[7] R. MacGinty and J. Darby, *Contemporary Peacemaking* (Basingstoke: Palgrave Macmillan, 2002), 157.

[8] R. L. Graff-McRae, 'Popular Memory in Northern Ireland', in *War Memory and Popular Culture*, eds. M. Keren and H. H. Herwig (Jefferson, NC: McFarland and Company, 2000), 41–56.

The ability to highlight continuities with what has gone before appeals directly (in this case through 'ghosts of the past') to give structure to understanding and interpretation of the contemporary social world. There are important consequences from this, not least is the centrality of shared mutual cultural understanding in maintaining the imagined community.[9] A core part of this process is 'the inter-generational transmission of values' through which children learn sectarian narrative of the national past 'at their mother's knee'.[10] Indeed, recent findings[11] suggest that over half of all their respondents (54 per cent of Protestants and 55 per cent of Catholics) believed that their parents had greatest influence on their knowledge of Northern Ireland's history.

Much of this popular memory[12] is deeply embedded in symbolism, political myth and popular culture, where cultural expressions of identity, variants of foundation myths and deep seeded community narratives are reproduced, celebrated and displayed on a regular, often daily basis.[13] A key focus for the chapter will therefore be a detailed consideration of the construction of loyalist popular culture. It will reflect on how popular culture is used in the construction and reconstruction of a loyalist memory and identity of these through case studies of the Orange Order, loyalist marching bands and importantly through the production of loyalist songs[14] and prose.

Popular culture is not just about pleasure, but it also represents values, identities and political interests[15] and is produced in relation to geography, place and cultural identities,[16] sometimes being shaped and operating at a highly localized level. In this context, popular cultures also provide for the transmission of collective memories and form part of the filter through which people understand their past and construct their future goals. These in different ways have become central to the 'culture war', in which large sections of loyalism now believe it is involved. This surrounds the perceived challenge to the construction of unionism in general and loyalism in particular, confronting solidarity based around the images, metaphors and shared symbolism, all of which are deeply located across the loyalist community.

---

[9] B. Parekh, *Report of the Commission on the Future of Multi-Ethnic Britain* (London: Profile Books, 2000).

[10] Stewart, *The Narrow Ground*, 16.

[11] J. Byrne, J. Bell, and U. Hansson, *Shared Living: Mixed Residential Communities in Northern Ireland* (Belfast: Institute for Conflict Research, 2006).

[12] R. L. Graff-McRae, 'Popular Memory in Northern Ireland', in *War Memory and Popular Culture*, eds. M. Keren and H. H. Herwig, 41–56.

[13] Bell, 'Mythscapes': Billig, *Banal Nationalism*.

[14] K. Radford, 'Red, white, blue and orange: an exploration of historically bound allegiances through loyalist song', *The World of Music*, 46, no. 1 (2004): 71–89.

[15] J. Street, *Politics and Popular Culture* (Cambridge: Polity Press, 1997).

[16] J. Connell and C. Gibson, *Sound Tracks: Popular Music Identity and Place* (London: Routledge, 2002).

Orange memory and narratives

One of the most visible groupings presenting a focus for loyalism is the Orange Order. Although membership numbers have reduced dramatically in recent decades, the Order continues to present itself as major guardians of loyalist memory and highlights its role in securing British identity on the Island. The Order continues to be both an outlet for distinctive social, religious and political identity and to act as a central marker of social belonging and ethnic identity,[17] underpinned by the assertion that the Orange Order continues to be central to the preservation of Protestant, Unionist and British values.[18]

In functioning as a political and community institution,[19] the Order provides a frame for cultural expression and political engagement within which narratives around memory and tradition are highly significant. The Orange narrative finds meaning through spoken and written words, artefacts, shared experiences and even sometimes in the physical environment by way of parades or monuments and memorials. All express a narrative that Orangeism draws upon to reproduce a particular set of collective memories that reinforces identity, and which becomes both 'the content and context for what they will jointly recall and commemorate'.[20]

Ritual and symbolism retain central meaning in the transmission of the Orange narrative as crucial ways of creating and solidifying narratives and transmitting collective memories over time. It is through such ceremony and repeated symbolic practices that continuity with the past is highlighted.[21] It is in this way that certain norms are enforced and regularly reinvented to meet current concerns.[22] Orange conventions and customs, such as public parades and closed meetings, buttress group solidarity through ritual expression that reinforces shared values and beliefs and send clear messages to both internal and external audiences.[23]

The importance of material objects in acts of remembrance should also not be understated.[24] A clear signifier of this can be seen in many of the public displays of Orangeism, within which physical expressions of collective memories offer a shared identity and direct link between past and present. Consequently, participating in ritual and commemorative events:

---

[17] J. W. McAuley and J. Tonge, '"For God and for the Crown": contemporary political and social attitudes among orange order members in Northern Ireland', *Political Psychology*, 28, no. 1 (2007): 33–54.

[18] *Orange Standard*, August 1999.

[19] Wright, 'Protestant ideology and politics in Ulster', 213–280.

[20] Middleton and Edwards, eds. *Collective Remembering*, 7.

[21] Material in E. Hobsbawn and T. Ranger, eds. *The Invention of Tradition* (Cambridge: Cambridge University Press, 1984); T. Ranger, 'The Invention of Tradition Revisited: The Case of Colonial Africa', in *The Collective Memory Reader*, eds. J. Olik, V. Vinitzky-Seroussi, and D. Levy (Oxford: Oxford University Press, 2011), 275–278.

[22] Connerton, *How Societies Remember*; N. Jarman, *Material Conflicts: Parades and Visual Displays in Northern Ireland* (Oxford: Berg, 1997).

[23] D. I. Kertzer, *Ritual, Politics and Power* (Yale: Yale University Press, 1988).

[24] Zerubavel, 'Social memories: steps to a sociology of the past'.

generates a collective re-enactment of the past. By such a re-enactment, the past, now mythified and decontextualized, is transformed into an 'unchanging and unchangeable substance' and becomes an indispensable part of the present.[25]

While Orange narratives consistently refer to the past, they do so in a precise way. This is not aimed at composing a detailed accurate account of past events, rather it is about constructing collective memories presenting a reading of this past to create of a common viewpoint, interpretation and understanding to form and reinforce the core of the group's social identity. The Orange narrative in large part focuses on events that carry emotional, political and social significance. While some cultural and political learning does take place in formal Orange Order settings, it is largely experienced through the reproduction of a narrative in informal settings that provide such knowledge, drawing as it does upon distinct historical reference points, mythology, folklore and sense of heritage.

This involvement with what Jeffrey Olick and Joyce Robins term the 'active past'[26] structures beliefs about what is to be done in the present. Hence, Orangeism consistently interprets the contemporary through past events by demonstrating the continuing relevance of the past to the group's current self-identity.[27] The Orange interpretation of history is used as a form of political reinforcement and to set contemporary political issues directly in the context of what has gone before.[28] Through this process, 'the myth of descent interprets present social changes and collective endeavours in a manner that satisfies the drive for meaning'.[29]

In turn, it is also valuable to recognize that memory cannot exist without people undertaking the act of remembering[30] and through executing collectively shared representations and understandings of the past.[31] Importantly, collective memory does not act as a precise review of past circumstances; rather, it reconstructs explanations through memory shaped by broader social forces, including commemorative displays and ritual, culminating in what Connerton terms a 'collective autobiography'.[32] This involves the prioritization of those memories that best allow for the endurance of fundamental beliefs.

---

[25] Connerton, *How Societies Remember*, 43.
[26] J. K. Olick and J. Robbins, 'Social memory studies: from "collective memory" to the historical sociology of mnemonic practices', *Annual Review of Sociology*, 24 (1998): 105–140.
[27] E. Kaufmann, *The Orange Order: A Contemporary Northern Irish History* (Oxford: Oxford University Press, 2007).
[28] J. Wertsch, *Voices of Collective Remembering* (Cambridge: Cambridge University Press, 2002).
[29] A. D. Smith, *Myths and Memories of the Nation* (Oxford: Oxford University Press, 1999), 62.
[30] D. E. Lorey and W. H. Beezley, eds. *Genocide, Collective Violence, and Popular Memory: The Politics of Remembrance in the Twentieth Century* (Wilmington, DE: Scholarly Resources, 2002).
[31] R. Wodak and J. E. Richardson, 'On the politics of remembering (or not)', *Critical Discourse Studies*, 6, no. 4 (2009): 231–235.
[32] Connerton, *How Societies Remember*, 13–14.

Tradition, memory and commemoration

It is through acts of commemoration that Orangeism inextricably links a particular
sense of social, political and collective identity, presenting a notion of tradition, practice
and ritual, through public memorial and ceremony to foster 'deep and horizontal
comradeship'.[33] Indeed, Orangeism offers support to the argument originally presented
by Halbwachs, suggesting that it is through groups that people are best able to obtain
and recollect memories,[34] and that through these shared memories, the social solidarity
and cohesion of the group is enhanced.

Accordingly, the creation of memory and the formation of tradition both take place
within a social context that directly links the individual to the group and contemporary
to historical experiences. Within this process, certain memories are relegated or
ignored, while others are given primacy in the imagined community of Orangeism.
These narratives are reinforced through specific actions and events, the power of which
rests in its 'ability to create, form, refashion and reclaim identity'.[35] Understood in this
way, one of the key functions of memory is to tie the community together from within
and to generate and replicate overarching values and shared perceptions, not only of
the past but also what is possible in the future.

Collective memories and reference to a common past remains core in constructing
knowledge of the wider social and political world. In so doing, Orangeism promotes
a broad British-Protestant way of life and emphasizes eternal vigilance against all
those continuously threatening Protestant Unionist political identity.[36] A vital part of
the Orange narrative therefore is projecting a Protestant community 'that has been
constantly under attack for 400 years'[37] and to highlight the role of the Order at the
heart of the cultural defence of Protestant unionism. It is a struggle, which for many
remains very much alive.

Memories of the future

For one section of loyalism, the only way to resolve the contemporary political and
cultural instability is by a re-emphasis of tradition in the face of what is perceived
as the continued assault on loyalist culture. Concern that loyalism is under coherent
psychological and cultural attack manifests directly around the issue of Orange
Order parades. The Orange parade as performance is underpinned by a narrative
that promotes heritage, the legitimization of tradition, the central place of religion,
respect for authority and strong support for the Union, Britishness and the Monarchy
within society.

---

[33] Anderson, *Imagined Communities*, 6–7.
[34] M. Halbwachs, *The Collective Memory*, translated by F. J. Ditter, Jr. and V. Y. Ditter (New York:
Harper Colophone Books, 1980).
[35] Rodriguez and Fortier, *Cultural Memory*: 7.
[36] *Orange Standard*, July 2007.
[37] *Orange Standard*, August 2008.

Social identification, remembering and forgetting alongside the use of accessible artefacts, rituals and a particular understanding of tradition combine to enable Orange members orient themselves in their social world. Orange discourse offers overt guidance to individuals as to how their personal and public lives should be conducted. Importantly, as Ron Eyerman and Andrew Jamison[38] explain, it is through such preordained ceremonies that participants are reminded of their place in the broader social and political movement, by locating them within what are seen as long-standing traditions.

While Orange Order members emphasize different elements, for most politics and religious involvement remain about the existence of the state. The core belief for many in the Order is that it must continue to act as a fortification to maintain the British way of life, and it is this that is at the nucleus of the Orange narrative that continues to stress the 'unbroken and unyielding' defence of the Protestant faith and Christian principles, loyalty to the Crown and to a state that guarantees civil and religious liberty for all.[39]

Members of the Orange Order draw on the perceived constants in this narrative, to make sense of current events and to reinforce responses that are seen to protect the overarching identity of Britishness. Indeed, for John Brewer and Gareth Higgins, this is part of a broader process through which heritage and tradition are used to constantly reproduce 'the same two antinomies that have governed Protestant identity since plantation, for marching is an expression of Britishness (against Irishness) and Protestantism (against Catholicism)'.[40]

Orange narrative thus provides a clear example in support of Samuel's claim that the past can increasingly be seen as a 'plaything of the present'.[41] As a result, in this way, the Orange Order, although it may seem archaic, demonstrates how the past increasingly impinges on popular consciousness and understandings of the present. Social memories not only shape how we understand both the past and present, but frame what we conceptualize as achievable futures,[42] through the 'dynamic social and psychological process' of drawing on social memories to create a 'collective narrative'.[43] Moreover, and somewhat contradictorily, social memory is concerned at the same time with process of both stability and change, referring to continuity and a conservation of the past, while reinterpreting past events to provide justifications for both social and political beliefs and the needs of the present and future actions.[44]

---

[38] R. Eyerman and A. E. Jamison, *Social Movements: A Cognitive Approach* (University Park, PA: Pennsylvania State University Press, 1991).

[39] *Orange Standard*, August 1999.

[40] Brewer and Higgins, *Anti-Catholicism in Northern Ireland*, 125.

[41] R. Samuel, 'Ulster Row over Powell's Definition of Loyalism', *Past and Present in Contemporary Culture* (London: Verso, 2012), 429.

[42] J. Brockmeier, 'Remembering and forgetting: narrative as cultural memory', *Culture and Psychology*, 8, no. 1 (2002): 15–43.

[43] Devine-Wright, 'A Theoretical Overview of Memory and Conflict', 28.

[44] Wertsch, *Voices of Collective Remembering*.

It is important to stress that individual memory exists inside of a collective framework. Our memories link us to other people and those who remember and commemorate in ways to bind them into a given community. People's lives, both in the past and present, determine what we should remember and the act of remembrance, sustained by books, photos, recordings, songs and folk memories and so on. Particular understandings of the past are often used, not just as justification to reinforce long-standing beliefs and attitudes, but also to legitimize actions in the present.[45] This gives shape to contemporary experiences, and the parameters of thought, in terms of both past and present.

Hence, loyalism often draws deeply on a narrative of the past that presents the contemporary conflict as merely the latest phase in a struggle to preserve, not just the existing constitutional position, but also a broader sense of their identity, which is seen as constantly threatened by other cultures and identities, primarily, of course, that of Irish nationalism and republicanism, which they continue to regard as alien, hostile and belligerent.

Founding narratives

Collective memories are part of a usable past, constructed to legitimize contemporary beliefs, attitudes and actions. Hence, identity 'is not something which is elemental, rather it is *produced* through the narratives people use to explain and understand their lives'.[46] It is often through reference to tradition and heritage that the justification for contemporary political actions is made. As Rafi Nets-Zehngut[47] explains when considering the Israeli-Palestinian conflict, in such situations collective memory is often compiled around major events. Through processes of inclusion or exclusion of certain episodes, groups identify and differentiate their experiences in particular ways.

This everyday formation of collective memories through the transmission of community narratives is vital in the diffusion of identity, because as Arthur writes, the 'political symbolism of whichever interpretation is adopted remains central to subsequent events'.[48] Anthony Giddens goes so far to suggest that an individual's identity rests in 'the capacity *to keep a particular narrative going*'.[49] Here, I wish to consider two examples of foundation myths within Ulster loyalism: the siege of Derry and the battle of the Somme.

---

[45] D. Páez, N. Basabe, and J. L. González, 'Social Processes and Collective Memory: A Cross-Cultural Approach to Remembering Political Events', in *Collective Memory of Political Events: Social Psychological Perspectives*, eds. J. W. Pennebaker, D. Páez, and B. Rimé (Hillsdale: Lawrence Erlabaum, 1997), 147–174.

[46] S. Lawler, *Identity: Sociological Perspectives* (Cambridge: Polity, 2008), emphasis in original.

[47] R. Nets-Zehngut, 'Major events and the collective memory of conflicts', *International Journal of Conflict Management*, 24, no. 3 (2013): 209–230.

[48] Arthur, *Government and Politics of Northern Ireland*, 3.

[49] A. Giddens, *Modernity and Self-Identity* (Oxford: Blackwell, 1991), 75, emphasis in original.

The Siege of Derry

Several writers have pointed to how emotionally central the feelings of siege are to many unionists and loyalists' sense of identity. Central to this is the foundation myth surrounding the 'Siege of Derry', a key encounter in the Williamite War waged between the Protestant William of Orange and the Catholic King James II.[50] Briefly, following the arrival in March 1689 of King James from France with a large professional army sent by Louis XIV, Jacobite forces made steady advances northwards. After a series of defeats in Dromore, Lisburn, Antrim and Belfast, the garrison based in Coleraine, alongside Protestants from all over the north, sought refuge in Derry.

The forces of James were, however, too lightly armed and poorly equipped to storm the city and had instead sought to enforce a blockade in the hope of starving those behind the walls into surrender. Having cut off Derry by land, the French constructed a boom across the river Foyle to ensure that supplies could not be landed from sea. As a result, most of those who died during the siege did so from disease and starvation rather than in military engagement. The blockade was eventually ended after 105 days when at the end of July relief ships broke through the boom to sail upriver to relieve the city.

Three incidents arising from the siege have become embedded into loyalist collective memory and folklore. The first was the closing by thirteen apprentice boys of the gates of Derry in the face of the advancing forces of King James II; the second was the actions (or perhaps more accurately inactions) of Lieutenant-Colonel Robert Lundy, the Governor of Derry, who appeared to advocate surrender of the City to Jacobite forces; and third was the breaking of the boom across the river Foyle, which ensured the beginning of the relief of the city. Both the 'shutting of the gates' and the 'relief of Derry' feature directly in annual commemorations of the events in August and December, respectively. As does Colonel Robert Lundy, the burning of whose effigy is an established part of the loyalist calendar and whose name has become embedded in the loyalist popular memory to represent a traitor or quisling.

If we return to Harbinson's account of his upbringing in the 1950s, he gives a sense of the centrality and importance of the communication of the narrative of the Siege of Derry, as he recalls:

> In school nobody ever told us about Marie Antoinette or Marshal Foch, but we knew Louis XIV and Robert Lundy the treacherous governor of Derry. We might not know the date of the French Revolution but we did know that in 1688, thirteen young men, apprentices in the city, closed the gates of Derry in the face of Catholic soldiers.[51]

The young Harbinson was also aware of the centrality of commemoration for the local community. Recounting seeing members of the Royal Black Institution on their way to commemorate the closing of the gates of Derry during the siege, he recalls

---

[50] I. McBride, *The Siege of Derry in Ulster Protestant Mythology* (Dublin: Four Courts Press, 1997).
[51] R. Harbinson, *No Surrender: An Ulster Childhood* (Belfast: Blackstaff Press, 1960), 126.

how he and many other children gathered together and 'sat out on the backyard walls, singing Orange ballads'.[52] Crucially, even at an extremely early age, Harbinson was plainly aware of the magnitude of such events within wider loyalist and unionist culture, recalling that:

> Although we enjoyed these celebrations as much as the grown-ups, we knew that serious feelings underlay the festivities. We had odd ideas on many things, but not about the reasons for these demonstrations.[53]

While today this is seen as central to the memory of loyalism and part of a story that is constantly reproduced, as Brian Walker[54] highlights, interest in the siege of Derry has changed considerably over time, and it was only the specific political relations that caused the larger Protestant and Unionist community to engage fully and exclusively in its commemoration. For example, at the annual burning of a model of Lunday Ian Paisley made reference to the apprentice boys in the following terms:

> Democratic Unionism has defended the Union at a time when other unionists were prepared to sell the Union. Like the gallant thirteen apprentice boys in Londonderry who shut the gates on the coming enemy so the DUP has prevented the destruction of the Union.[55]

The Somme

Populist memory and commemoration of the Great War has been, and remains, inseparable from broader ethno-political and sectarianized divisions. Within this fragmented memory, it is almost impossible to overemphasize the centrality and meaning of the Somme to loyalism, or its consequence as a central reference point in formulating contemporary loyalist identity[56] and ethno-history.[57] Hennessey gives some indication of this when he says:

> if any one event in the Great War might be selected as the moment which symbolized the psychological partition of Ulster Unionism from the rest of the island, it was probably the impact of the Battle of the Somme upon the Ulster Unionist psyche, and the Ulster Protestant community generally, coming as it did so soon after the Easter Rising.[58]

[52] *Ibid.*
[53] *Ibid.*
[54] B. M. Walker, *A Political History of the Two Irelands.*
[55] I. Paisley, 'Leader's Speech', DUP 25th Anniversary conference, Broughshane (DUP Press Release, 1996).
[56] K. Brown, 'Our Father Organization': 707–723.
[57] D. Officer and G. Walker, 'Protestant Ulster: ethno-history, memory and contemporary prospects', *National Identities*, 2, no. 3 (2003): 293–307.
[58] T. Hennessey, *Dividing Ireland, World War I and Partition, Ireland in 1914* (London: Routledge Press, 1998), 198.

Relationships between collective memory and collective identity are often codified and reproduced through the enacting of commemorative events, highlighting those people and actions deemed to be of greatest significance to the group. Such enactments replicate, reproduce and perpetuate core myths and memories and act to ensure that memory is transmitted by way of 'a whole set of cultural practices through which people recognize a debt to the past' [and that] 'these cultural forms store and transmit information that individuals make use of'.[59]

So, for example, Orange banners illustrating events at the Somme are commonplace, while memorials and parades extensively mark the battle, as do murals with stylized images of troops going 'over the top' at the Somme, or commemorating the four Victoria Crosses won by members of the 36th Division in the first 48 hours of the battle. Elsewhere, commemoration of the Great War in general, and the Somme in particular, is inseparable from broader ethno-political and sectarian divisions in Ireland. Although at its outbreak the War found support from nationalist and unionist political leaders, and both Catholics and Protestants joined the British Army in sizeable numbers, the experiences at the War's end and their position in subsequent commemorations differed vastly.

The complexity and politicization of these memories were compounded following partition of the Ireland and the efforts of both states to build distinctive and largely mutually exclusive identities. In particular, both populist memories and official commemorations were constructed in ways to all but eliminate the (predominately Irish Catholic) 16th Division from the *historiography* of the Great War in the South.[60] Because of their perceived Britishness, they became part of what some have called 'the Great Oblivion' or a 'national amnesia'.[61] In the North, however, the 16th Division were marginalized because of their 'Irishness', while during the same period, the Ulster Division were lauded as an overt example of patriotism and blood sacrifice for the Union to form a core pillar of Northern Irish Protestant Unionist identity.[62]

This was complicated yet further by the onset of the Troubles and the claim by the paramilitary that formed around 1966 of direct lineage to those of the UVF assembled in 1913, and who subsequently fought with the 36th Ulster Division in the First World War. Recent memorialization by loyalist paramilitaries has led to a vast number of highly localized and populist memorials appearing in the past three decades, illustrating in part the depth to which the commemoration of the Great War became directly associated

[59] M. Schudson, 'Dynamics of Distortion in Collective Memory', in *Memory Distortion: How Minds, Brains and Societies Reconstruct the Past*, ed. D. Schacter (Cambridge, MA: Harvard University Press, 1997), 346–347.

[60] E. Byrne, 'The forgotten Irish soldiers who fought for Britain in the first world war'. Available at: http://www.theguardian.com/world/2014/apr/05/irish-soldiers-who-fought-for-britain; accessed 16 April 2014.

[61] K. Jeffrey, 'Ireland and the First World War: The Historical Context'. Available at: http://www.qub.ac.uk/sites/irishhistorylive/IrishHistoryResources/ArticlesandLectures/IrelandandtheFirstWorldWar/; accessed 1 March 2012.

[62] F. Brearton, 'Dancing unto death: perceptions of the Somme, the Titanic and Ulster Protestantism', *The Irish Review*, 20 (1997): 89–103.

with the broad Unionist and loyalist community.[63] The commemoration of this became an almost exclusively Unionist and loyalist event. In the post-conflict period, many have joined Somme associations to link directly to the past and express future unswervingly to the formation of British/unionist identity,[64] but which link to contemporary loyalism.

Within the populist culture of many Protestants, the entire events of World War are condensed into the single event of the Somme,[65] whereby Ulster's ungrudging sacrifice is the key building bloc in the 'paradigmatic model of the ideal Ulsterman'.[66] Another indication of this can be found in the following speech at a commemoration event organized by the East Belfast Historical and Cultural Society:

> In the First World War thousands of Ulstermen left these shores and fought for King and Country. On the 1st July 1916 these men as part of the 36th Ulster Division launched [an] attack by British forces against the enemy. Thousands died in a matter of hours. They fought for our freedom, they fought and died that we might live in peace they fought and died that we would remain part of the UK. 90 years later we must never forget that sacrifice. It must be ingrained in our memory and we must do everything in our power to follow their example of loyalty; courage and sacrifice so that in 90 years time future generations will reflect kindly on this generation.[67]

Events at the Somme[68] now form such a central reference point within loyalist identity that as a foundation myth it has for many become at least equivalent to that of 1690, and for some, it attains even more central significance. As such, the Somme is conflated with the Boyne and elevated across loyalism achieving 'near-sacred status in popular memory'.[69] Much of the core narrative is identified and transmitted in the following loyalist song entitled, 'From the Shankill to the Somme':

> At the age of sixteen years,
> Well he left his home in tears,
> His mother watched as he walked out the door,
> And as his family bade farewell,
> and his neighbours wished him well,
> From the road his dad and brother took before.

---

[63] C. Switzer, *Unionists and Great War Commemoration in the North of Ireland 1914–1939* (Dublin: Irish Academic Press, 2007).

[64] D. Officer, 'For God and for Ulster': The Ulsterman on the Somme', in *History and Memory in Modern Ireland*, ed. I. McBride (Cambridge: Cambridge University Press, 2001), 160–183; B. Graham and P. Shirlow, 'The Battle of the Somme in Ulster Memory and Identity', *Political Geography*, 21, no. 7 (2002): 881–904.

[65] D. Bryan, *Orange Parades: The Politics of Ritual, Tradition and Control* (London: Pluto, 2000); N. Jarman, *Material Conflicts: Parades and visual Displays in Northern Ireland*, (Oxford: Berg, 1997).

[66] Officer, 'For God and for Ulster': 82.

[67] East Belfast Historical and Cultural Society, 'Speech at the Grand Opening of the Thorndyke Street Murals' (Belfast: EBHCS, 2004): 3.

[68] C. Switzer, *Ulster, Ireland and the Somme: War Memorials and Battlefield Pilgrimages*, (Dublin: The History Press Ireland, 2013).

[69] N. Jarman, *Material Conflicts*, 72.

Chorus: And as the ship set sail for France,
He gave Belfast one more glance,
As the ship began to move away from shore,
He could see there on the land, the proud YCV flute band,
And he could hear them play 'The Sash My Father Wore'.

Oh, from the Shankill Road they went,
Oh, their young lives to be spent,
On the first day of July so long Ago,
And for the deeds that they have done,
And the glories they have won,
We remember as long as the bright red poppy grow.

When they charged from Thiepval wood,
They were in a fighting mood,
As they made their way across the fields of fire,
And as they stormed the great redoubt,
You could hear those brave men shout,
To have them lie beneath the twisted shells and wire
We remember as long as the bright red poppy grow.

Commemoration and popular cultures

Collective memories provide frameworks through which individuals engage with and re-enforce group identities. All of this emphasizes that memory and memorial needs individuals and groups to be active in carrying out and participating in acts of remembering and commemoration.[70] Hence, representations and perspectives on the past of the past can be altered to explain and make a better 'fit' with the contemporary.[71] As David Cooper[72] suggests:

History has certainly been sharply etched into the consciousness of the people who live in Northern Ireland. Dates such as 1607 (the Flight of the Earls), 1690 (the Battle of the Boyne), 1798 (the United Irishmen's Rebellion) and 1916 (the Easter Rising) are still all too keenly remembered, and the names of places where battles were lost and won centuries ago remain tokens of everyday conversation, even in the primary school playground.

[70] P. Pinkerton, 'Resisting memory: the politics of memorialisation in post-conflict Northern Ireland', *The British Journal of Politics and International Relations*, 14, no. 1 (2012): 131–152.

[71] Middleton and Edwards, *Collective Remembering*.

[72] D. Cooper. 'On the twelfth of July in the morning … or the man who mistook his sash for a hat', *Folk Music Journal*, 8 (2001): 67–89.

Following the outbreak of the Troubles, overlapping senses of loyalist identity manifested at the macro level through an emphasis on a distinct sense of Britishness (and crucially an antagonism to Irishness) and at the micro level through expressions of communal belonging. Crucially, loyalist reference to, and the ordering of, memories help individuals and groups construct understandings of political life. Loyalists draw on distinctive memories that are meaningful to them, which help them understand and respond to events and often seek to commemorate and replicate the events on which the memories draw. Central to this process is the weight given to perceived continuities between past and present organized through encounters with distinct political-cultural memories.[73]

The numbers of Protestants who participate in commemorative events is not inconsiderable (see Table 5.1). The resulting senses of fit, draws on collective memories, narratives and interpretations to produce contemporary understandings of unionism and loyalism.[74] Partly, as we shall see, this is because the construction of collective memory involves processes of both remembering[75] and forgetting.[76] The resulting ideas and narratives 'give shape to our experience, thought and imagination in terms of past, present and future'.[77]

Table 5.1 Have you ever taken part in historical anniversaries/commemorations?

Event	Total (%)	Protestants (%)	Catholics (%)
Not taken part in any	42	21	59
Remembrance Sunday	35	66	11
Boyne/12th of July	23	51	3
Battle of the Somme	9	18	2
Bloody Sunday	9	3	16
Hunger Strikes	8	0	17
Easter Rising	7	3	13
Relief/Siege of Derry	6	13	1
Closing of the Gates	3	7	1
Internment	1	0	3

Source: Adapted from Bell et al. (2010).

---

[73] K. Trew, O. Muldoon, G. McKeown, and K. McLaughlin, 'The media and memories of conflict in Northern Ireland', *Journal of Children and Media*, 3, no. 2 (2009): 185–203.

[74] See J. W. McAuley, *Ulster's Last Stand? Orangeism and Britishness in Northern Ireland* (Dublin: Irish Academic Press, 2010).

[75] Schwartz, 'The social context of commemoration'.

[76] J. Wertsch, 'Collective Memory', in *Memory in Mind and Culture*, eds. P. Boyer and J. V. Wertsch (Cambridge: Cambridge University Press, 2009), 117–137.

[77] Brockmeier, 'Remembering and forgetting', 15–43.

It is Prager[78] who suggests memories are best understood as cultural products, affected by the wider culture, but also the result of relationships to Self and the outside world. Following on from this, Connerton argues that it is so difficult to disentangle the past from the present, not just because present circumstances 'tend to influence – some might want to say distort – our recollections of the past', but also because 'past factors tend to influence, or distort, our experience of the present'.[79] Importantly, outcomes of this process can also involve the silencing of competing narratives of memory.[80]

Broadly, the dominant collective memory of the Great War in loyalist communities served several purposes to legitimize the Britishness in Northern Ireland; as a means to laud the events as a core pillar of Northern Irish Protestant Unionist identity; and for some to legitimize paramilitary organizations and operations within the loyalist community itself. Thus, following Partition, the memory of the past was enlisted in the cause of contemporary politics of the day. It was militarized in the course of the Troubles, and it remains a touchstone of collective loyalist identities to this day.

Hence, the formation of loyalist collective memory is also found through the Remembrance (Armistice) Day commemorations observed each year on 11 November. However, in Northern Ireland, active participation in the day, indeed even the wearing of Poppies, is seen as a highly politicized act, symbolizing direct association with the unionist community and affiliation to Britishness. Although in very recent years there has been some softening of the position,[81] displays of commemoration of those who have died in the British forces are still opposed or at best ignored by many Irish nationalists and republicans. It was for this reason that when in 1987 the Provisional IRA exploded a bomb, killing eleven people at a Remembrance Sunday ceremony in Enniskillen, the shock waves were felt far beyond those directly involved. It was seen as attack on entire Protestant unionist community and their history of sacrifice.

Loyalist narrative and memory

Loyalism draws on an overarching meta-narrative that rolls together the Enniskillen bombing, Siege of Derry, the Battle of the Boyne, the sacrifice of the Great War and other events to mark a continuity of deed, thought and politics across loyalism. Loyalist narrative brings together particular strands of social memory, representations and identities, all of which are held together by an accepted knowledge and chronology of events (both real and assumed), as these subjective histories are told, re-told and transmitted across generations.

As Jens Brockmeier[82] explains, these narratives help position everyday events and experiences in larger discursive frames, which provide the context for explaining and

---

[78] Prager, *Presenting the Past: Sociology and the Psychoanalysis of Misremembering*.

[79] Connerton, *How Societies Remember*, 2.

[80] De Cillia, Reisigl, and Wodak, 'The discursive construction of national identities'.

[81] Walker, *A Political History of the Two Irelands*.

[82] Brockmeier, 'Remembering and forgetting'.

understanding such events.[83] The imagined community of loyalism is reconstructed and reproduced through direct reference to collective memories and which are made meaningful in the contemporary world. Importantly, these memories have everyday meaning in the ways people attach relevance to particular events in their past in understanding the present.[84] Hence, memory must be made living and part of everyday experiences.[85] As Jeanette Rodriguez and Ted Fortier argue, 'people carry a memory and that the memory itself is also a carrier'.[86]

Hence, memories and representations do not just function to support social identities, rather membership of a particular group also regulates those social identities. Through this engagement with active, living memory,[87] loyalists seek to answer core questions surrounding the identity of Self and their social and political relationships with others.[88] None of this is to suggest that individuals do not have memories that are unique, or that some memories will be shared with others and some not.[89] But it is to emphasize that collective and individual memory are multi-layered. Social memory is always facilitated through individuals,[90] importantly, however, although memories are shared not everyone remembers past events in the same way. It is also important to recognize that the past is not a given or a fixed entity to be passed on. Rather, the past is continually reinterpreted and re-evaluated and often this remembering occurs directly in relation to factors related to the present.

The resulting memories provide one instrument through which people authenticate and revalidate both Self and group identity.[91] Paul Arthur[92] suggests, for example, differences of interpretation as to whether the seventeenth-century plantations are viewed as a homecoming of the 'Celtic people of Scotland reinvigorated with the reformed faith' as emphasized by Adamson,[93] or as a straightforward case of unadorned colonial conquest and abuse, has clear political consequences for the present. The interpretation of the past frames comprehension and action in the present, and such knowledge is passed from generation to generation. Thus, the collective memories of groups in conflict predictably rewrite and reinterpret an exclusive history, to legitimize and ennoble the Self and one's own community, while highlighting the unjust nature of the values and actions of the Other.

---

[83] J. Bruner, *Acts of Meaning* (Cambridge, MA: Harvard University Press, 1990).

[84] Hirsch, *Genocide and the Politics of Memory*.

[85] J. W. Pennebaker and B. L. Banasik, 'On the Creation and Maintenance of Collective Memories'.

[86] Rodriguez and Fortier, *Cultural Memory*, 7.

[87] B. Schwartz, 'The social context of commemoration'.

[88] D. McAdam, S. Tarrow and C. Tilly, *Dynamics of Contention* (Cambridge: Cambridge University Press, 2001); J. K. Olick, '"Collective memory": a memoir and prospect', *Memory Studies*, 1 (2008): 23–29.

[89] Zerubavel, 'Social memories: steps to a sociology of the past', 283–299.

[90] J. Nerone and E. Wartella, 'Studying social memory', *Communication*, 11 (1989): 85–88; Olick, *The Politics of Regret – On Collective Memory and Historical Responsibility*.

[91] A. Assmann and L. Shortt, 'Memory and Political Change: Introduction', in *Memory and Political Change*, eds. A. Assmann and L. Shortt (Basingstoke: Palgrave Macmillan, 2012), 1–16.

[92] Arthur, *Government and Politics of Northern Ireland*.

[93] Adamson, *Cruthin; Identity of Ulster*.

Perfect loyalist memory

One clear representation of how the past can influence the present and the Loyalist sense of being is found in the large mural at Thorndyke Street in East Belfast. Some 130-feet long it is made up of twelve main panels, each of which is around 30-feet tall. It is a physical representation of the collective memories of loyalism. Indeed, it is possible to argue that it projects an idealized understanding of loyalist political memory. This is brought into further relief by recognizing that those who commissioned the work did so to convey the story of Ulster Protestants and to counter those: 'Republicans [who] peddle the myth that … the Protestant/ Loyalist/ Unionist community have no culture and no history'.[94]

Given this overt goal, it is important to consider which historical events are selected and drawn upon to represent the collective memories of loyalism. The mural depicts the following in order: 'the Ulster Covenant; the Ulster Scots (Scots-Irish) Connection; Oliver Cromwell in Ireland; the Siege of Derry; the Orange Order; the Home Rule Crisis; the Battle of the Somme – 36th Ulster Division; the 1970s on – the sectarian Irish Republican campaign; a united community – 1974 UWC strike; the "B" Specials; Cluan Place; and the United Kingdom – Loyalty to Queen and to God'.

There are probably few surprises in the events identified as loyalist history, but it is important to point to how these are linked by a seamless narrative that draws on these collective memories to directly yoke past and present. Accordingly, at the official opening of the mural, in September 2004, the main orator drew particular attention to the panel depicting the Siege of Derry, declaring that 'Republicans continue to attack our homes, our culture and all that we hold dear'.[95] As Halbwachs reminds us essential to collective memory is that it 'retains from the past only what still lives or is capable of living in the consciousness of the groups keeping the memory alive'.[96]

This can be seen in the following statement from the UVF, which highlights what they see as a distinct heritage, drawing on loyalist history and discrete collective memories as follows:

> Great names and great events from Ulster's history pass through our thoughts, including that of William of Orange or his General, Duke Schomberg. Who can ever forget the bravery of the thirteen Apprentice Boys, who defied authority and manned the walls of the Maiden City for 105 days of starvation and deprivation? Giants of great stature such as Edward Carson, Sir James Craig, along with their comrades in Colonels Crawford and Wallace, immediately spring to mind … the signing of Ulster's Solemn League and covenant in 1912, with the formation of the Ulster Volunteer

---

[94] East Belfast Historical and Cultural Society, Thorndyke Street Murals, East Belfast, Belfast, EBHCS, 2006.

[95] *Ibid.*

[96] Halbwachs, *The Collective Memory*, 25.

Force with 100,000 armed, trained and disciplined men, ready to face and fight the might of the Empire ... Simply to remain British.[97]

Loyalist marching bands

Loyalists have sought to resist what they regard as the marginalization of their narratives by reinforcing their 'own' sense of identity. Often this occurs through the production of loyalist popular culture, and increasingly significant with this aspect of loyalist life is band culture. A growing form of expression for loyalist popular culture has been seen in the development of the marching band.[98] Orange music and marching bands have a long tradition within the Protestant Unionist community evolving from the fife and drum popularized by British military forces in the late eighteenth century to become established as part of a broader Orange parading tradition.[99]

As inter-communal violence became embedded in Northern Irish society in the early 1970s, the form, accent and organization of many loyalist bands changed.[100] As generational change manifested in personnel changes in existing bands and the formation of newer ones, there were also striking adjustments in musical range.[101] Further, the 1980s also saw another dramatic change in style, with the:

> subversion of the military marching style in the exaggerated swagger and rhythmic shuffle of the fluters; the weaving dancers of the cymbal players who jaunt, crissing and crossing, through the ranks of the rest of the band ... the vigorous, synchronised swirling of the flags by their bearers; the drum majors providing a touch of pure circus as they hurl their stocky decorated batons high into the sky above the crowd.[102]

Moreover, the adoption of a widening repertoire of popular tunes witnessed the encouragement and growth of audience participation with supporters marching on the pavements alongside the bands. Perhaps more importantly such bands became an 'increasingly visible and assertive manifestation of loyalist identity',[103] and often

---

[97] *Combat*, November 1990.

[98] D. Cairns, 'The object of sectarianism: the material reality of sectarianism in Ulster loyalism', *Journal of the Royal Anthropological Institute*, 6, no. 3 (2000): 437–452; N. Jarman, 'For God and Ulster: Blood and Thunder Bands and Loyalists Political Culture', in *The Irish Parading Tradition*, ed. T. G. Frazer (Basingstoke: Macmillan, 2000), 158–172.

[99] D. Bryan, T. G. Fraser, and S. Dunn, *Political Rituals: Loyalist Parades in Portadown* (Coleraine: University of Ulster, 1995).

[100] D. Bell, 'Acts of union: youth sub-culture and ethnic identity amongst Protestants in Northern Ireland', *The British Journal of Sociology*, 38, no. 2 (1987): 158–183.

[101] G. Ramsey, 'Practice: class, taste and identity in Ulster loyalist flute bands', *Ethnomusicology*, 1 (2011): 1–20.

[102] D. Bell, *Acts of Union: Youth Culture and Sectarianism in Northern Ireland* (London: Macmillan, 1990), 124–125.

[103] G. Ramsey, *Music, Emotion and Identity in Ulster Marching Bands: Flutes, Drums and Loyal Sons* (Oxford: Peter Lang, 2011), 113.

they were more overtly loyalist in form. Around the same time, many bands adopted a much more paramilitary style, developing a distinct image that often including replica military uniforms or combat fatigues.[104] Indeed, Neil Jarman[105] identifies how the newer marching bands not only suggested overt support for the loyalist paramilitaries, but also were seen as offering a place of opposition to mainstream Orangeism.

Hence, the emergence of a 'blood and thunder' band culture marked not just a re-configuration of populist loyalism, but also an ideological cleavage, as the new forms of politicized expression brought by the bands came into direct opposition with the more established Orange Order leadership. Up to this point, the majority of loyalist bands were directly supported by, and organized by Orange Order lodges, engagement with whom gave bands the opportunity for most of their public performances. The growing divergence between the traditional Orange leadership, emphasizing what they saw as the respectable nature of the Order's membership, compared to what they regarded as the 'rough and rowdy', more proletarian blood and thunder bands and their followers, was readily apparent. This variance has continued until today, where the vast majority of loyalist bands stand outside the direct control of the traditional organizers of Orange Order events and the involvement of bands in Orange parades form only a very small proportion of their annual activities.

Contemporary blood and thunder culture revolves around an organized calendar of events, competitions and parades organized by the bands themselves, which fall far outside the auspices or authority of the loyal Orders. These now form a distinct part of the wider loyalist commemorative culture, including band parades and competitions (for marching, turnout and musical ability), alongside parades held in tribute to, or the memory of local paramilitaries and wider cultural events such as the commemoration of Remembrance Day (with or without paramilitary involvement).

The actual number of loyalist marching bands is difficult to quantify. Darach MacDonald[106] identifies 584, while Jaqueline Witherow[107] suggests around 700 active marching bands in currency (the vast majority describing themselves as Protestant and Loyalist). In recent years, television coverage by BBC Northern Ireland has consistently reported about 800 bands on parade (although this number would be including some visiting overseas bands, largely from Scotland and occasionally from Canada), while a recent NI Youth Forum report identified 640 bands in existence.[108]

Whatever the precise figure for active band membership, it is clear the number of people involved is considerable, with the *Belfast Telegraph* reporting that Loyalist

---

[104] Bell, *Acts of Union: Youth Culture and Sectarianism in Northern Ireland*, 100.
[105] Jarman, *Material Conflicts*; 'For God and Ulster'.
[106] D. MacDonald, *Blood and Thunder: Inside an Ulster Protestant Band* (Cork: Mercier Press, 2010).
[107] J. Witherow, 'Band development in Northern Ireland: ethnographic researcher to policy consultant', *Anthropology in Action*, 13, no. 1/2 (2006): 44–54.
[108] Northern Ireland Youth Forum 'Sons of Ulster: Exploring Loyalist Band Members Attitudes towards Culture, Identity and Heritage' (Belfast: NIYF, 2013).

band number was at an all-time high at somewhere around 30,000 members.[109] Certainly, contemporary loyalist band culture directly engages large numbers of participants and supporters across the loyalist working-class population. Band culture has expanded and grown in importance to be repositioned 'at the heart of loyalist political culture',[110] within which 'members express a loyalist identity though embodied action rather than through conversation'.[111]

Involvement in band culture now stretches far beyond participation in those commemorative events or church parades traditionally undertaken with the Orange (or other Loyal Orders) to the organization of their own workshops, competitions and other social events. Crucially, from the 1980s onwards, the ability of the Order to uphold control over bands lessened, as both the number of bands and independent band parades grew, asserting values and behavior beyond the existing structures.

Perhaps most importantly, as the number of parades increased, so the bands became increasingly important in the lives of their members (mainly young working-class Protestant men), as did the assertion that parading was a necessary assertion of a threatened and marginalized culture. All this is deeply entwined with social class.[112] Gordon Ramsey[113] demonstrates how the behaviour, aesthetics and preferences of band members can be seen as the outgoings of a particular class faction in positioning themselves as defenders of loyalist (and perhaps more broadly Protestant and Unionist) identity.

Politics of commemoration

Remembrance and commemoration in Northern Ireland is highly politicized, moreover, as Becker reminds us, public events 'leave a deep imprint on those who experience them'.[114] Events of commemoration are saturated with political action, so much so that they remain fundamental in understanding the continuation, regulation and transformation of the conflict. Its function and outcome remains fraught and contested, as far from being suspended in academic debate, the effects of competing claims on ideological and physical space continue to structure everyday politics. It is this group that provides the mechanisms and context for the individual to recall some events and to forget others. Hence, memories are acquired at a societal level and that it is also at this level that people 'recall, recognize, and localize their memories'.[115]

---

[109] *Belfast Telegraph*, 'Loyalist band numbers at new high', 7 October 2013.
[110] Jarman, 'For God and Ulster', 159.
[111] Ramsey, 'Practice: class, taste and identity in Ulster loyalist flute bands', 18.
[112] Northern Ireland Youth Forum, 'Sons of Ulster'.
[113] Ramsey, *Music, Emotion and Identity in Ulster Marching Bands*.
[114] Becker, 'Memory gaps, Maurice Halbwachs, memory and the Great War', 102–113.
[115] Halbwachs, *The Collective Memory*, 38.

It is, in part at least, through commemoration that the contemporary is fashioned by way of the past.[116] In this context, one primary consideration for the Orange Order is the remembrance of those members who were killed throughout the Troubles. The numbers involved are sizeable; of all the RUC officers killed during the conflict, approaching one in five were Orange Order members. As Edward Stevenson expresses it:

> The truth ... is that this Institution bore the brunt of the IRA's sectarian campaign of cold-blooded murder, brutality and mayhem. Over 300 of our members, many of whom served in the security forces, were callously targeted and ruthlessly killed at the hands of republican terrorists.[117]

For Orangeism, this indicates the continuing selfless actions undertaken by Orangemen in defence of their country[118] in the face of sectarianized republican violence, as the following statement clearly indicates:

> We pay tribute to the 337 members of our loyal Institution who were callously murdered throughout the Troubles. The crime of the vast majority of our brethren – in the eyes of republicans – was to don the uniform of their country in response to a vile terrorist campaign. Others were simply targeted for being in possession of an Orange collarette.[119]

Here, we can usefully draw on the work of Margaret Somers,[120] who argues that we can best understand the construction of such public narratives as a social process that transcends the individual to become cultural stereotypes and interpretations.

One way in which both paramilitary and their associate political groupings have sought to gain creditability is through a narrative projecting themselves as defenders, either physically or ideologically, of the loyalist and sometimes the broader unionist community. Hence, while the centrality of the Battle of the Somme in structuring loyalist identity has been clearly established above, loyalists see this as but one link in the chain of continuing commitment and sacrifice. It is not uncommon, therefore, for loyalists to directly link the loss of life experienced by the 36th Ulster Division to other conflicts across the history of the British Empire, to events at the battle of the Boyne, via the loss of life in the Belfast air raids of 1941, to those who died in military service in the Second World War, to those who lost their

---

116 Connerton, *How Societies Remember*, 70–71.

117 Grand Orange Lodge of Ireland, 'Speech Made by the Grand Master of the Grand Orange Lodge of Ireland', Edward Stevenson, at the Dungannon Demonstration, *GOLI Press Release*, 12 July 2012.

118 *News Letter*, 7 April 2006.

119 Grand Orange Lodge of Ireland, 'Grand Master leads Armistice Day tributes, 2013'. Available at: http://www.grandorangelodge.co.uk/news.aspx?id=100413#.U-ic0yjmbfh; accessed 23 February 2014.

120 M. R. Somers, 'Narrativity, narrative identity, and social action: rethinking English working-class formation', *Social Science History*, 16, no. 4 (1992): 591–630.

lives during the Troubles, and even through to those who have died in much more recent conflicts such as Afghanistan or Iraq.

Such events are seen as part of a collective history, the recalling which provides security and a coherent understanding of the Self and the community. Moreover, through these memories, it is possible to highlight continuity with the past, witnessed through an understanding that 'the loyalist people have ... paid a heavy price for the privilege of being British ... [through] our sacrifices in two world wars'.[121] As elsewhere, the memories of such core events are maintained through narratives often determined by contemporary political tensions and conflicts of the present.[122]

The following loyalist song entitled 'Ulster Volunteer' gives a clear example of the construction of loyalist identity, by joining together of loyalist paramilitary membership, the fight for Empire, resistance to Hitler and the more recent Northern Ireland conflict into a seamless series of events:

> Dear friend if you will listen, a story I will tell
> About a band of loyal men, we all know so well.
> In two world wars they fought and died through blood, sweat and tears
> To keep us free from tyranny, the Ulster Volunteers.
>
> Now the IRA for many years has savaged this fair land
> With bomb and gun and hatred, they are the devils band.
> They've murdered little children, but their end is drawing near
> For they know they'll never match the men of the Ulster Volunteer.
>
> Now the might of Hitler's forces, in Nineteen-Forty-One
> Had conquered all before them, no one could stop the hunt.
> When the British empire stood quite firm, we knew we need not fear
> For we knew the Lord was on our side, and the Ulster Volunteers.
>
> Now the U, it stands for Ulster, a place of great renown.
> The V, it stands for Victory, for we will not back down.
> The F, it stands for Freedom, for which we fight till death.
> When you put them all together you've got UVF.
> So all you loyal Protestants, who listen to my song.
> In England and in Canada, and Scotland or Hong Kong.
> If ever you are troubled, you need never shed a tear
> For we will march to victory with the Ulster Volunteers.

[121] *Loyalist News*, 30 September 1972, cited in G. Bell, *The Protestants of Ulster* (London: Pluto Press, 1976), 9.

[122] Kinnvall, *Globalization and Religious Nationalism in India*; 'European trauma: governance and the psychological moment', *Alternatives: Global, Local, Political*, 37, no. 3 (2012): 266–281.

Dominant loyalist narratives

The broad terrain for loyalist and Unionist memory is one of a covenantal people constantly under threat of attack. The resulting narrative rests on:

> the vicissitudes of the first settlements, and memories of earlier golden ages after the Battle of the Boyne and the siege of Londonderry... coupled with a deep-rooted belief in ethnic election as God's covenanted people... [resulting in] a powerful attachment to Ulster as the ancestral and promised homeland of the Protestant settlers.[123]

Within this broad frame, some parts of the narrative are more important than others, forming what Judith Butler refers to as 'normalising fictions',[124] while some have called them master scripts,[125] or meta-narratives.[126]

Bronwyn Davies and Rom Harre[127] outline how individuals may be located through such narratives that position both Self and others and the relationships between them. As Phillip Hammack explains meta-narratives represent:

> a story which is so central to the group's existence and 'essence' that it commands identification and integration into the personal narrative. Master narratives exist at the level of all social categories... and are predicated on a doctrine of essentialism... which serves to imbue them with a 'natural' rather than 'social' character.[128]

While not always overtly so, political and social relationships alongside what are regarded as legitimate or illegitimate cultural practices are embedded in the everyday. Hence, the social and political actions of loyalists are motivated and guided by the dominant narrative into which they are rooted,[129] actively using these narratives as cultural resources to construct and understand the present.[130]

Loyalist memories and representations help shape the loyalist sense of identity, and a narrative that provides both the language and boundaries for people to construct symbolic representations of what is remembered (and, of course, what is forgotten). This represents a broader theme whereby people engage with narratives, to 'make decisions about which aspects of them to appropriate and which to repudiate'.[131] These public-shared narratives take in both the individual and the collective. As Connerton

---

[123] Smith, *Myths and Memories of the Nation*, 273.

[124] J. Butler, *Gender Trouble* (London: Routledge, 1990).

[125] L. R. Bloom, *Under the Sign of Hope: Feminist Methodology and Narrative Interpretation* (Albany: State University of New York, 1998).

[126] M. R. Somers, 'Narrativity, narrative identity, and social action: rethinking English working-class formation'.

[127] B. Davies and R. Harre, 'Positioning: the discursive of selves', *Journal for the Theory of Social Behaviour*, 20, no. 1 (1990): 43–63.

[128] P. L. Hammack, 'Narrative and the politics of meaning', *Narrative Inquiry*, 21, no. 2 (2011): 311–318.

[129] Somers and Gibson, 'Reclaiming the epistemological "other"', 67.

[130] Davies and Harre, 'Positioning: the discursive of selves'.

[131] Hammack, 'Narrative and the politics of meaning', 313.

suggests through these processes, 'groups provide individuals with frameworks within which their memories are localised'.[132]

Within recent years across loyalism, there are countless examples of local manifestations of commemoration. This can of course take place at different societal levels, ranging from the international, such as the commemoration of those killed in wars, Remembrance Day in the UK and ANZAC day in the antipodes,[133] to other forms of commemoration that are much more restricted, perhaps even limited to a specific community or identified neighbourhood. These draw heavily on common interpretations and representations to reinforce the past as legitimate and meaningful. They also provide a framework on which individuals can hang their own memories and then engage in broader processes of identification with, and re-enforcement of, group identities. One expression of this is found in the following, entitled 'The Ulster Volunteers – Our 60 Year Tribute':

> When statesmen now to treason bow, and loyalty betray,
> And traitorous knaves being Rebel slaves,
> our rights would take away,
> To serve their Queen and Country,
> a gallant band appears,
> While cowards quail,
> Come let us hail,
> The Ulster Volunteers.
>
> Let Rebels frown to put them down,
> and peaceful homes invade,
> Oh never yet by idle threat,
> were Ulstermen dismayed,
> They take their stand for native land,
> and know no paltry fears,
> These loyal boys who fear no noise,
> The Ulster Volunteers.
>
> True in the days,
> when many change for profit or for dread,
> True to the same old sacred Cause,
> for which our fathers bled,
> They'll guard the rights that William won,
> in famed and by-gone years,
> Then let us toast, our pride, our boast,
> The Ulster Volunteers.

---

[132] Connerton, *How Societies Remember*, 37

[133] See material in *Nation, Memory and Great War Commemoration: Mobilizing the Past in Europe, Australia and New Zealand*, eds. S. Sumartojo and B. Wellings (Bern: Peter Lang, 2014).

Here, we find an example of the formation of social solidarity through processes that bring together different memories (individual, social and collective) to form the central building blocs within the overall formation of the distinct ethno-political identity of loyalism. Crucial are the ways in which collective memories are used to frame individual political identities and understandings of how their community relates to the wider social and political world. Hence, collective memory helps construct a social reality that is transmitted through the conscious efforts of groups.[134]

This has led some to favour the term social memory, which often finds expression through everyday explanations of the world and collective memories, preserved through what Pierre Nora[135] has called the sites of memory, such as museums, archives, cemeteries, festivals, anniversaries and monuments. This recognizes how 'memory is sometimes located in collectively created monuments and markers: books, holidays, statues, souvenirs.'[136] Loyalism produces its own sites of memory (wall murals and Orange banners, to name but two) that are seen as integral to the transmission of a cultural history with distinct social boundaries. Such institutional forms of memorialization express distinction and difference and a form of cultural politics,[137] perhaps the clearest example of which is seen in the Orange Order and those loyalists who see themselves engaged in a culture war. It is also a site of contest for those it excludes or silences, such as the labourist tradition within the Protestant working class.

Who shares loyalist memory?

One important question arising from the above is who shares (or is allowed to share) collective memories. Loyalist collective memory is maintained and reproduced 'through a community of interests and thoughts'[138] and by drawing on specific understandings of the past to configure specific forms of collective memory. Collective memory is central to the narratives of past experience constituted by specific groups to empower particular forms of identity. The institutions that support collective memories, in turn, help to create, sustain and reproduce the imagined community of loyalism by identifying individual experiences as part of a continuity of history, place and social belonging.[139]

Take, for example, the commemoration to the UVF at Cherryville Street, in East Belfast. This stands on the original site of Willowfield Unionist Hall, opened by Sir Edward Carson on May 16th 1913 as a drill hall and rifle range for the UVF, which

---

[134] N. Russell, 'Collective memory before and after Halbwachs', *The French Review*, 79, no. 4 (2006): 792–804.

[135] P. Nora, 'Between memory and history: Les Lieux de Memoire', *Representations*, 26 (1989): 7–25.

[136] Schudson, M. 'Dynamics of Distortion in Collective Memory', in *Memory Distortion: How Minds, Brains and Societies Reconstruct the Past*, ed. D. Schacter (Cambridge, MA: Harvard University Press, 1995), 346–364.

[137] J. Winter, *Sites of Memory, Sites of Mourning* (Cambridge: Cambridge University Press, 2014).

[138] Connerton, *How Societies Remember*, 47.

[139] Anderson, *Imagined Communities*.

was demolished in 1983. The centrepiece of the contemporary memorial highlights those members of the UVF 2nd Willowfield Battalion who died in the First World War. Alongside this, however, are memorials to the contemporary 'Fallen Volunteers of 3rd Battalion, East Belfast Brigade, UVF', commemorated in a granite plaque reading: 'In solemn remembrance we salute the brave men of Ulster without favour or reward they fought militant Republicanism on it's [sic] own terms.' Within loyalism, it becomes crucial to 'remember those who gave their lives and hold their memory for future generations so that their loyalty, courage and sacrifice will never be forgotten'.[140]

This link to a broader loyalist narrative is clear, reinforcing the view that the 'maintenance of Ulster as an integral part of the United Kingdom was purchased with the blood of our forbears'.[141] Loyalist collective memory 'retains from the past only what still lives or is capable of living in the consciousness of the groups keeping the memory alive'.[142] This remembered past, however, only remains meaningful to the present through 'the self-conscious memory of individual members of a group'.[143] The resulting loyalist narrative performs several roles not least of which is to provide a point of stability when individuals and groups are struggling to make sense of situations they see as socially and politically uncertain. In this context, group narratives offer recognizable images and reassurances, which act in reinforcing existing worldviews.

Conclusions

Memory as discussed in this chapter remains a central component of identity, which is constantly constructed and reconstructed. Shared group memories have been understood and classified in a number of different ways and from within differing disciplinary perspectives.[144] In broad terms, however, all recognize collective memories as binding together identified communities through mutually recognized presentations, representations, understandings and interpretations of the past.

One of the major ways in which loyalist collective memory is reproduced, shared and reinforced is through popular culture and populist narratives. As with all forms of popular culture, it is possible to identify constantly recurring themes, of which three such as defence, sacrifice and suffering are central. Narratives carry memories forward from one generation to another and one historical period to another.[145] Consequently,

[140] *News Letter*, 12 July 2007.
[141] *Ibid.*
[142] Halbwachs, *The Collective Memory*.
[143] S. A. Crane, 'Writing the individual back into collective memory', *The American Historical Review*, 102, no. 5 (1997): 1372–1385.
[144] See, for example, J. K. Olick and J. Robbins. 'Social memory studies: from "collective memory" to the historical sociology of mnemonic practices', *Annual Review of Sociology*, 24 (1998): 105–140; J. Wertsch, 'Collective Memory', in *Memory in Mind and Culture*, eds. P. Boyer and J. V. Wertsch (Cambridge: Cambridge University Press, 2009), 117–137.
[145] Epstein, 'Remember to Forget: The Problem of Traumatic Cultural Memory', 186–204.

while loyalism's ties to and memories of the past are constantly reproduced, at the same time they are redefined in terms of contemporary identities and political responses. None of this is to suggest that these group narratives are read or interpreted entirely consistently or that group members act upon the narrative in uniform ways. One grouping offering particular readings of the broader loyalist narrative and the focal point for the production and reproduction of distinct popular cultural forms can be found amongst loyalist paramilitarism.

6

Paramilitarism and Commemoration

Within loyalism, it is important to recognize how a sense of community is used not just as a focus of identity and social organization, but also as a site for different forms of political intervention and action. One manifestation of this was seen in the type of paramilitarism that emerged following growing political tensions across Northern Ireland in the mid- to late 1960s. However, as we shall see, the same broad grouping also at times provided the platform for the development of an alternative narrative within loyalism and for different sites for political intervention and organization,[1] including the development of a distinct and politicized form of popular culture and a set of narratives that often run counter to mainstream unionism.

Loyalism began to take contemporary form following reactions by sections of working-class Protestants to the growth of the civil rights movement. It was given further direction by the outbreak of widespread communal sectarian violence, the break-up of unionist political hegemony and the emergence of Provisional republicanism. Throughout this sequence, loyalists began increasingly to articulate fears that the worsening security situation marked more than just another episode of sectarian violence, but rather a coherent attempt to undermine the existing political structures and even the very existence of the state itself.

Although loyalist paramilitarism reflected only one part of a wider community riposte to the conflict, it is important to acknowledge how that response was located both ideologically and structurally directly within the loyalist community and its understanding of the political situation. Brian Lennon[2] suggests that the social relations existing within traditional closely knit working-class loyalist communities were central in motivating sizeable numbers of (mostly) young men to become involved in such organizations. In particular, many felt they were needed as defence against militant republicanism. Some saw violence (or the threat of violence) as the main to achieve their goals, while others no doubt joined as part of the broader sectarianized response seen across Northern Ireland at the outbreak of widespread societal conflict.

---

[1]   R. Reed, 'Blood, thunder and rosettes: the multiple personalities of paramilitary loyalism between 1971 and 1988', *Irish Political Studies*, 26, no. 1 (2011): 45–72.

[2]   B. Lennon, *Peace Comes Dropping Slow* (Belfast: Community Dialogue, 2004).

Loyalist paramilitarism interpreted and reacted to events in particular ways but within parameters bound by existing narratives of past experience. It is important to recognize, as Duncan Morrow clearly does, that:

> ... the actions of the few were not the actions of independent mad men, but were carried out with the instruction of some, the encouragement of more and the tacit sympathy of many. At the very least, those called victims and survivors were victims of acts carried out by a few which on behalf of many more. This violence did not spring randomly from the hearts of a few, but grew from a soil that was made fertile by the experiences and fears of communities and generations. The tragic truth is that the prosecution of individuals for specific acts stirs up and tests the sympathies and actions of whole communities and political communities.[3]

As loyalism began to become more structured in its response, two main paramilitary organizations emerged: the UDA founded in 1971 grew out of the wide network of vigilante groups that had appeared in loyalist districts and the UVF, which, although it had surfaced in 1966 (and was consciously named after the early twentieth-century organization), began to organize and recruit heavily in the early 1970s. The dynamic behind growing paramilitary membership continued to draw on existing notions of community, especially through narratives of community defence. It also gave expression to the conviction felt by many Protestants that the constitutional position was under direct threat, and that the government response was weak. The belief that Northern Ireland faced a challenge that was not being effectively met by state forces, which were unable or unwilling to effectively engage republicanism, was deeply felt.

This found outlet in a number of ways and a wide variety of loyalist groupings, all of which believed that increased loyalist militancy was necessary to defend the Protestant population, to ensure the continuance of the existing constitutional position.[4] There was also a 'fear that a "doomsday" situation was approaching in which "Ulster" would be thrust out of the Union and placed at the mercy of the IRA'.[5] Hence, many recruits to the paramilitary organizations saw their actions as a legitimate response in a time of perceived threats. The following passage from former UVF member Alistair Little indicates clearly his own motivation:

> The security forces were unable to prevent the bombing, and their increasingly intrusive attempts to gain intelligence about paramilitary activity on both sides of the conflict were causing resentment not only on Catholic estates, but also in my community.... Increasingly, people on our estate began to feel that not only did they have to find ways of defending themselves from the violence of the IRA, but

---

[3] D. Morrow, 'The weight of the past on the way to the future'. Community Relations Council Victims Conference, 29 October 2007.

[4] Ruane and Todd, *The Dynamics of Conflict in Northern Ireland*.

[5] T. P. Coogan, *The Troubles: Ireland's Ordeal 1966–1996 and the Search for Peace* (Boulder, CO: Roberts Rinehart Publishers, 1997), 283.

the very people we looked to for security were making our lives more difficult .... When any RUC or UDR men were shot dead, my friends and I mourned and promised revenge.[6]

The resulting organizational forms, strategies, tactics and targeting processes undertaken by loyalist paramilitarism across the conflict have been dealt with in some detail elsewhere.[7] While a comprehensive history of loyalist paramilitarism lies beyond this book,[8] broadly, as the voices within paramilitarism expressing the need to directly confront republicanism grew louder, loyalists too became engaged in a bloody and often sectarianized street war. Loyalist paramilitarism operated within a sphere of activity of what Lyndsey Harris[9] calls, its own 'strategic environment', with their own values, meaning that for some violence was best understood as a logical response to broader political events.[10]

From around the mid-1980s, the more militaristic actions conducted by loyalist paramilitaries were wrapped in a discourse highlighting a duality of taking the war to the enemy and a loose narrative of counterterrorism. Attacks on the Catholic/nationalist/republican community were seen as one way of driving a wedge between the IRA and its support. By the 1990s, the slackness of the boundaries in the definitions used meant that there was such a loose understanding of the notion of 'legitimate target' that it was all but meaningless, as the concept of collective punishment[11] became more substantial in guiding the actions of loyalist paramilitarism.[12]

Loyalist paramilitaries were responsible for a catalogue of horrific violence, directly accountable for 991 deaths between 1969 and 1998[13] and for a further 98 deaths between 1994 and 2010.[14] While in no way seeking to marginalize or underplay the magnitude of loyalist violence, the remainder of this chapter has a different focus.

---

[6] A. Little [with R. Scott] *Give a Boy a Gun: From Killing to Peacemaking* (London: Darton, Longman and Todd, 2009), 53.

[7] See, for example, J. Cusack and H. McDonald, *UVF* (Dublin: Poolbeg, 1997); H. McDonald and J. Cusack, *UDA: Inside the Heart of Loyalist Terror* (London: Penguin, 2004); P. Taylor, *Loyalists* (London: Bloomsbury, 2000).

[8] See material in J. W. McAuley and G. Spencer, eds. *Ulster Loyalism after the Good Friday Agreement* (Basingstoke: Palgrave Macmillan, 2011).

[9] L. Harris, 'Duck or Rabbit? The Value Systems of Loyalist Paramilitaries' *Irish Protestant*: 305–318; 'Exit, Voice, and Loyalty: Signalling of Loyalist Paramilitaries in Northern Ireland' *Transforming the Peace Process in Northern Ireland*: 79–98; 'Quis Separabit? Loyalist Transformation and the Strategic Environment', *Ulster Loyalism after the Good Friday Agreement*: 87–104.

[10] P. Shirlow and K. McEvoy, *Beyond the Wire: Former Prisoners and Conflict Transformation in Northern Ireland* (London: Pluto, 2008), 9–10.

[11] M. L. R. Smith, *Fighting for Ireland? The Military Strategy of the Irish Republican Movement* (London: Routledge, 1997).

[12] T. McKearney, *The Provisional IRA: From Insurrection to Parliament* (London: Pluto Press, 2011), 135.

[13] D. McKittrick, S. Kelters, B. Feeney, and C. Thornton, *Lost Lives: The Stories of the Men, Women and Children Who Died as a Result of the Northern Ireland Troubles* (Edinburgh: Mainstream Publishing, 1999).

[14] R. Monaghan and P. Shirlow, 'Forward to the past? Loyalist paramilitarism in Northern Ireland since 1994', *Terrorism and Political Violence*, 16, no. 3 (2011): 439–461.

Throughout the past forty years, those involved in loyalist paramilitarism have also sought (and found) various outlets for political expression and organization, independent of established unionism.[15] They have been responsible for the production of identifiable forms of popular culture, involving commemoration and memorialization, which draw heavily on distinct collective memories across loyalism.

New loyalism and the new politics?

Despite earlier attempts throughout the 1970s and 1980s, loyalist paramilitaries had failed to garner any significant level of electoral support.[16] Nonetheless, by the early 1990s, paramilitary politics had been reorganized and developed to a point where both the PUP, most closely associated with the UVF, and the Ulster Democratic Party (UDP), which was connected with the UDA, were again presenting themselves as an alternative source for unionist votes, with a modicum of success. Billy Hutchinson explains political developments of the time, and the emergence of the PUP in particular, as follows:

> ... there has been a war going on here for 25 years that has been fought by working-class people. The establishment parties have kept clear of it. They've never, ever got involved in it. They've always made sure that they've stayed out of jail. Whenever it came to actually trying to resolve the problem, nothing happened.[17]

In similar light, Gary McMichael, the then leader of the UDP, declared that his party intended to provide the loyalism with real leadership 'because ... for the past 25 years ... our community has been plagued with political leaders who refuse to lead'.[18]

Although never cohesive, the main political perspectives projected by the PUP and to a lesser extent by the UDP drew on common themes identified across paramilitarism and broader Protestant working-class experiences, to promote a different form of more pluralism politics.[19] The PUP in particular brought onto the unionist agenda a more gendered and class aware politics, promoting a leftist perspective on social and

---

[15] J. W. McAuley, 'Not a Game of Cowboys and Indians' – the Ulster Defence Association in the 1990s', in ed. A. O'Day *Terrorism's Laboratory The Case of Northern Ireland* (Dartmouth: Aldershot, 1995): 137–158; 'The Emergence of New Loyalism', in *Changing Shades of Orange and Green*, ed. J. Coakley, 106–122; 'Fantasy Politics? Restructuring Unionism after the Good Friday Agreeement', *Eire – Ireland*, 39, no. 1/2: 189–214; 'Whither new loyalism? Changing loyalist politics after the Belfast Agreement', *Irish Political Studies*, 20, no. 3 (2005): 323–340; J. W. McAuley and S. Hislop, 'Many roads forward': politics and ideology within the Progressive Unionist Party', *Études Irlandaises* 25, 1 (2000): 173–192.

[16] I have covered this period in some detail in J. W. McAuley *Ulster's Last Stand?*

[17] *An Phoblacht*/Republican News: 10, no. 2, February, 1995.

[18] *The Irish Times*, 18 May 1996.

[19] J. W. McAuley, 'Mobilising Ulster Unionism: new directions or old?', *Capital and Class*, no. 70 (2000): 37–64; Whither new loyalism? Changing loyalist politics after the Belfast Agreement'.

welfare issues.[20] Moreover, as Kevin Cassidy[21] suggests, those involved sought to act autonomously from most existing Unionist representatives and displayed little of the deference usually displayed by the Protestant working class towards their traditional political leaders.

Such views were prominent when some three decades after O'Neill's famous 'Crossroads' speech, the editorial of the UVF magazine *Combat* provided a rejoinder to O'Neill's remarks, claiming that once again Unionism was at a crossroads, setting out the position as follows:

> The world is changing, Europe is changing and Northern Ireland is changing. Important decisions must be made within Unionism to equip itself for these changes. Gone are the days when simple majority was enough to dictate policy. Structures and institutions now exist within Northern Ireland that warrant changes in the process of political impressioning. Long gone are the days when a pan class, pan ideological Unionism could be raised to exert its will effectively against Government coercion or Republican aggression.[22]

Transforming narratives

New loyalism openly articulated concerns over the effects of social marginalization experienced within many working-class Protestant communities. That the established unionist political leadership did not recognize such issues, and loyalism did seek to find a new civic form of political expression and representation, gave much momentum to new loyalism. Although Shirlow has criticized use of the term,[23] the expression undoubtedly retains legitimacy around the attempts by those involved to reposition loyalism and to draw on collective memories in different ways (for example, by emphasizing the Labour, communal, and leftist traditions within working-class Protestant history).

Certainly, the narrative that emerged from new loyalism was not just self-critical of the nature of unionism, but politically pluralistic in outlook,[24] actively promoting the view that the existing sectarian social relations upon which Northern Ireland social structure rested should be challenged and could be altered.[25] Part of that narrative challenged the notion of a specific Ulster people as projected with traditional loyalist

[20] B. Graham, 'The past in the present: the shaping of identity in Loyalist Ulster', *Terrorism and Political Violence*, 16, no. 3 (2004): 483–500.

[21] K. J. Cassidy, 'Organic intellectuals and the new loyalism: re-inventing Protestant working-class politics in Northern Ireland', *Irish Political Studies*, 23, no. 3 (2008): 411–430.

[22] *Combat*, July 1999.

[23] P. Shirlow, *The End of Loyalism?* (Manchester: Manchester University Press, 2012).

[24] Shankill Think Tank, *A New Beginning*, Island Pamphlets no. 13, (Newtownabbey: Island Publications, 1995).

[25] J. W. McAuley and J. Tonge, 'Politics and Parties in Northern Ireland: the convergence of ideological extremes', *Etudes Irlandaises*, 27, no. 1 (2002): 177–198.

discourse and sought to replace it with ideas of the democratic citizen as a core basis for loyalist identity.[26] Indeed, as Stephen Howe[27] points out, the new loyalist narrative increasingly downplayed nationality at the expense of emphasizing the idea of community.

Another key grouping determining the direction of loyalism at street level was made up from former combatants, whose experiences helped reshape their political input often following a reassessment of why they participated in the conflict. At an everyday level, this has led to a redesign and softening of some traditional militaristic tendencies.[28] Some former combatants have sought to develop a deeper sense of community engagement with republicans.[29] Groupings involving former combatants have, with varying levels of success, sought to change social relationships both within and across loyalist communities, driven broadly by a desire to ensure that 'ethno-sectarian segregation between communities is not bolstered by the promotion of oppositional discourses'.[30]

Cultural and heritage work is thus seen as an opportunity for working-class loyalists to effectively engage with other actors, in this case importantly the government and the republican community.[31] None of this is to suggest that such views are uncontested, from both within and without the paramilitary groupings. The rate and speed of transformation was far from constant, differing not just between the UDA and the UVF, but also within them. The political positioning within the UDA grouping was particularly convoluted and determined by localism,[32] and it was only following protracted consultations with its membership through an initiative called 'Loyalism in Transition' that conflict transformation was established within the UDA grouping.[33]

The demise of new loyalism?

The emergence of new loyalism had important implications for both the readings of collective memories and the political repositioning of sections of loyalism. Those involved engaged reasonably wide sections of the Protestant working class in a range

---

[26] Finlayson, 'Loyalist political identity after the peace', 47–75.

[27] S. Howe, 'Mad Dogs and Ulstermen: The Crisis of Loyalism (part one)' Available at: http://www.opendemocracy.net/debates/article.jsp?id=6anddebateId=33andarticleId=2876; accessed 1 March 2012; 'Mad Dogs and Ulstermen: The Crisis of Loyalism (part two)' Available at: http://www.opendemocracy.net/democracy-protest/loyalism_2885.jsp; accessed 1 March 2012.

[28] L. A. Smithey, 'Conflict Transformation, Cultural Innovation and Loyalist Identity in Northern Ireland', in *Culture and Belonging in Divided Societies*, ed. M. H. Ross (Philadelphia: Pennsylvania University Press, 2009), 85–106.

[29] Inter Action Belfast, *The Role of Ex-Combatants on Interfaces* (Belfast: Inter-Action Belfast, 2006).

[30] Shirlow, *et al.*, *Abandoning Historical Conflict*, 171.

[31] Smithey, *Unionists, Loyalists, and Conflict Transformation in Northern Ireland*.

[32] I. S. Wood, *Crimes of Loyalty: a history of the UDA* (Edinburgh: Edinburgh University Press, 2006).

[33] M. Hall, *Loyalism in Transition 1: Learning from others in conflict* (Belfast: Island Pamphlets, 2006): *Loyalism in Transition 2: Learning from others in conflict* (Belfast: Island Pamphlets, 2007).

of voluntary, political and social activities.[34] But the new loyalism political project as originally evident has increasingly been diluted and its energy dissipated. Much of this has to do with unresolved relationships with those paramilitary organizations that have failed to leave the stage.

The UDA now represents such a diverse grouping that any form of political coherence across it is all but impossible, while sections of the UVF has moved beyond its commitments to conflict resolution it demonstrated at the time of the Belfast Agreement. Its relationship to the PUP is still apparent, but so too is the resurgence of militancy amongst the UVF in an attempt to reassert local community control. Witness the resignations of Dawn Purvis as leader of the PUP, and those of other leading members, following a murder in Belfast by the UVF in June 2010. Explaining her decision, Purvis claimed that she could no longer lead the PUP if it meant she was 'expected to answer for the indefensible actions of others'.[35] Since then the party has gone through a series of leaders all of whom have struggled to capture its original dynamic.

In core working-class districts the dissolution of paramilitary structures have not gone according to plan, resulting in discord surrounding how political processes are framed across loyalism. Throughout the peace process, and since, key activists, many of them involved previously in direct conflict, have engaged in cross-community work. The construction of a different narrative justifying support for political renegotiation and demilitarization within the context of a class aware politics has, however, failed to gain long-term support amongst sections of loyalism.

As we have seen, the loyalist narrative can at times be more homogenized, while at other times, it can be heterogenic, for example, when new loyalism directly sought to provide a counter-interpretation within loyalism through alternative constructions of what the loyalist worldview might look like. Like all collective social identities, the sense of a loyalism is based on broader social processes identifying what are seen as common interests and experiences, beliefs and values of the group.[36] This involves projecting what the group stands for and how it wishes others to see it. As such, collective memory acts as the link between expressions of social identity and collective action. Central here is the production of distinct forms of loyalist popular culture involving commemoration that draw heavily on identifiable collective memories and narratives that are common across loyalism.

Paramilitarism, commemoration and popular culture

Given that all social groups have a past, memory intervenes directly in how members understand the present, thus connecting them with history in a particular way and

---

[34] E. Cairns, T. Van Til, and A. Williamson, *Social Capital, Collectivism – Individualism and Community Background in Northern Ireland* (Report to the Office of the First Minister and Deputy First Minister, Coleraine: University of Ulster, 2003).

[35] *Belfast Telegraph*, 4 June 2010.

[36] J. Bruner, *Acts of Meaning* (Cambridge, MA: Harvard University Press, 1990).

represented and interpreted through distinct narratives.[37] Memories associated with historical events are often formed and reformed many years after the event took place, perhaps even many years after anyone can have any lived memory of the events. More importantly, such collective memories are constructed, prolonged and communicated within and across the group.[38]

One core aspect of the paramilitary narrative surrounds legitimacy within their own communities and the validity of their actions during the Troubles and beyond. Paramilitaries have sought to construct this through the reinforcement of their 'own' popular culture and the production of materials that bond and forge a sense of community. Popular culture is distinguished through its reliance on a formulaic repetitive structure,[39] and it is in the course of such repetition that popular culture evolves into standardized symbols that become and are accepted and meaningful amongst those who are constantly in contact with it.[40] Loyalist popular culture encompasses a wide range of material, including performance, written and recorded outputs, all of which are produced as cultural artefacts recognizing and reinforcing perceived ethno-political differences and historical commonalities.

For the grouping set around the contemporary UVF, a key strategy in seeking legitimacy has been to seek to construct ideological and representational linkages with the UVF of 1913, the stance against Home Rule and the mobilization undertaken in the defence of Empire during the First World War. This has taken several forms, including murals depicting a continuity of resistance, the involvement in organizing Somme anniversary parades, memorial organizations, which commemorate not just First World War UVF volunteers, but also promote the memory of paramilitaries who died in the contemporary Troubles, and the formation of various clubs and organizations to celebrate and commemorate UVF history.

Another example is found in popular songs as a means of transmitting social memory across generations and strengthening social bonds traversing generations.[41] Such songs draw on collective memories that drive a social dialogue in the development of popular cultures.[42] These coalesce into a collectivity, where they are distilled and refined to define the remembered occurrences of the social group. Take the following song 'Will You Stand', which is sung in loyalist pubs and clubs across Northern Ireland:

---

[37] W. Kansteiner, 'Finding meaning in memory: a methodological critique of collective memory studies', *History and Theory*, 41, (2002): 179–197.

[38] R. Eyerman, 'The Past in the Present: Culture and the Transmission of Identity', in *The Collective Memories Reader*, eds. J. K. Olick, V. Vinitzky-Seroussi, and D. Levy (Oxford: Oxford University Press, 2011).

[39] C. Barker, *Cultural Studies: Theory and Practice* (London: Sage, 2003).

[40] J. Storey, *Cultural Theory and Popular Culture: An Introduction* (Abington: Routledge, 2013).

[41] R. Eyerman, 'Music in movement: cultural politics and old and new social movements', *Qualitative Sociology*, 25, no. 3 (2002): 443–458.

[42] See, for example, Orange Cross Committee, *Orange Cross Book of Songs, Poems and Verse* (Belfast: Orange Cross Committee, no date).

Oh! Will you stand?
Oh! Will you stand?
With the Ulster Volunteer Force as a patriotic band
Would you fight unto the death, would you join the UVF?
If you can you're a man then you'll stand.

Chorus: And when the sound of the battle is over
It's shoulder to shoulder we'll stand
To remember the brave young Ulster soldiers
Who fought for the flag of the Red Hand?

Oh! Will you stand?
Oh! Will you stand?
Would you fight for God and Ulster?
And to keep it British Land?
With rifle and grenade, would you serve the Old Brigade?
If you can you're a man then you'll stand.

Oh! Will you stand?
Oh! Will you stand?
Would you bear and swear allegiance?
To the Flag of the Red Hand
Would you fight and never fear with the Ulster Volunteers?
If you can you're a man then you'll stand.

Chorus: Oh! Will you stand?
Oh! Will you stand?
Would you travel the road where the brave and bold must go?
Would you wear the black cockade, would you serve the Old Brigade?
If you can you're a man then you'll stand.

Commemoration and collective identity

If we accept that we are defined in part both by what is remembered and what is forgotten, the resulting sense of identity is often corroborated and reinforced by acts of remembrance, memorial and commemoration. Part of this involves a direct attempt to transmit values across generations, such as in the following song 'Daddy's Uniform':

Oh Daddy what's that uniform in the wardrobe over there?
Has it any history or medals for to bear?
Has it seen the battlefields like bygone days of yore?
Oh Daddy is that the Uniform that you so proudly wore?

Chorus: See its buckles shining bright from the shoulder to the waist,
I also see three letters emblazoned on its breast,
The U it stands for Ulster,
The V for Volunteer,
The F it stands for the Force,
That fights and never fears.

My memory it strays back again to nineteen forty one,
When Ulster's shores were threatened,
By the Jackboot of the Hun,
And Ulster's people rallied round,
They knew they need not fear,
For they knew God was on their side,
And the Ulster Volunteers.

So son, please take my Uniform and go and fight the foe,
And fight just like your father did so many years ago,
For Ulster it is calling and we must never fear,
So take my Gun my only son and join the Volunteers.

Crucially, over the last four decades, loyalist paramilitary commemoration has moved from largely private to public space; from restricted often semi-illegal or illegal settings and into the public gaze. During the Troubles, fear of attack or of being raided by security forces meant that most commemorative acts took place in private or semi-private locations such as pubs and clubs, within identifiable loyalist districts. Other more public events, such as paramilitary funerals, did take place, but most often these were within formally agreed parameters with the security forces. As Kris Brown observes, some of these public commemorative events have become extremely complex and large scale in their organization involving 'street theatre, tableaux, motorised floats, and the wearing of the period costume of earlier … Loyalist groupings'.[43]

Witness, for example, Loyalist commemorations at the centenary anniversary of the formation of the UVF, which was marked by a parade re-enacting of one of the key events of the Home Rule crisis, which saw many participants in period costume. During the parade, the PUP leader, Billy Hutchinson, dressed in period dress of top hat and tails, read parts of Edward Carson's original speech. One of the passages he chose is significant in highlighting contemporary loyalist values:

If you are prepared to hand yourselves over to the men, who in the past have shown themselves the most hostile element in the whole United Kingdom, to the Throne and the Constitution, then of course we must give way. But I promise you;

---

[43] K. Brown, '"Our father organization": the cult of the Somme and the unionist "Golden Age" in modern Ulster Loyalist commemoration', *The Round Table – The Commonwealth Journal of International Affairs* 96, 393 (2007): 707–723.

that so long as you stand firm; I and those associated with me, will most certainly stand firm and we will never, ever, surrender.[44]

The social and political functions of song can also vary and change over time. Take this where the lyrics have adopted a timeless quality 'No 1 Platoon':

I'll remember, I'll try, it was nearly July,
As we walked down the road I'll remember the year,
There was me, there was Sam, Jimmy Sloan and McCann,
Would enlist in the Volunteers.

And the man says to me, 'Boy I hope you will see',
'And remember this day all the things you've been taught',
It could be now or then, but we'll fight once again,
For the things that our grandfathers fought.

Chorus: And I swore like the rest to the badge on my breast,
To the gun in my hand I will fight for my land,
With my hand held high I took that vow,
And I joined Number One Platoon.

And deep down inside my heart fills with pride,
I remember the men who have fought through the years,
I could name quite a few but to me and to you,
They were Ulster Volunteers.

And to all here today just some words I must say,
To remember this day,
All the things you've been taught,
It could be now or then, but we'll fight once again,
For the things that our grandfathers fought.

The Ulster Covenant and collective memory

One of the largest public manifestations of loyalist collective memory in recent times was seen in September 2012, when some 30,000 marchers and over 200 bands took part in a parade to commemorate the centenary of the Ulster *Solemn League and Covenant*, which had originally been signed by around 500,000 people (218,206 men and 228,991 women in Ulster and a further 19,612 in Britain). It is difficult to overstate

---

[44] Carson cited in Chicago Tribune, September 28, 1913; Hutchinson cited in the *Belfast Newsletter*, September, 2013.

the importance of the event in the formation of Loyalist collective memory. Indeed, some argue that the recent history of loyalism, including its paramilitary strands, is directly framed and seeks their legitimacy by the text of the Ulster Covenant.[45] The Ulster Covenant has grown in significance for many Ulster loyalists indicated by the following song celebrating the event:

> The day is fast approaching and the hour is drawing nigh,
> Republicans are encroaching so cunningly and sly,
> But we'll follow in the footsteps of those men so adamant,
> And keep the rights our fathers gained and our Ulster Covenant.
>
> Let foes of Britain tremble when they think of Ulster's sons,
> Who never will surrender or flee from Rebel guns.
> We can depend on one another but not in our Government
> They have sold out to those that hate us and our Ulster Covenant.
>
> Let them think on Gallant Derry's Walls and on Aughrim's plains,
> Where crimson blood by valiant hands each valley deeply stained.
> Likewise with Enniskillen our ancestors did cement,
> And sealed in blood our bill of rights and our Ulster Covenant.
>
> Strong men will come to lead us, there'll be no traitors in our rear,
> The Loyalists of Ulster no danger need they fear,
> Our religion is our bulwark and our cause is Heaven-sent,
> God bless Carson and Craigavon and our Ulster Covenant.

Rituals generate strong messages, particularly within a society fragmented and split by deep social and cultural differences. So at the anniversary of the signing of the Ulster Covenant, the drums that were played a century ago during Carson's original UVF inspection were included in the parade, and a central part of the commemoration involved the direct re-enactment of events of the previous century. The depth of collective memory evoked and the perceived continuity involved was not lost across sections of unionism and loyalism, Edward Stevenson, the Grand Master of The Orange Order positioning events directly as a commemoration of: 'the steadfastness and Loyalty of our forefathers', while looking forward: 'to the next one hundred years of Northern Ireland within the United Kingdom'.[46]

The importance of commemorative ceremonies rests not just in participation or the event, but also because they highlight continuity and in so doing shape communal memory. In response to the question 'what is being remembered in commemorative ceremonies?', Connerton offers the following:

[45] Mitchell, 'Principles of Loyalism'.
[46] *News Letter*, 29 September 2012.

Part of the answer is that a community is reminded of its identity as represented by and told in a master narrative … Its master narrative is more than a story told and reflected on; it is a cult enacted. An image of the past, even in the form of a master narrative, is conveyed and sustained by ritual performances.[47]

This can also be the case in the commemoration of individuals as well. Part of the story told by loyalism involves the commemoration of particular individuals. One such example is found in Brian Robinson, a loyalist paramilitary who was shot dead after his motorbike was rammed by undercover British Army patrol, minutes after he had killed a Catholic man, Patrick McKenna in a random sectarian attack in the Ardoyne area of Belfast. Many within the UVF later alleged that Robinson had been 'executed' by soldiers marking the only so-called shoot-to-kill incident involving a loyalist paramilitary, and that he 'was summarily executed for the expediency of appeasement to Nationalists.'[48]

Consequently, Robinson's death was commemorated on a large UVF mural in the Woodvale Road in Belfast, through an annual band parade, which has become a central feature in the loyalist calendar and in the following loyalist song:

Let me tell you of a story of fame and gallantry,
What the name of Brian Robinson it means to you and me,
It's a name that stand for courage and it stands for liberty,
On the 2nd day of September come and drink this toast with me.

So now here's to Brian Robinson a brave and loyal man,
And to every Ulster Volunteer who has fought for the Red Hand,
They have made the greatest sacrifice and we have seen the best,
So lift your glass to Brian and to the men of the UVF.

And to the men behind the wire for they have stood the test,
Let's not forget their sacrifice for they are Ulster's best,
Let us fight now for their liberty and freedom from Long Kesh,
With the cry 'For God and Ulster' free the men of the UVF.

Another feature of Ulster loyalists' is their recasting of American and British popular songs as their own anthems of identity.[49] Here we have an example of Mike, and the Mechanics hit 'The Living Years', which is transformed into 'The Prison Years'.

---

[47] Connerton, *How Societies Remember*, 70–71.
[48] *Combat*, 25 September 1989.
[49] D. Wilson, 'Ulster Loyalism and Country Music, 1969–85', in *Country Music Goes to War*, eds. C. K. Wolfe and J. E. Akenson (Lexington, KY: University Press of Kentucky, 2005), 192–207.

I can still recall the moment, when my father went away,
They locked him up in Long Kesh,
For being Loyal so they say,
I heard he was a hero, in the UVF it seems,
They told me to be proud of him, to hold on to his dream.

So I took the oath and joined them, the men in Sweeney's Team,
The years went by so quickly, and they set my father free,
We'd hardly been together, when the Bastards got to me,
I became a Loyalist Prisoner, as my father had before,
I learned the price of freedom, at the slamming of the door,
And my love for Ulster lived with me, even in these days.

Chorus: Say it loud, Say it clear,
I'm a soldier, an Ulster Volunteer,
Proud to be, a YCV,
And to serve with the men in Sweeney's team.

My father came to see me, as often as he could,
His knowledge was astounding, his advice was always good,
Remember where you come from, keep your head held high,
Be proud of your history, Ulster's flag must fly,
And if you don't give up don't give in, you'll win the fight some day.

I wasn't there that evening, when my father passed away,
And though he hadn't spoken, I knew just what he'd say,
Be true to your religion,
Remember Queen and Crown,
Always love your comrades, never let them down,
That's what he would have told me, in the living years.

Conclusions

The acts and thoughts of those involved in loyalist paramilitarism can be plotted on a wide continuum. The actions behind much of the initial wave of loyalist paramilitary activity involved ideological and physical defence of community, which was quickly reframed as loyalist paramilitaries began to organize and engage in more aggressive forms of political violence. As conflict became embedded in Northern Irish society and political violence took pattern and shape, some within the paramilitary groupings were convinced of the need for wider involvement in welfare and housing issues and for some form of political representation.

Much of this reflected the need to try to ensure legitimacy within their immediate communities and the desirability of broadening this to engage more fully across the arena of civil society. None of this proved straightforward, however. Both during the Troubles and in the post-conflict period, the processes involved in the development of loyalist political thinking were never linear and often complicated by factionalism, driven by clashes surrounding ideology, personalities or sometimes mainly pragmatic considerations. This eventually gave rise to a changed emphasis amongst the leadership of the paramilitary groups involved, and the expression of the distance many felt from the established unionist politicians, as well for some more traditional concerns.

In the contemporary period, many loyalists believe their politics and politicians have been further marginalized, and they also consider that their core narrative has been rendered subservient to Republican accounts of the Troubles. Social and physical representations of collective memory help maintain the imagined community and contribute to the formation of a defined collective. In their response, the significance of social and cultural memories goes far beyond that of the individual. Sections of loyalism represented by paramilitarism have undergone crucial processes of transformation at several key points throughout their recent history, which has given rise to competing accounts of that community's collective experiences. The political outgoings of those memories have manifested in other ways, and as we shall see in Chapter 7, remain for some central to the contemporary political agenda through the emergence of what is seen as a culture war and the attempt to hollow out loyalist identity.

7

(In)security, (Dis)connection and Culture Wars

Loyalism is deeply located within sections of the Protestant working class and over the past four decades has in large part been driven by the reactions of that grouping to political events, and their response to rapidly changing social circumstances they have faced at the community level. Writing in the mid-1980s, Desmond Bell[1] outlined what he saw as the major challenges facing loyalism, such as economic, in particular, the problems brought about through deindustrialization; spatial, especially those issues arising from the break-up of long established working-class communities; and political, in particular, the form loyalist politics was to take following the demise of the Unionist controlled Stormont administration.

Over a quarter of a century after the publication of Bell's work, it remains remarkably accurate as a synopsis of the main issues facing many working-class loyalism. These views were mirrored by the newspaper columnist Nick Garbutt, who in reviewing the political landscape shortly following the 2011 Assembly election suggested that large sections of loyalism had now become so socially disenfranchised and alienated that they formed what could best be described as a 'lost tribe' within Northern Irish society.[2] The concepts of social and political disconnection have become widely reoccurring themes within the lexicon of loyalism. It builds upon the terrain of political and social alienation which has been in widespread currency since at least around the time of the AIA,[3] set in the wider context of what many unionists regarded as the 'demonisation of the Protestant Community'.[4]

This chapter identifies community as site for political engagement and in particular seeks to distinguish how throughout the contemporary period, several political groupings have claimed they best speak for and represent the interests of the loyalist community. It highlights the emergence of the notion of 'culture wars' and its increasing currency as an organizational focus for key sections of loyalism. Finally, we return briefly to the notion of ontological security we can see how in different

---

[1] Bell, 'Acts of union: youth sub-culture and ethnic identity amongst Protestants in Northern Ireland'.
[2] *Newsletter*, 19 May 2011.
[3] S. Dunn and V. Morgan, *Protestant Alienation in Northern Ireland: A Preliminary Survey* (Coleraine: Centre for the Study of Conflict, University of Ulster, 1994); C. Knox, 'Alienation: An Emerging Protestant Phenomenon in Northern Ireland', *Ulster Papers in Public Policy in Management, No. 53* (Jordanstown: University of Ulster, 1995).
[4] G. Gudgin, 'The Demonisation of the Protest Community; presentation to the Ulster Society on Thursday 26 September 1996' (Lurgan: Ulster Society, 1997).

ways all have sought to reintroduce a stable narrative[5] across loyalism following a period of political dislocation.

At various times, a wide range of political organizations and groupings have claimed to represent the authentic voice of loyalism, seeking to attract support by directly addressing the insecurity of that community. These range from the Vanguard movement of the 1970s,[6] to the contemporary position expressed by the anti-Agreement Traditional Unionist Voice and the more recent Protestant Coalition. Throughout the most recent period, however, it is the DUP that has claimed the mantle of Sir Edward Carson and to best represent the authentic voice of working-class loyalism.

Indeed, the modern electoral and political importance of the DUP was built upon unconcealed and explicit opposition to all those seen as in any way to threaten the Union. The party projected a narrative that the very future existence of Northern Ireland was at stake and that all attempts at political settlement, up to and including the 1998 Belfast Agreement, undermined the Union. The DUP presented the view that the political sphere was being set by an untrustworthy British government rapidly conceding ground to a pan-nationalist front, against which the only effective opposition was organized around the leadership of the DUP. Take, for example, the following from Peter Robinson, the then DUP Deputy leader:

> I have been in this Party from its birth and there has not been a moment when we have not been in the forefront of the battle. There has not been a period where the Party has not been engaged in the struggle to save the Union .... we are still here, still in the midst of the fray, still contending and still unwavering.[7]

For much of the period the DUP consistently repeated its claim to be the only party that could ensure the stability of the Union that would directly challenge, not just by the rise of militant republicanism but also by the workings of a treacherous Westminster administration in cahoots with pan-nationalism.[8] Subsequently, however, the DUP supported a modified version of the 1998 deal, having negotiated changes in the 2006 St Andrews Agreement and accepted the political bona fides of Sinn Féin. As the DUP was seen to move away from traditional loyalist narrative and from a vehicle largely set in place to express the 'politicized Protestantism' of Paisley's Free Presbyterian Church, to a modern political party, they moved from self-styled unionist opposition, positioned as 'outsiders' to one at the heart of a working devolved government.

The DUP now heads the Executive in a power-sharing arrangement with Sinn Féin and holds the majority of seats in the Northern Ireland Executive, while also providing the First Minister of Northern Ireland. But the rise of the DUP has not been uncontested. Loyalism is capable of and framing the conflict in a particular way that

---

[5] Kinnvall, 'Globalization and religious nationalism: self, identity, and the search for ontological security'.

[6] L. Gardner, *Resurgence of the Majority* (Belfast: Ulster Vanguard Publications, 1971).

[7] P. Robinson, 'Speech to DUP Annual Conference, Omagh, 1998'. Available: http://www.dup.org; accessed 21 September 1999.

[8] Tonge, et al., *The Democratic Unionist Party*.

mobilizes security amongst one group, while generating further distance from, and antagonism towards, groups seen to represent the Other. This is realized through an internalized discourse that provides core reference points for both individual and group identification.[9] To succeed, unionism must draw on existing collective memories in some recognizable way, and it must do so in a way whereby it is seen to reconfirm core principles. Hence, some see compromise by the DUP as weakness.

It was John Reid, when Secretary of State for Northern Ireland, who was prompted to say that it was important Northern Ireland did not become a 'cold house for Protestants'. Sometime after, in 2003, a later Secretary of State Paul Murphy announced that 'despite great progress in Northern Ireland, some people feel they have been left behind ... many in this category are from loyalist communities'.[10] This has remained central to the loyalist political agenda. Accordingly, in its editorial of 10 December 2008, the *News Letter* felt required to ask the question: 'Are working-class Protestants out in the cold – again?', highlighting what it acknowledged as the 'sense of detachment' and disconnection from the peace process expressed by many.

Community activists, alongside sections of paramilitarism, former paramilitarists and their political representatives all continue to suggest that in loyalist communities the 'lustre of the peace process has long dulled',[11] and that these communities 'are not reaping the benefits of the new era'.[12] Hence, contemporary loyalist politics is structured not just by its long-standing covenantal frame, but also in relation to economic decline, social deprivation, educational underachievement and everyday, albeit, often low-level sectarianized conflict. Throughout Northern Ireland, social bonding remains largely restricted to ones 'own' community,[13] and that intra-community cohesion remains high.[14]

Across Belfast, areas of loyalist and republican deprivation can, and do, exist side by side. Increasingly, however, loyalist reaction is to directly compare the two, usually to argue that republican community is better off and is winning the struggle to impose their culture. Equally observable is the level of social division between communities, where high levels of distrust constantly reinforce social distance from the Other, strengthening social links and weakening the possibility of social bonding.[15] Much of

[9] Wertsch, *Voices of Collective Remembering*; 'Collective Memory', in *Memory in Mind and Culture*, eds. P. Boyer and J. V. Wertsch (Cambridge: Cambridge University Press, 2008), 117–137.

[10] P. Murphy, '£3m fund set to boost hard-hit communities'. Available: http://www.4ni.co.uk/northern_ireland_news.asp?id=5676; accessed 12 May 2009.

[11] B. Hutchinson, 'Why Loyalism Feels Cut Adrift'. Available at: http://eamonnmallie.com/2012/10/why-loyalism-feel-cut-adrift-billy-hutchinson-explains/; accessed 14 June 2013.

[12] *Belfast Telegraph*, 20 July 2009.

[13] D. Bacon, 'Revitalising Civil Society in Northern Ireland: Social Capital Formation in Three Faith-Based Organisations (FBOs)', paper presented at the 7th Researching the Voluntary Sector Conference (London: NCVO Headquarters, 2001).

[14] E. Cairns, T. Van Til, and A. Williamson, *Social Capital, Collectivism*.

[15] E. Cairns, A. Lewis, O. Mumcu, and N. Waddell, 'Memories of recent ethnic conflict and their relationship to social identity', *Peace and Conflict: Journal of Peace Psychology*, 4, no. 1 (1998): 13–22; U. Niens, E. Cairns, and M. Hewstone 'Contact and Conflict in Northern Ireland' in *Researching the Troubles: Social Science Perspectives on the Northern Ireland Conflict*, eds. O. Hargie and D. Dickson (Edinburgh: Mainstream Publishing, 2003), 85–106.

this has been distilled and concentrated into the notion of a 'culture war', and a distinct loyalist identity, which is seen as under coordinated attack from Irish republicanism.

Loyalism's culture wars

Although in Northern Irish society much of the everyday politics dealing with the past trends directly focuses on violence and increasingly on victimhood, it is important to recognize that they too draw upon collective memories to construct a very broad understanding of the direction of conflict. One consequence of this is that differences between physical assault on group members and attacks on what are seen as the symbolic or cultural artefacts of group identity are blurred. Many loyalists, for example, now believe that having failed in its military campaign, Irish republicanism has undertaken a strategy to hollow out British cultural symbolism, having 'now moved into the next phase of the plan to break Protestant resistance so as they can achieve their end goal'.[16]

The point was made directly by PUP leader Billy Hutchinson in claiming 'Sinn Féin lost the war for a united Ireland and what they are now doing is fighting the cultural war'.[17] Hence, across loyalism, many see themselves as openly engaged in a new form of cultural conflict.[18] Take for example, the following response from the Orange Order to the vandalizing of a war memorial in Coleraine in March 2014:

> lodge members quite rightly see this as an attack on their community ... and on the memory of those who fought and died in service, not least those members of the lodge who served in the First World War.... Attacking the memory of those who gave their life in conflict is one of the lowest actions that anyone can take. This systematic and premeditated attack needs to result in immediate police attention and action to apprehend those responsible and bring them to justice.[19]

This view has been gaining increased currency for some time. Accordingly, when in November 2001 the then secretary of state, John Reid, declared that the unionist community 'believes its traditions, culture and way of life are under threat [and] that Catholic confidence in the peace process has been bought at their expense', it was greeted in the following days *News Letter* 'Morning View' editorial by the claim that the view offered a 'clear, concise and insightful understanding of unionist and Protestant perceptions'.[20]

---

[16] *Orange Standard*, August 2004.
[17] UTV News, 'SF "fighting cultural war" – Hutchinson'. Available at: http://www.u.tv/News/SF-fighting-cultural-war-Hutchinson/891157d6-1378-408f-9a6f-508541cd17f9; accessed 28 March 2014.
[18] *Orange Standard*, July 2007; *Orange Standard*, March 2008.
[19] UTV News, 'Hate attack on Orange war memorial'. Available: http://www.u.tv/News/Hate-attack-on-Orange-war-memorial/ba9ab99f-7c8a-4f58-88ad-5a43c848456a; accessed 28 March 2014.
[20] *News Letter*, 22 November 2001: 8.

This is compounded by the changed social relations that have emerged following the decline of the physical environment in Protestant working-class areas, alongside which are important feelings of social abandonment, negative feelings towards the presence of former republican combatants in government, and what is seen as an increasingly confrontational approach of sections of republicanism manifest in the cultural battleground. This is understood as a direct attack on loyalist culture, manifest in issues such as parade re-routing, which has led sections of the broader Protestant/ Unionist/Loyalist community to feel:

> ... that some elements of nationalism are intent on humiliating it, and it fears that an historical inevitability, rather than democracy, dictates the political and constitutional future of the Province. Protestants also believe that Catholic confidence in the peace process has been bought at their expense.[21]

The worldview of many loyalists includes the belief that they now face an almost 'daily onslaught on their British heritage and culture'.[22] As a consequence, this led one commentator to suggest that '... by the mid-1990s Protestant urban communities found themselves nearly a generation behind in the business of grassroots cultural education'.[23] In late 2008, for example, the UDA felt obliged to issue a statement that members were now engaged in peaceful struggle on 'a new battlefield of cultural politics' to be fought out on the terrain of media presentation, education, politics, social and community work and business.[24]

Such ideas have gained traction across much of unionism, and what is seen as the continued 'cultural agitation'[25] by republicanism, causing UUP leader Mike Nesbitt to call on Sinn Féin to call off their culture war.[26] At the heart of the notion of culture wars is loyalist anxiety surrounding concerning perceived threats to their sense of identity. Although loyalist fears do encompass concerns about physical security, it also involves less concrete, but no less valid, trepidation surrounding the possible obliteration of the cultural icons and sites of loyalism.

Cultural contestation has of course been current ever since the formation of the state, but in the contemporary period, it and much broad political differences have been distilled into the notion of culture wars. What is different is the central part that culture war now occupies within the contemporary loyalism narrative that the conflict had entered a new political and cultural phase.[27] This corrals many of the concerns

---

[21] *Ibid.*
[22] BBC News, 'Northern Ireland Orange Order leaders warn of cultural war', 12 July, available: http://www.bbc.co.uk/news/uk-northern-ireland-23267038; accessed 12 November 2013.
[23] M. W. Dowling, 'Confusing culture and politics: Ulster scots culture and music', *New Hibernia Review*, 11, no. 3 (2007): 51–80.
[24] *News Letter*, 11 November 2008.
[25] Grand Orange Lodge of Ireland, 'Speech Made by the Grand Master of the Grand Orange Lodge of Ireland, Edward Stevenson, at the Dungannon Demonstration'.
[26] *Larne Times*, 2 February 2013.
[27] Hall, *Loyalism in Transition 1*; *Loyalism in Transition 2*.

highlighted above as part of a much broader narrative that spells out the dangers they have overcome and continued struggle emphasizing the group's shared culture.

It is important to recognize how widespread the engagement in the culture war is perceived. Cultural difference is reproduced at several levels: symbolically through public emblems and symbols[28]; at the every day, through what newspaper one reads, or what sport one follows; through a divided civil society; and sometimes through violent confrontation or attacks. It is also reproduced directly through popular culture products. The range of loyalist commemorative and promotional material is now vast. Specialist shops throughout Northern Ireland offer material, ranging from books, films, CDs, DVDs, newspapers, commemorative flags (for example, the formation of the UVF in 1913), clothing, especially embossed T-shirts and polo shirts, ties, commemorative metal and wooden carved plaques, framed photographs, badges, key rings, mugs, postcards, tea-towels, postcards, stickers and booklets.

Set alongside other highly publically visible physical manifestations of the collective memory, such as murals or commemorative gardens, personal tattoos and even gravestones of paramilitary members, these are central in reminding people of particular memories and interpretations of events.[29] As such, the range of artefacts and icons are seen and used as essential parts of the arsenal in a cultural conflict, where consistent exposure to popular culture adds to processes that shape attitudes often by representing shorthand, and therefore, easily understood and transmitted, forms of complex sets of beliefs.

Even in low-level conflicts, group self-esteem can be felt challenged, and the need to defend it quickly forefronted. In more intense conflicts, the difference between physical attacks and symbolic attacks become blurred. This often involved overt assaults on the perceived cultural symbols of the other community, such as chapels, churches, Gaelic Athletic Association clubs, Orange halls and commemorative War monuments the latter seen as part of what concerted attack on the cultural iconography of loyalism.

While it may seem reasonably straightforward to distinguish between physical and symbolic attack, it becomes much harder to separate the two in the mindset of those who see themselves engaged in the heat of a real conflict. Both physical and symbolic attacks invoke feelings of vulnerability, often alongside feelings of humiliation or defeat that link past losses to present dangers. Fears can be about individual or family, but they can equally represent deep concerns surrounding the extinction of a group and its culture, especially when some loyalists see Republicans as 'engaging in a cultural war to erode all symbols of Britishness'.[30]

A core example can be seen in the flags dispute.[31] Recent social unrest in Northern Ireland, following a decision to fly the Union flag only on designated days at Belfast

---

[28] P. Devine-Wright and E. Lyons, 'Remembering pasts and representing places: the construction of national identities in Ireland', *Journal of Environmental Psychology*, 17, (1997): 33–45.

[29] Zerubavel, 'Social memories: steps to a sociology of the past'.

[30] BBC News, 'Northern Ireland Orange Order leaders warn of cultural war'.

[31] S. McBride, 'Heated meeting hears loyalist claims of abandonment over flag'. Available: http://www.newsletter.co.uk/news/politics/latest/heated-meeting-hears-loyalist-claims-of-abandonment-over-flag-1-5041902; accessed 28 March 2014.

City Hall[32] (a crucial site in unionist social memory), demonstrates the potential for these culture wars to undermine the prospects for reconciliation in a divided society.[33] The following comments were typical of the views of flag protestors:

> ... the whole flag thing ... they're trying to take away our Britishness ....
>
> ... the Provos tried to bomb and shoot us into an all-Ireland for years and they couldn't do it. Now they're trying to do it in a different way by taking away our culture.
>
> There's still a war going on, but this time its without bullets and bombs.
>
> We have given everything, the RUC and the UDR they've been disbanded, all the emblems of the Queen are gone, now they're trying to take away our flag.[34]

The protests brought parts of Northern Ireland to a standstill, as demonstrators blocked major roads, clashed violently with police and caused widespread disruption to the everyday lives of many.[35] In the view of Mervyn Gibson, the Grand Chaplin of the Orange Order, however:

> ... the flag protestors did this generation a great service by waking us from our slumber – apathy, pessimism and defeatism were walking us into a united Ireland. Rather than waking up to fight each other, we need to concentrate yet again on defeating republicanism, this time in the current cultural war. Let this generation not be found wanting, do not fight the war on yesterday's battlefield – fight the war on today's battleground.[36]

As Gibson's response to the street protests of 2013 and 2014 indicates, one articulation of loyalist identity is being expressed by a small but significant faction through a response to a perceived cultural erosion and loss and of their British identity. Many loyalists who would not condone the violence emerging from such protests still share the senses of loss and insecurity expressed by loyalist demonstrators.[37] This marked a repositioning of sections of loyalism, whereby 'one saw an increasing popularity of loyalist parades, and an accompanying shift ... away from its traditional "Ulster-British" ideology to a more narrowly monocultural and rebellious position'.[38]

---

[32] E. Mastors and N. Drumhiller, 'What's in a flag? The protestant community's identity, symbols, and protests in Belfast', *Peace and Change*, 39, no. 4 (2014): 495–518.

[33] B. McCaffrey, 'Flag report says loyalism feels abandoned by unionist parties', *The Detail*, Issue 227. Available at: http://www.thedetail.tv/issues/297; accessed 15 December 2013.

[34] Interviews with flag protestors, Newtownards Road, 22 November 2013.

[35] H. McDonald, 'Belfast union flag dispute is lightning rod for loyalist disaffection'. Available: http://www.theguardian.com/uk/2013/jan/06/belfast-union-flag-dispute-loyalist; accessed 28 March 2014.

[36] BBC News, 'Northern Ireland Orange Order leaders warn of cultural war'.

[37] McDonald, 'Belfast union flag dispute is lightning rod for loyalist disaffection'.

[38] Dowling, 'Confusing culture and politics: Ulster scots culture and music', 54.

Such feelings were also apparent in August 2011, when the *Belfast Telegraph* ran a special three-day feature under the banner of 'Why people in Protestant Working-Class areas feel left behind'. The responses highlighted the belief that ordinary Protestants had been abandoned by mainstream unionist parties; the loss to loyalism of key political leaders such as Gary McMichael, or the late David Ervine, Gusty Spence and Billy Mitchell, and the inability to replace such quality of leadership from within; the piecemeal approach to the socio-economic problems in working-class Protestant communities; the increased lack of job opportunities; demise of traditional apprenticeships; educational underachievement; media demonization; and the marginalization of loyalist culture exemplified by the banning or re-routing of Orange marches.

Core geographical areas such as East Belfast highlight the economic decline of traditional Protestant working-class communities. Any direct link to secure work in heavy industry is little more than a fading memory, reflected directly in the resulting levels of unemployment and lack of job opportunities in traditional industries. The waning in traditional work and the rise of unstable labour patterns was compounded by the break-up of traditional housing and physical infrastructures and paralleled by the growth of social problems.[39] Moreover, those living in working-class Protestant districts are certainly not immune from wider social forces, indicating not only the decline of social class, but also the rise in the individualization of economic inequality that has been experienced globally and has gone some way to dismantle the sense of working-class community and common consciousness.[40]

The consequences of this are profound. The reliance on what was seen as an unbreakable intergenerational link to industrial work (and shipbuilding and its related industries in particular) meant that the culture that emerged placed little emphasis or merit on educational qualifications as a route to employment or a means to a more secure future. Following the effects of deindustrialization and globalization, the contemporary period has seen many young people from loyalist districts with low educational achievement cut adrift, which would previously most likely be assured of some form of employment. Many are seen at best as subsidiary to the demands of the contemporary Labour market and confined to inner urban areas.[41]

Public spending as a percentage of GDP has increased by 14 per cent since 1998 to 71 per cent, and wages, especially in the private sector, remain low by UK standards. Around one in six workers in Northern Ireland are now classed as low paid,[42] part of what has been termed 'a lost generation economically'. In economic terms, there is little to suggest to urban working-class loyalists that the peace dividend has been shared in

[39] R. Sennett, *The Culture of the New Capitalism* (New Haven: Yale University Press, 2006).

[40] U. Beck, *Risk Society: Towards a New Modernity* (London: Sage, 2000).

[41] E. McCann, 'Peace brings no dividend to the poorest in the North', *The Irish Times*. Available: http://www.irishtimes.com/news/politics/peace-brings-no-dividend-to-the-poorest-in-the-north-1.1739265?utm_source=dlvr.it&utm_medium=twitter; accessed 27 March 2014.

[42] J. Campbell, 'Northern Ireland's poorest "still struggle after downturn"'. Available at: http://www.bbc.co.uk/news/uk-northern-ireland-26721962; accessed 25 March 2014.

a society where living standards still remain 20 per cent below the UK average.[43] The rapidly changed economic base experienced by sections of the loyalist community, the Troubles and its legacy have also occasioned major social problems across Northern Ireland, including widespread family disruption, further community fragmentation and the break-up of established family and kinship networks.[44]

Particularly in interface areas, political and social schisms increasingly structured everyday life, as the existing social structure fragmented. One consequence was that young people left existing communities in sizeable numbers leaving an older generation with much less of extended family network to provide support. The point is reinforced by Orr[45] in a survey conducted in East Belfast during the mid-1990s, which indicated that of those regularly attending the local ten churches, only 28 per cent lived in the neighbourhood. A further 31 per cent used to live locally but had moved to other districts returning only on Sundays to attend worship. Moreover, of the thirty-two people deemed to be church leaders, only three lived in the area. Despite the obvious strength of appeal to a common ethno-political-religious identity, intra-Protestant class and social divisions remain extremely meaningful. For many loyalists, the social and political gap between themselves and middle-class Protestants, the mainline Protestant churches and the established Unionist political parties is an everyday reality.

Political disconnection

That those living within Protestant working-class areas often feel they 'lack the capability and capacity to [bring about] political change'[46] has been widely noted. This is compounded by the deeply embedded perspective within many working-class Protestant districts that 'they are not well represented by elected politicians',[47] (and the DUP in particular), adding to mounting evidence that a section of loyalism is now completely disengaged from the political institutions, and that they are completely unrepresented by the existing unionist representatives.[48]

An absence of an elected voice from working-class Protestant communities and the distance from the DUP and UUP both highlight the disengagement from politics. As Billy Hutchinson puts it:

> ... the new distribution of power at Stormont has left working class Unionists, and increasingly working class Catholics with no political voice .... the larger parties in the new distribution of power manipulate working class voters to satisfy the concerns of the better off.[49]

[43] Nolan, *Northern Ireland Peace Monitoring*.
[44] Manktelow, 'The needs of victims of the troubles in Northern Ireland'.
[45] Orr, *New Loyalties*.
[46] *Newsletter*, 19 May 2011.
[47] *Ibid.*
[48] Intercomm and J. Byrne, 'Flags and Protests', 33–34.
[49] Hutchinson, 'Why Loyalism Feels Cut Adrift'.

Within many Protestant working-class districts, it is apathy that best defines the dominant relationship to politics and the political process, illustrated by the extremely low turnout at elections in working-class loyalist areas throughout Northern Ireland. Partly, this can be explained by the weakness of organic leadership, causing feelings of disconnection and mistrust from the mainstream unionist parties. There remains widespread suspicion towards the Other community within the new political era, with a working devolved Assembly and a discernible level of distrust of those unionist politicians willing to work with Sinn Féin and of the intentions of the British government.

Many perceive the DUP as having moved to centre ground of politics. This was recognized in part Tony Blair's former chief of staff Jonathan Powell, who perhaps came closest to the continuing concerns of this section of the population in commenting that the loyalist community had not got enough political support, arguing that:

> Sinn Féin have looked after their communities, the working class Catholic communities, the SDLP have looked after their communities and the middle class Catholics.... The DUP have looked after the middle class unionists but no-one has looked after the working class Protestants trapped in their ghettos. No-one has provided an economic future for them, no-one has given them leadership, so they are trapped with those gangs the UVF and the UDA.[50]

In suggesting that sections of loyalist working-class communities continue to experience wide senses of alienation, Jonny Byrne concludes:

> The absence of political leadership compounds the siege mentality and reinforces the sense of isolation. In the eyes of many loyalists, the only way to secure their culture, history and sense of identity is to replicate the past, take to the streets and hope that mass demonstrations will redress the hurt and sense of loss.[51]

In part, this represents broader societal changes and the notion that many sections of western societies have increasingly been made to feel insecure through a series of significant and unpredictable social changes including, large-scale migration, changes in labour and workforce practices, the break-up of long-established community and family patterns, the increase in globalization, the cultural and political impacts of mass consumerism and the rise in individualism.[52] At this level, the situation in many working-class Protestant districts mirrors the situation elsewhere, for example, in those urban communities in England and Sweden that feel left behind and which in recent years have dissolved into unrest and violence.

---

[50] BBC News, 'Jonathan Powell in appeal over loyalist communities', Available: 21 April, http://www.bbc.co.uk/news/uk-northern-ireland-22237958; accessed 12 June 2013.

[51] Intercomm and J. Byrne, 'Flags and Protests', 17.

[52] J. Young, *The Exclusive Society: Social Exclusion, Crime and Difference in Late Modernity* (London: Sage, 2007).

At another level, of course, events in such loyalist communities must be seen through the specific prism of Northern Irish society and the clamour for greater feelings of ontological security from within sections of loyalism. This sense of social and political alienation has occurred in parallel with the evaporation of economic opportunity, the security of employment in the industrial workplace, raised levels of unemployment and social deprivation and the resulting increase in welfare dependency experienced in many working-class loyalist districts, alongside an undeveloped civil sphere within loyalist districts. Much of the above points to increasing feelings of powerlessness in working-class Protestant communities, where:

> ... feelings of 'disconnection' came across strongly... In particular there was a feeling of disconnection, or sense of loss from the peace process in the sense that local politicians are particularly inept at dealing with local issues that mattered/matter to the working class Protestant community, and that they and their 'identity' had somehow been 'sold out' with the signing of the Good Friday Agreement.[53]

Conclusions

A strong sense of identity is seen to enhance emotional, social and physical security, especially through association with other like-minded individuals. Many loyalists feel ever more marginalized and disconnected from the new post-conflict Northern Ireland, recoiling at what they regard as the diffusion of their core symbols, baulking that their identity is increasingly seen as insignificant and flinching at what they see as 'a conveyor belt of concessions' to republicanism[54] and the perceived unevenness of the rolling out of the political process following the Belfast Agreement.

Social, political and cultural loss find expression throughout unionism, but it is most directly felt in working-class loyalist areas, within which the sense of disconnection has deepened to the point where long-term community activist Jackie Redpath suggests that 'feelings of loss have now become culturally and psychologically embedded'[55] within working-class Protestant communities. The subsequent fear of loss of identity and feelings of disconnection at the economic, social and political levels is integral to understanding recent loyalist protest and violence. Much of this has been distilled into issues surrounding parades, emblems and the legacy of the violent past. It is because of this mounting culture of fear and feelings of social and political disconnection in the political and cultural areas that some loyalists feel most threatened. Those that seek most strongly to defend their identity through the cultural war have taken to the streets.

---

53 R. McAlister, 'The struggle to belong when feeling disconnected: the experience of loyalist east Belfast', paper presented at the International RC21 conference, Amsterdam, 7–9 July 2011: 5–6.
54 *The Times*, 24 January 2002: 19.
55 J. Redpath, 'Left Behind and Locked Out', 15 August 2011. Available at: http://greatershankillpartnership.org/news-blogs/shankill-inside-out/171-blog-left-behind-and-locked-out.html; accessed 3 March 2003.

8

Ulster Loyalism and Futures Past

It was Samuel who once expressed the thought that history 'notoriously takes wing at dusk, that twilight hour when shadows lengthen, silence thickens... when... thought flies heavenward and ghostly presences make themselves felt'.[1] So does the recent focus on loyalism suggest that it has entered its endgame, or that the loyalism has now been neutered as a political force? The answer to this is in large part determined by how we understand loyalism. Peter Shirlow[2] in his account of post-ceasefire loyalism compartmentalizes loyalists into a clear binary of those prepared to engage in violence and those not. He identifies the main thrust of contemporary loyalism by largely focusing on the progressive processes of conflict transformation involving former loyalist combatants.

But this is a limited view; other social forces exist beyond paramilitarism, which seek to determine and define loyalism. Important as the actions of ex-combatants may be to the future of loyalism, it cannot be determined merely by an understanding of the political direction taken by paramilitary groupings. Nor can loyalist ideology be reduced to those ideas produced from within paramilitarism, whether progressive or otherwise. One of the current dynamics within loyalism is, for example, provided by the post-conflict loyalist generation, which is not necessarily a chronological category but draws on long established parts of loyalist collective memory to produce a populist response expressing fear for the future and abandonment.[3]

Central here is Bauman concept of fear, which he argues 'is the name we give to our *uncertainty*: to our *ignorance* of the threat and of what is to be done...'.[4] It is clear how such notions of an uncertain future feature strongly in the contemporary loyalist response, not from fear of losing the 'fighting' war, but rather of conceding the peace through 'symbolic failure' and defeat in the culture wars. For sections of loyalism, the fear is that its symbols of identity, such as flags, marches and murals, are increasingly dismissed as adverse aspects of civic space and that this view is becoming entrenched.

---

[1] Samuel, 'Four Nations History', 21.

[2] P. Shirlow, *The End of Ulster Loyalism* (Manchester: Manchester University Press, 2010).

[3] R. Greenslade, 'Belfast's rioting loyalists feel abandoned by their politicians'. Available: http://www. theguardian.com/commentisfree/2013/jan/07/belfast-rioting-loyalists-politicians-union-flag; accessed 28 March 2014.

[4] Z. Bauman, *Liquid Fear* (Cambridge: Polity Press, 2006), 2, emphasis in original.

Repositioning loyalism?

These views that loyalist culture is seen as detrimental to any new social formation need to be located in the contemporary construction of loyalist identity. As Reinhart Koselleck[5] explains in *Vergangene Zukunft* [Futures Past], at certain points both present and future are directly influenced by dominant versions of the past. Following the outbreak of the Troubles, loyalists drew on heavily on existing collective memories as core reference points to guide political reactions. At the macro level, this was uncontested, loyalists emphasizing the need to protect a distinct sense of Britishness. At the micro level, however, senses of unionist identity and belonging were more fluid, often resting on a highly localized memories and experiences to create different and often exigent senses of belonging within loyalism.

These different levels have remained within loyalism.[6] While recognizing they share common features, John Brewer[7] has highlighted how different social settings give rise to differing idioms of loyalism, manifest, for example, in differences between rural loyalism and what he terms, 'urban interface Loyalism' (those whose sense of loyalist identity is formed through experiences of living on sectarian interfaces found in Belfast). Political expressions of loyalism remain firmly grounded beyond the ideas and political organization offered by mainstream unionism, where working-class Protestants have consistently sought to find different forms of outlets for their social values and political beliefs.

As we have seen from many of the issues encountered throughout this book, contemporary loyalism expresses a broad assemblage of Self. The resulting range of identity and cultural reference points has all influenced key areas of loyalist thinking, from the inception of the Troubles until the present day. Loyalism represents a highly localized interpretation and expression of socio-economic, political and spatial relations. The combined effect of massive social changes brings about further confusion surrounding status, roles and rewards, which as Young[8] highlights increases feelings of ontological insecurity manifest in a growing lack of confidence in one's own identity, and the perceived need to defend that identity, often in its most essentialized form.

How loyalists interpret and use collective memories to frame and structure their past explains, in part at least, why loyalists have responded to contemporary political events in a distinct manner. It also begins to explain how loyalism, on the one hand, can take more progressive forms and, on the other, coalesce around more fundamental expressions of identity. Hence, in part, the story told above concerns the strengthening of traditional discourses and the emergence of loyalist street demonstrators around flags and parades. It also explains why progressive voices

---

[5]   R. Koselleck, *Futures Past*, translated by Keith Tribe (Cambridge, MA: MIT Press, 1979).
[6]   See A. Finlay, 'Defeatism and northern Protestant "identity"', *Global Review of Ethnopolitics*, 1, no. 2 (2001): 3–20.
[7]   Brewer, 'Culture, Class and Protestantism in Urban Belfast'.
[8]   J. Young, *The Vertigo of Late Modernity* (London: Sage, 2007).

have seemingly been marginalized, seen by many as marking a break, rather than continuity, with the loyalist past.

Notions of marginalization, disconnection and detachment find increasing validity across significant sections of loyalism, including but stretching far beyond loyalist paramilitarism and/or its former combatants. Sections of the broader loyalist community, who have increasingly questioned the peace dividend, have come to believe that their symbolism is increasingly challenged, and that they occupy a restricted social and political position in the post-conflict Northern Ireland. As a result, many loyalists have sought security in a return to long-established loyalist narratives and established discourses. The identifiable content of loyalist history and the strength of the cohesive narrative provide a platform for the construction of the Other and the social relations of 'us' and 'them'. This in turn makes transformation and new forms of identification and political expression extremely difficult.

Novick says we prioritize some memories over others because we see them as so central to our collective identity, and 'those memories, once brought to the fore, reinforce that form of identity'.[9] There are a growing number of studies focusing on the influence of memory on conflict and its possible resolution or continuation.[10] If, for example, we return to Halbwachs,[11] it is possible to recognize how collective memory provides a common range of reference points, which future generations can use to 'think with' and draw upon to produce their version of contemporary reality. As we have seen throughout this book, Loyalists draw heavily on pre-existing narratives and collective memories to understand their everyday lives and actions.[12]

What one remembers is, in part at least, defined by the identities one takes on,[13] and amid rapid social and political change, people draw heavily on established memories to find reassurance by linking with the past. The values established through this collective social memory are often reinforced through commemoration, for example, through making 12 July a public holiday, public symbolism such as flags, as indicators of a common past. All of this remains crucial to the central identity of both individuals and social groups alike. One result is an avowal of the past through direct engagement with collective memory to affirm the loyalist politics of the present. As Connerton reminds us more generally:

> What binds together recent memories is not the fact that they are contiguous in time but rather that they form part of the whole ensemble of thoughts common to

[9] P. Novick, *The Holocaust and Collective Memory* (London: Bloomsbury, 1995), 5.

[10] See, for example, C. McGrattan, *Northern Ireland 1968-2008 The Politics of Entrenchment* (Basingstoke: Palgrave Macmillan, 2010); C. Mitchell, 'The limits of legitimacy: former loyalist combatants and peace-building in Northern Ireland', *Irish Political Studies*, 23, no. 1 (2008): 1–19; K. Simpson, 'Political strategies of engagement: Unionists and dealing with the past in Northern Ireland', *British Politics*, 8, no. 1 (2013): 2–27.

[11] Halbwachs, *On Collective Memory*, 45–51.

[12] Bruner, *Acts of Meaning*.

[13] J. R. Gillis, ed. *Commemorations: The Politics of National Identity* (Princeton, NJ: Princeton University Press, 1994); 'Memory and Identity: The History of a Relationship', in *Commemorations: The Politics of National Identity*, 3–26.

a group, to the groups with which we are in relationship at present or have been in some connection in the recent past.[14]

Heritage, truth and victimhood

One of the clearest manifestations of issues involving collective and social memory is found in the politics of the past, dealing with the legacy of the conflict.[15] A common interpretation of a shared past events is, of course, at the core of a more progressive society, but in practice this is an area that has proved to be particularly fraught in Northern Ireland. Partly, this is because as Marcel Baumann recognizes, it involves 'understanding the other's "understanding" of violence', and that 'both sides fought a campaign which from their own perspective was just and legitimate'.[16]

As Jenkins[17] underlines, 'tradition' and 'heritage' are two of the key phrases through which loyalism finds expression. These are meaningful for loyalists not because they seek to establish the 'truth' about past events, but rather they form part of an interpretative relationship with the past, through a complex matrix of individual, collective and community narratives. Consequently, discourses of tradition and the notion of coherent and stable links with the past are deeply imbued across loyalism and the core narratives identified above:

> are more than ways of giving meaning to the world, they imply forms of social organisation and social practices which structure institutions and constitute individuals as thinking, feeling and acting subjects.[18]

It is possible to argue for the existence of some commonality across conflict experiences and within deeply divided societies and there has been some excellent material produced identifying the politics of peace processes across a wide range of societies such as South Africa, Israel and Palestine, the Balkans and Sri Lanka.[19] If we are to understand the form of the conflict in Northern Ireland, its transformation and the possibilities for a shared future, the contradictions around defining those who can and who cannot legitimately be regarded as victims, we must return to the specific constructed collective memories. Both past exposure to conflict and

---

[14] Connerton, *How Societies Remember*, 36.

[15] A. Assmann, 'From collective violence to a common future: four models for dealing with a traumatic past' (2011). Available at: http://www.ysu.am/files/02A_Assmann.pdf; accessed 10 May 2013.

[16] M. M. Baumann, 'The trouble with the peace science's "trouble makers"', *Peace Review*, 20 (2008): 455–461.

[17] Jenkins, *Social Identity*, 107–123.

[18] G. Jordan and C. Weedon, *Cultural Politics: Class, Gender, Race and the Postmodern World* (Oxford: Blackwell, 1995), 14.

[19] J. Darby, *The Effects of Violence on Peace Processes* (Washington, DC: US Institute of Peace Press, 2001); Steenkamp, *Violence and Post-War Reconstruction*; J. Tonge, *Comparative Peace Processes* (Cambridge: Polity Press, 2014).

the legacy expressed through collective memories of political violence help mould political views and identity.[20]

It is often restriction from, or inclusion into, particular social and political categories that offer legitimation to particular groups for their actions, or for that group justifies the reasons why they became engaged in conflict.[21] The gulf in interpretation between conflicting groups heightens in-group feelings of victimization while denying any victim status to the out-group. Moreover, the need to deal with traumatic events of the past can of course be particularly destabilizing in post-conflict societies.[22] This is especially true when it is recognized that the political circumstances brought about by any peace accord are not fixed and the peace process must be managed.[23]

Both the Catholic/Nationalist/Republican and Protestant/Unionist/Loyalist communities still largely perceive themselves as victims of the other group. In conflict and immediate post-conflict situations, it is not uncommon for competing groups to construct interpretative frames, discourses and narratives that are used to legitimize their cause and to claim moral superiority over other groups.[24] This process involves narratives that draw directly on wider traditions and collective memories. But these are in themselves divisive. Unresolved issues concerning the definition of who can be termed victims and who called survivors, as well as the apportionment of 'guilt' or 'blame' for historical crimes, continue to be contested within and between both communities.

As a result, different groups understand the same past in different ways. Nationalists also have concerns over alleged collusion between the UK government and loyalist paramilitaries.[25] Unionists largely believe that those who committed, or were involved in, acts of violence should be excluded until there is some form of full admission to past deeds. Memories and representations of the past are always contested to a greater or lesser degree,[26] and these memories are likely to become increasingly conflictual if a group believes that members have been systematically victimized. Witness the events of 27/28 June 1970 outlined in chapter 4.

---

[20] J. Darby and R. MacGinty, *The Management of the Peace Process* (Basingstoke: Macmillan, 2000); Cairns, Lewis, and Mumcu, 'Memories of recent ethnic conflict and their relationship to social identity'.

[21] S. Rosland, 'Victimhood, identity, and agency in the early phase of the troubles in Northern Ireland', *Identities: Global Studies in Culture and Power*, 16, no. 3 (2009): 294–320.

[22] J. Lederach, *Building Peace: Sustainable Reconciliation in Divided Societies* (New York: United States Institute of Peace, 1997).

[23] J. Brewer, *Peace Processes: A Sociological Approach* (Oxford, Polity, 2010); Borer, T. A., J. Darby, and S. McEvoy-Levy, *Peacebuilding after Peace Accords* (Notre Dame USA: University of Notre Dame Press, 2006).

[24] D. Bar-Tal, 'Sociopsychological foundations of intractable conflicts', *American Behavioural Scientist*, 50, no. 11 (2007): 1430–1453.

[25] A. Cadwallader, *Lethal Allies: British Collusion in Ireland* (Cork: Mercier Press, 2013); Rolston, 'Dealing with the past: pro-state paramilitaries, truth and transition in Northern Ireland', 652–675.

[26] C. Koonz, 'Between Memory and Oblivion: Concentration Camps in German Memory', in *Commemorations: The Politics of National Identity*: 258–280; R. Wagner-Pacifici and B. Schwartz, 'The Vietnam veterans memorial: commemorating a difficult past', *The American Journal of Sociology*, 97, no. 2 (1991): 376–420.

This is far from straightforward. Although there is widespread support for the view that victims should be remembered,[27] and they should be at centre in any process of remembering, there is little agreement over who the victims actually are. It has proved impossible to find any consensus on how a victim is defined. Much of the argument has revolved around support, or opposition, for the formation of some form of Truth and Reconciliation Commission based on the model established in South Africa.[28] The 'Healing through Remembering' report,[29] for example, recommends an approach based on storytelling, a process whereby all those wishing to record their experiences of the conflict should be allowed to do so. But several writers have pointed to a broad attitude found across unionism and loyalism suggesting a particular wariness of engagement in any truth recovery process,[30] seeing in it the potential for a rewriting of history by republicans that seeks to blame unionists for the conflict's origins, to focus disproportionately on violence undertaken by the state[31] and the underplaying of the actions of militant republicanism.

Cheryl Lawther shows how both DUP and UUP members hold similar views, namely that a distinction must be upheld between 'the service and sacrifice of members of the security forces' and those 'who were setting out to plan murder'.[32] Peter Robinson claims the DUP 'has always prioritised the needs of innocent victims', adding that 'we will not contemplate any rewriting of the terrorist campaign or compromise the truth of what happened here by asking those who engaged in terrorism to agree a joint narrative'.[33] Indeed, the DUP has pledged to prevent Sinn Fein from having any role in writing or determining the history of the Troubles, further declaring that the party 'will never compromise this by asking those who have engaged in terrorism to agree a joint narrative'. Robinson further added, the 'facts are the facts; Sinn Fein's agreement or lack thereof to those facts will not change the truth of the past'.[34]

---

[27] Cairns, Van Til, and Williamson, *Social Capital, Collectivism – Individualism and Community Background in Northern Ireland*.

[28] M. Smyth and K. Thomson, *Working with Children and Young People in Violently Divided Societies* (Belfast: CCIC and the University of Ulster, 2001).

[29] Healing Through Remembering, *Making Peace with the Past: Options for truth recovery regarding the conflict in and about Northern Ireland* [written by Prof. Kerian McEvoy], (Belfast: Healing Through Remembering, 2006).

[30] C. Lawther, 'Unionism, truth recovery and the fearful past', *Irish Political Studies*, 26, no. 3 (2011): 361–382; A. Edwards, 'Fearful of the past or "remembering the future and our cause"? A response to Cheryl Lawther', *Irish Political Studies*, 27, no. 3 (2012): 457–470; C. Lawther 'Unionism, truth and the challenge of the past: a response to Aaron Edwards', *Irish Political Studies*, 27, no. 3 (2012): 471–478.

[31] K. Simpson, *Unionist Voices and the Politics of Remembering the Past in Northern Ireland* (Basingstoke: Palgrave Macmillan, 2009); *Truth Recovery in Northern Ireland: Critically Interpreting the Past* (Manchester: Manchester University Press, 2009).

[32] C. Lawther, 'Denial, silence and the politics of the past: unpicking the opposition to truth recovery in Northern Ireland', *The International Journal of Transitional Justice*, no. 7 (2013): 167.

[33] Cited in S. McBride, 'DUP: No role for Sinn Fein in writing story of Troubles', *Belfast News Letter*, 1 May 2014.

[34] *Ibid.*

Edward Stevenson, Grand Master of the Orange Order, mirrored such views when he said:

> The past simply cannot be re-written. Nor can it be twisted at will to suit the false anecdotes of the republican propaganda machine. The truth – and nothing but the truth – must always prevail for the sake of those who suffer the most.[35]

This can also be set in a slightly broader context that sees the peace process as rested on a policy of appeasement with the republican movement, which has distorted the democratic process.[36] Thus, the deep sense of loss and of anger on the part of families and friends of those killed in Northern Ireland is counterpoised against the presence of Sinn Féin in government, and a system that is seen to give former paramilitaries, other combatants and civilians, equal status and to focus on the actions of the state.

For many, this position is formulated not just on political grounds, but also through a rationale that openly refutes any moral equivalence between the actions of the paramilitaries, both loyalist and republican, and those of the security forces. This proves crucial in mobilizing not only political but also moral support. Take the following from the DUP MP, Jeffrey Donaldson:

> ... the current system is weighted heavily towards state killings, with inquests, ombudsman investigations, costly public enquiries, etc. We need a new process for dealing with the past that holds the paramilitary organisations to account and enables the innocent victims to pursue their quest for truth and justice. This new process must ensure there is no hierarchy of victims and that the rights of innocent victims are recognized and their suffering is properly acknowledged.[37]

The point is reinforced in the following from the Edward Stevenson:

> Let me state categorically there can be no moral equivalence whatsoever between the victim makers and the thousands of security personnel, civilians and their relatives whose lives they set out to destroy. Those who deliberately chose to pull the trigger or detonate the bomb, without thought for the consequence of their depraved actions, will forever be terrorists in the factual narrative of the Troubles.[38]

Across the Protestant/Unionist/Loyalist bloc, the dominant understanding of the truth is one in which 'the actions of unionist political elites or the security forces did not contribute to or perpetuate the conflict in Northern Ireland'.[39] Overall, loyalists

---

[35] Grand Orange Lodge of Ireland, 'Grand Master leads Armistice Day tributes'. Available at: http://www.grandorangelodge.co.uk/news.aspx?id=100413#.U-ic0yjmbfh; accessed 23 February 2014.

[36] *Orange Standard*, May 2001.

[37] J. Donaldson, 'Loading the dice against state killing will not solve the legacy of the past'. Available at: http://eamonnmallie.com/2014/06/loading-the-dice-against-state-killers-is-not-dealing-with-the-legacy-of-the-past-by-jeffrey-donaldson/; accessed 5 June 2014.

[38] Grand Orange Lodge of Ireland, 'Grand Master leads Armistice Day tributes, 2013'.

[39] Lawther, 'Denial, silence and the politics of the past', 49.

fear in processes for dealing with the past that sacrifice made by loyalists would be minimized 'at the expense of prioritizing "republicans" demands for truth and justice'.[40] This perspective is made apparent in the following statement:

> Republicans show no sign of washing their bloody hands and demonstrating remorse for their cowardly actions, which left 550 children from the Orange family without a father. Many of these families await and deserve justice. However, the recent 'On the Runs' controversy exposed the underhand and dirty side deals exchanged between our Government and the republican movement. A price for peace some might say; but to others a shameful betrayal to the innocent victims.[41]

Still under siege?

In September 2006, the then Secretary of State Peter Hain gave a keynote address focusing on the need for 'unionism to shed its fears'. In it he claimed that contemporary unionism (in which he incorporated loyalism) lacked the confidence to move forward because it continued to carry uncertainties raised not just by the Troubles, but by events that took root as long ago as 1641. He went on to suggest that unionists should recognize that 'the siege has been lifted', and the 'Union was as secure as it had ever been'. He concluded that unionism should be culturally proud, but overall they were failing to properly comprehend political and social changes in the Province, and that 'the constitutional issue is settled and can only ever be revisited through peaceful and democratic means'.[42]

Although Hain begins to identify the cultural terrain upon which many loyalists now see themselves politically engaged, he fails to fully recognize how the peace process, and more importantly the parallel political process, have been perceived and experienced at the community level. While for some the Agreement marked the end of the militant Republican campaign and the endorsement of Northern Ireland's constitutional position, other loyalists felt the Agreement:

> represented the distillation of the forces that had been ranged against them since the 'Troubles' began in 1969: a duplicitous British government; an avaricious Irish state; a violent Irish republicanism within Ireland; and a hostile and meddling international community beyond it. It is difficult for people who are insecure about the future to embrace the very change that they fear could destroy them, especially if it is couched in such pathological ambiguity.[43]

---

[40] Lawther, 'Denial, silence and the politics of the past', 154.
[41] Grand Orange Lodge of Ireland, 'Speech Made by the Grand Master of the Grand Orange Lodge of Ireland, Edward Stevenson, at the Dungannon Demonstration', *GOLI Press Release*, 12 July 2014.
[42] *News Letter*, 11 September 2006.
[43] Cochrane, *Unionist Politics and the Politics of Unionism since the Anglo-Irish Agreement*: 201.

This strong sense of losing past privileges[44] and disillusionment with politics is far from a short-term phenomenon.[45] As Jenkins points out, ever since the suspension of the Stormont parliament in 1972, sections of Ulster Protestants have felt that they live their political lives in a state of high political insecurity and increased psychological uncertainty.[46] Hence, the imperative of considering the notion of siege mentality must be taken more seriously than many appear to do in understanding loyalist identity. This involves part of the process of identification highlighted throughout this book and deeply held belief by members of the group that they are socially and politically isolated,[47] and ontologically insecure.

This touches on what Elliott[48] refers to as that deeply engrained part of the Protestant psyche, by which collective memories of planter and native are constantly revived, alongside the deeply held belief that the Protestant unionist in-group stand alone, or almost alone, surrounded by a unsympathetic and antagonistic social and political world. This echoes a constant refrain from loyalism, in particular, it reflects the understanding by group members that out-groups or the Other consistently organize to confront their group (either physically, culturally or emotionally).

But this sense of the notion of siege is not merely located in Hain's insecure past, it exists as a meaningful social category through which to understand contemporary political issues. The intensity of loyalist identity draws much of its form from the constant reproduction of core cultural narratives. While they are individually produced, they also exist in common understandings[49] and narratives which are at the same time both general and specific, both global and local.[50] Such constructed histories illustrate important social processes, within which priority and primacy given to certain memories 'because they seem to us to express what are central to our collective identity'.[51] The widespread cultural reproduction of loyalism confirms social processes, whereby 'we remember past events has a profound impact on what we do and how we will live'.[52]

The processes of selective remembering identified above are applicable much more widely, clearly illustrated in this example by Jill Edy, who in discussing the construction of popular memory surrounding the Watts riots and the protests at the 1968 Republican Party convention in the USA suggests:

[44] *The Times*, 24 Jan 2002, 19.
[45] B. C. Hayes, I. McAllister, and L. Dowds, 'The erosion of consent: Protestant dissillusionment with the 1998 Northern Ireland Agreement', *Journal of Elections, Public Opinion and Parties*, 15, no. 2 (2005): 147–167.
[46] R. Jenkins, *The Limits of Identity: Ethnicity, Conflict, and Politics* (Sheffield University: Sheffield Online Papers in Social Research, no date).
[47] Bar-Tal and Antebi, 'Siege mentality in Israel'.
[48] Elliott, *When God Took Sides*.
[49] Somers and Gibson, 'Reclaiming the Epistemological "Other"'.
[50] S. Phibbs, 'Four dimensions of narrativity: towards a narrative analysis of gender identity that is simultaneously personal, local and global', *New Zealand Sociology*, 23, no. 2 (2008): 47–60.
[51] Novick, *The Holocaust and Collective Memory*, 5.
[52] Rodriguez and Fortier, *Cultural Memory*, 7.

When a moment in time is controversial, every narrative possibility seems to be offered up to account for events. Such richness cannot survive for long ... the past must shrink to fit its niche ... Social relations of power will trump some stories out of existence, if such stories are ever publicly related in the first place. But more even than this, our own beliefs about the nature of reality mitigate against the survival of multiple, competing stories about the past.[53]

Many cultural meanings come ready packaged in stories and artefacts that are readily and freely available in a variety of social contexts, sometimes formal, more often less so.[54] Much of our cultural knowledge is learnt tacitly and not consciously held. Nonetheless, it is embodied and reproduced in everyday practices, rituals and behaviour. Within this, there is a heavy accent on continuity, in terms of both membership and in proliferating shared cultural values and mutual interpretations.

Another crucial way in which existing narratives and collective memories are used within loyalism is as metaphors to provide guidance, perhaps even instruction for the future. Narratives summon the past in reaction to the understood needs of the present, by 'placing the present in the context of the past and of the community'.[55] Such normative accounts provide the group with an agreed understanding of what has gone before. These include stories of victory, and less commonly defeat in past conflicts, and the clear identification of continuities from the past. This reinforces the perspective projected by Connerton[56] concerning how connections to the past are always draw upon in ways that are deemed useful in shaping the perceived needs of the present.

Throughout the book, we have seen many examples of how within loyalism, participation in social events involving ritual and commemoration play central roles in sustaining knowledge and in reproducing the core narratives of loyalism. Groups engage memories in intricate and often complex ways to selectively focus on significant events to understand and respond to social and political issues in the present. As George Gaskell reminds us, 'the main function of collective memory is to conserve the coherence of the social group and to reassure its identity in the present and in the future'.[57] As is apparent from much of the above, these narrative accounts are different from any academic history of the group, working to frame and give form to individual and collective identities rather than seeking to recall any precise happenings in the past.

Elsewhere, one example of this process is found in the Holocaust memorial in Germany, where James E. Young points out that in creating deliberate acts of

---

[53] J. A. Edy, *Troubled Pasts: News and the Collective Memory of Social Unrest* (Philadelphia, PA: Temple University Press, 2006), 123.

[54] J. Assmann and J. Czaplicka, 'Collective memory and cultural identity', *New German Critique*, 65 (1995): 125–133.

[55] Smith, *Myths and Memories of the Nation*, 62.

[56] Connerton, *How Societies Remember*.

[57] G. Gaskell, 'Attitudes, Social Representations and Beyond', in *Representations of the Social*, eds. K. Deaux and G. Philogène (Blackwell: Oxford, 2001), 232.

remembrance and commemoration '*memory must be created for the next generation*'.[58] In the context of Northern Ireland, the following speech given by Edward Stevenson at a Remembrance Day commemoration event in 2013 is worth quoting at some length, as it provides another clear example of how memory is fashioned for future generations:

> The torment and suffering of the innocent victims has been cruelly exacerbated in recent weeks and months by the sickening and increasingly strident glorification of a bloody terrorist campaign by republicans. Even the most impartial observer could only look on with horror at the galling spectacle of apologists for murder openly celebrating the abhorrent activities of IRA terrorists ... (and) the equally repugnant sight of an IRA bomber unveiling a plaque in memory of his partner in crime only days ahead of the 20th anniversary of the Shankill bomb atrocity.[59]

Both unionist and the nationalist blocs recognize the significance of the violent conflict that emerged from 1969 onwards, most often they give very different explanations to the cause and offer differing (sometimes diametrically opposed) narratives to suggest its major perpetrators and those who may be regarded as victims of the conflict. This occurs not just from within loyalist collective consciousness, but also through relationships with other broader groupings, in this case, largely in opposition to those categorized as Irish nationalists or republicans. In categorizing themselves in terms of what they have in common, and how they differ from others, loyalists form a recognizable community.

The ways in which loyalist group belonging and sense of community are maintained remain core to establishing identity and consequently the social boundaries between groups. These relationships are constantly reinforced and consolidated by memories of the past. The remembering of events through wider but competing narratives is one reason that makes dealing with the past so problematic. Hence, for example, the level of effort put into commemoration by paramilitary groupings. The selection and reinforcement of collective memories helps formulate and reinforce a distinct sense of a loyalist community and create space between 'their' memories and those of other groups.

Throughout the book, we have engaged with four major and connected approaches to community, involving space and face-to-face interactions; through imagined connections; as social boundaries that operate to include some and exclude others; and as a site for political intervention. Understanding the significance of community in this way identifies those fundamental features through which loyalist's gives particular meaning to the formation of social and cultural identity. This process of constructing

---

58 J. E. Young, 'Memory and Monument after 9/11', in *The Future of Memory*, eds. R. Crownshaw, J. Kilby, and A. Rowland (Oxford: Berghahn Books, 2010), 84, emphasis in original.
59 Grand Orange Lodge of Ireland 'Grand Master leads Armistice Day 2013 tributes'.

a shared identity occurs through the building of a dominant narrative of a collective history, the purpose of which is:

> to enable individuals to position their personal life-stories within the larger, more significant national story. Identification not knowledge is its raison d'être. It allows individuals to identify with something outside, and greater than, personal experience. It binds individuals into a broader interdependence.[60]

Crucial to the making of this interdependence are the roles of commemoration and memory. But equally important is the forgetting of those incidents that are difficult to place within, or which run counter to the dominant narrative. This has fundamental political implications for reconciliation and conflict transformation, as memory is used to justify political viewpoints and actions or legitimatize particular political identities.[61] Moreover, while the often emotionally powerful narratives of loyalism link and bond its followers through an identifiable sense of collective identity, it is not necessarily straightforward or consistent in its construction or presentation.

This is part of the broad process by which groups bring influence to bear upon members to conform.[62] Often, this process is reinforced in conflict situations when there is greater stress on heightened group solidarity and the agreement about the meaning of events. In such circumstances, any expression of social or political dissent from within the group is quashed, while the blame on others for the cause and continuance of conflict is heightened.[63] As part of this process, any questioning from within the group is perceived as disloyalty and the dominant narrative is readily accepted and reinforced.

Increasingly fractions of loyalism believe that the symbolism and iconography so central to their sense of identity is subject to what Smith[64] terms 'ethnocide', in an attempt to destroy the cultural icons that are seen to rest at the heart of the loyalist community. At a minimum, many loyalists see their culture regarded as being of little worth in wider society and perceived as a major obstruction to creating a positive post-conflict Northern Ireland society. Such views are reinforced within loyalism by the perception that the peace process, the resulting political process and the subsequent Assembly policy of a 'shared future' strongly bias Irish nationalism and republicanism. For many loyalists, this is 'reinforced through the belief that restrictions on band music, parades and bonfires are part of a republican strategy to diminish the role and significance of loyalism in the "new" Northern Ireland'.[65]

---

[60] Parekh, *Report of the Commission on the Future of Multi-Ethnic Britain*, 16–17.
[61] Darby, *The Effects of Violence on Peace Processes*.
[62] K. A. Cerulo, 'Identity construction: new issues, new directions', *Annual Review of Sociology*, 23, (1997): 385–409.
[63] R. A. LeVine and D. T. Campbell, *Ethnocentrism: Theories of Conflict, Ethnic Attitudes, and Group Behavior* (New York: Wiley, 1972), 21.
[64] A. D. Smith, *Nationalism and Modernism* (London: Routledge, 1991).
[65] Intercomm and Byrne, 'Flags and Protests', 17.

Importantly, in this context, core sections of loyalism have, in a perceived time of threat, increasingly sought to return to and reinforce those cultural traditions that are seen to rest in established narratives and collective memories. Notably, therefore, as Rodriguez and Fortier suggest, while 'personal memory is the cornerstone supporting collective or social memory, memory cannot be understood apart from social forces' and the broader affiliations to social groups: 'help construct the manner in which memory will be interpreted'.[66] Loyalist narratives frame responses concerning what may or may not be possible, and what is or is not, what is deemed as a legitimate response to particular circumstances and what is seen as incomprehensible regarding the future.

In this context, the strength of the interpretation of those memories expressed through the discourses of new loyalism now seems unable to sustain its transformative narrative or to provide satisfactory explanations of contemporary events to sections of loyalism. Misztal[67] refers to these as 'communities of memory' and uses them to define collective identity. At the heart of all contemporary loyalist narrative is the preservation and continued cohesion of the group. These narratives are grounded in collective remembering and communally interpreted experiences that often provide the basis for political mobilization and organization. It is Frank Ankersmit[68] who makes clear how certain groups, by drawing on particular understandings of history and the past, identify who they are in the present and what they think they can or cannot become in the future.

In this sense, the loyalist narrative, in part at least, provides not only an interpretative framework for the present, but projects notions of an idealized future, structuring responses and framing the possibilities for change, of those political changes that are possible and those that are not. At the moment, it is what loyalists think they cannot be which dominates their action and reaction and their vision of what is to come. The continuing strength and dominance of the traditional loyalist narrative limits change, and the cumulative force of the categorization of the Other serves to limit the possibilities for political flexibility or change. Even as many loyalists may concede that the direct struggle about the legitimacy of the state has receded, witness the lack of loyalist paramilitary reaction to dissident republicanism, others have entered a new phase of conflict over cultural symbols such as flags and parading, which intensifies everyday expressions of loyalty and commitment to Ulster as an exclusive social category.

Forever loyalist?

From within the loyalist gaze, the cause of many of the contemporary social problems rests not just in the continuing cultural and political confrontation with republicanism, but also at the feet of Westminster, the devolved administration in Northern Ireland,

---

[66] Rodriguez and Fortier, *Cultural Memory*, 7.

[67] Misztal, *Theories of Social Remembering*, 155.

[68] F. R. Ankersmit, 'The sublime dissociation of the past: or how to be(come) what one is no longer', *History and Theory*, 40, no. 3 (2001): 295–323; *Sublime Historical Experience* (Stanford, CA: Stanford University Press, 2005).

alongside the unionist political leadership. All are seen to have ushered loyalists into a marginal position, where they are seemingly prepared to leave them. What some now see as the continued distancing and lack of direction by the political leadership (including the PUP and UPRG) means that cultural conflict has become more centred in the loyalist political agenda.

These communal understandings are seen as defence against ontological insecurity, drawing directly on collective memories that have been organized and adjusted in order to fit current expectations.[69] The lines of engagement are drawn in a culture war, the boundaries of which are set by collective memories that have become fully intertwined with other experiences, such as those of economic decline and social deprivation. Central in understanding why the issue of the Union flag flying over City Hall has produced the intensity of reaction it has is an understanding of how this is indicative of the broader feelings of disenfranchisement and marginalization identified throughout this book.

Core sections of loyalism are 'struggling to find a place in the new Northern Ireland'.[70] Prominent amongst the loyalist street protests of late 2012 and early 2013, for example, was a large banner reading: 'We will not be the generation to fail Ulster'. It has been suggested that the desire for separation and deep sectarian views are commonly expressed amongst younger members of the social networks they studied in Protestant Unionist Loyalist areas.[71] Moreover, some 'younger people who have not experienced the harsh realities of the "troubles" are now romanticising about this period and may see a continuation of violence as a source of excitement'.[72]

What needs to be assessed is whether this new political grouping coalescing around cultural protests is a short-term expression of disconnection or marks some form of broader more enduring realignment in loyalist politics. An important focus must be on whether the resulting senses of identities are either fluid or frozen[73] at any given historical point. Sections of contemporary loyalism seek to construct and project identity through the filter of the need for greater ontological security. Core sections of loyalism now see themselves as politically, socially and culturally marginalized, as one prominent loyalist blogger recently put it: 'Loyalism has become a derogatory and pejorative term over the years, none more so than today, there is probably not a worse time in the history of this country to be labelled a "Loyalist" than today'.[74]

For many loyalists, there is the feeling that political stability and ultimately their sense of security can only be achieved by an immobilization (perhaps even the

[69] B. C. Hayes and I. McAllister, *Conflict to Peace: Politics and Society in Northern Ireland over Half a Century* (Manchester: Manchester University Press, 2013).

[70] Meredith, 'How loyalism became a dirty word'.

[71] Identity Exploration Limited and Trademark, *Community Identities and a Shared Future for N. Ireland, Final Report* (Dunmurry: Identity Exploration Ltd, 2011).

[72] *Ibid.*, 45.

[73] J. Todd, T. O'Keefe, N. Rougier, and L. Cañás Bottos, 'Fluid or frozen: choice and change in ethno-national identification in contemporary Northern Ireland', *Nationalism and Ethnic Politics*, 12, nos. 3–4 (2006): 323–347.

[74] Jasonburkehistory 'What does it mean to be a loyalist'.

backward turn) of existing social and political relations in Northern Ireland. Such views re-enforce, and in turn are reinforced, by the loyalist sense of community, the loyalist interpretation of collective memories, the loyalist narrative of ethno-political difference and the struggle to find ontological security. A sense of remaining faithful to a specific encircled past, commemorating the sacrifices of previous generations, and more recent victims reproduces long-standing social and political divisions through a commitment to unchanging senses of belonging.

In a situation of conflict, the community turns to what it feels it trusts and knows as the basis of ontological security, reinforcing the view of the dangerous Other as the reason for, and perpetrator of, the conflict, of which the culture war is merely the latest skirmish. There have been growing challenges to the validity of a culture war, but in one sense, any attempt to determine its authenticity remains irrelevant. When large numbers of loyalist group members accept as true that many have negative intentions towards them, their responses are structured accordingly.

Here, it is important to be clear that there exists no single loyalism; indeed, given its historical fragmentation into different organizations and groups each placing a somewhat different emphasis of the various themes identified, there never has been a homogeneous or unvarying sense of loyalism. Hence, the DUP, the PUP, blood and thunder bands, flag protestors, former combatants, the UDA and the Orange Order all in different ways draw upon collective memory to produce differing understandings of loyalism. While these diverse strands of loyalism are united by their reliance on a distinct historical narrative, this is interpreted in somewhat different ways to produce differing political positions.

There remain fundamental questions concerning how far identities are unchanging and the way collective memories understood as constant? How permanent are the ways in which working-class Protestants draw on core points of history to formulate loyalist identity? Does the strength of reliance on a particular understanding of these collective memories mean that loyalist identity is permanently circumscribed?

Central here is a recognition that the interpretations of collective memories are not continuous, and as with all such memories, these are transmitted within a particular historical, social and political context. While memories are profoundly social and may frame beliefs and orientate intensions,[75] the interpretations of these collective memories are subject to constant processes of negotiation and re-negotiation[76] and the product of political conflicts and social contestations in the present. The strength of collective memory in determining the contemporary can of course inhibit social and political change, provide a focus to repel the resolution of conflict and inhibit reconciliation between the parties. Hence, for Bartlett, the consequence is that 'it is hard to feel optimistic' and 'only possible to feel a sort of nervous confidence' when considering the future of loyalism.[77]

---

[75] B. Schwartz, *Abraham Lincoln and the Forge of National Memory* (Chicago, IL: Chicago University Press, 2000): 251.

[76] Misztal, *Theories of Social Remembering.*

[77] T. Bartlett, *Ireland: A History* (Cambridge: Cambridge University Press, 2010), 579.

However, no matter how seemingly predetermined identities are, impermanent and collective memories are conditional and not fixed. Interpretations can and do change.[78] It is an obvious truism that we cannot change the past. What can be altered, however, is how the past is remembered and interpreted, and what effect this interpretation has on contemporary events.[79] In this sense, it is not that the memory is or is not accurate that is important, rather it is what it does which is imperative.[80]

The social identity of both the individual and the group can, and do, change over time, and this may involve a re-emphasis, re-selection or reinterpretation of collective memories as was seen with the emergence of new loyalism. But collective memory is always activated by the events.[81] It would be wrong to suggest that the processes of social and political dislocation and the strength of construction of the oppositional Other somehow ended with the political settlement brought about by the Belfast Agreement.

The range of the social processes of remembering (and forgetting)[82] identified throughout this book still informs the active past, the construction of identities and how these are expressed, clearly enunciating how memory is dynamic social force. Such collective memory draws directly on narratives surrounding *major events* seen as: 'relevant to group members' lives [and] that cannot be disregarded'.[83] It is Brian Hanley who reminds us directly that both 'communities hold their conflicting "memories" dear, and rival political organizations have invested much in their own reading of the outbreak of the Troubles'.[84] The strength of the homogeneous construction of loyalist identity draws on collective memories to reinforce distinct attitudes, social values and allegiance to one's own group, while at the same time clearly identifying the Other.

It is important to highlight how throughout this book it has been demonstrated that to be meaningful, loyalist collective memory must be active, represented and communicated through contemporary social relations and perhaps most importantly passed through narratives.[85] Learned memory, as opposed to actual experienced memory, plays an important role in motivating and mobilizing loyalists. Here,

---

[78] S. Radstone and K. Hodgkin, eds. *Regimes of Memory* (London: Routledge, 2003).

[79] D. Bell, 'Introduction: Memory, Trauma and World Politics', in *Memory, Trauma and World Politics*, ed. D. Bell (Basingstoke: Palgrave Macmillian, 2006), 1–30.

[80] D. Bell, 'Agonistic democracy and the politics of memory', *Constellations: An International Journal of Critical and Democratic Theory*, 15, no. 1 (2008): 148–166.

[81] Edkins, *Trauma and the Memory of Politics*.

[82] A. Assmann, 'To Remember or to Forget: Which Way Out of a Shared History of Violence?', in *Memory and Political Change*, eds. A. Assmann and L. Shortt (Basingstoke: Palgrave Macmillan, 2012): 53–71.

[83] D. Bar-Tal and D. Labin, 'The effect of a major event on stereotyping: terrorist attacks in Israel and Israeli adolescents' perceptions of Palestinians, Jordanians and Arabs', *European Journal of Social Psychology*, 31, (2001): 268.

[84] B. Hanley, 'Tragic period that transformed NI', 13 August. Available at: http://news.bbc.co.uk/1/hi/ northern_ireland/8195962.stm; accessed 7 June 2013.

[85] Connerton, *How Societies Remember*, 38.

mobilization can be understood as involving broad process of persuasion,[86] through which individuals identify with the objectives of the group and approve its actions.[87]

In conflict, collective memory is used to increase cohesiveness within the in-group, to solidify boundaries between that group and the Other[88] and to lionize ones own group, while at the same time dehumanizing members of the Other through narratives that attribute negative intentions and hostile actions to the other group.[89] Thus, within conflict situations, much collective memory focuses 'on the other sides responsibility for the outbreak and continuation of the conflict and its misdeeds, violence and atrocities; on the other hand, they concentrate on self-justification, self-righteousness, glorification and victimization.'[90]

In times of overt conflict, collective memory and time are collapsed to respond to existing political and social connections. Collective memories provide the cultural calligraphies through which members not only view their collective past but also identify the social and political dynamics of today. They steer the group through its collective aims for the future. Social identity should never be regarded as a fixed possession, but rather as a fluid, although not necessarily rapid, social process. Within this understanding, the individual and the social are seen as inextricably related and their social world constituted through the actions of the group. This means, of course, that all existing formations of identity, no matter how firm or stable they may appear, exist as a shifting rather than an enduring set of social relationships.

There have always been various components of loyalist identity, different aspects of which have been more central or marginalized at different points in time. Take the following from the playwright Graham Reid offering the following account of part of his own family history:

> The Reids were burnt out, or forced out of Ardoyne in 1935. Apparently my Father played 'THE SASH' loudly on a wind-up gramophone, as an act of defiance as they left the area. Yet he was never an Orangeman, voted Labour all his life and cried when Joe Stalin died!... My Grandfather Reid was a foreman painter in the shipyard. He worked on the TITANIC... He signed the Covenant, was a member of the original UVF and fought on the Somme... my other Grandfather... a real

---

[86] Bar-Tal, *Intractable Conflicts*.

[87] B. Klandennans, 'The Formation and Mobilization of Consensus', in *From Structure to Action: Comparing Social Movement Research across Cultures*, eds. B. Klandennans, H. Kriesi, and S. Tarrow (Greenwich: JAI Press, 1998), 173–196.

[88] A. J. Lambert, L. N. Scherer, C. Rogers, and L. Jacoby, 'How Does Collective Memory Create a Sense of the Collective', in *Memory in Mind and Culture*, eds. P. Boyer and J. V. Wertsch (Cambridge: Cambridge University Press, 2009), 194–222.

[89] G. Elcheroth and D. Spini, 'Political Violence, Intergroup Conflict, and Ethnic Categories', in *Intergroup Conflicts and Their Resolution: A Social Psychological Perspective*, ed. D. Bar-Tal (New York: Psychology Press, 2011), 175–194.

[90] Bar-Tal, 'Collective Memory of Physical Violence', 84.

tough man ... joined the British Army before the Covenant. When I asked him if he'd signed he said 'no'. Although he agreed with it he felt that as an 'oathbound' soldier he couldn't sign it.[91]

In this short passage, Reid highlights several aspects of the broad matrix of working-class politics and society, including the influence of class, sectarianism, workplace and commitment to Britain in constructing working-class Protestant identity. The question remains to what extent this identity can be re-imagined, or perhaps more accurately to what extent there is any desire or momentum to do so within the contemporary Protestant working class.

The labour tradition highlighted by Reid above was partly absorbed by PUP, although, in turn, much of this has been marginalized within contemporary discourse following the inability of the values of new loyalism to embedded in loyalist culture. Over the past four decades, the socio-economic standing of many Protestant working-class communities has declined dramatically, direct patronage from the ruling Unionist group is a distant memory, and many within such communities now regard themselves as increasingly marginalized across the interconnected arenas of politics, culture and physical space.

Feelings of political and cultural alienation are now deeply engrained within loyalist consciousness.[92] There is now considerable evidence that many loyalist communities believe that they experience increasing levels of cultural threat.[93] Taken alongside their belief that loyalists are being made scapegoats for wrongs of the past, this has formed the basis for further disconnects between working-class loyalism and the political representatives of unionism.[94] Social identity rests on a process of self-categorization achieved in part through shared social representations, collective memory and narrative. These reinforce common origin and highlight mutual past events to illuminate present experiences and sense of identity.

The loyalist narrative highlights a perceived exclusive past, providing senses of commonality and continuity crucial to the construction of a meaningful social identity, resting in a shared present, but which itself is an extension of a common past. In the current phase, loyalists have drawn on collective memories in ways that sees them express their cultural politics and sense of identity and in a more essentialized form, part of which seeks to confirm (or re-confine) the broad parameters of Northern Ireland society within a distinct Protestant–British cultural and political ethos.

[91] G. Reid, 'Author's Note' in *Love Billy*, programme (Belfast: Lyric Theatre, 2013), 11, emphasis in original.

[92] N. Southern, 'Protestant alienation in Northern Ireland: a political, cultural and geographical examination', *Journal of Ethnic and Migration Studies*, 33, no. 1 (2007): 159–180.

[93] S. Pehrson, M. A. Gheorghiu, and T. Ireland, 'Cultural threat and anti-immigrant prejudice: the case of Protestants in Northern Ireland', *Journal of Community and Applied Social Psychology*, 22, no. 2 (2012): 111–124.

[94] A. Kane, 'No voice for Loyalist working-class', *Newsletter*, 4 July 2011

Bibliography

Adair, J. [with G. McKendry] *Mad Dog*. London: John Blake, 2007.

Adamson, I. *Cruthin: The Ancient Kindred*. Newtownards: Nosmada, 1974.

Adamson, I. *Identity of Ulster: The Land, the Language and the People*. Belfast: Pretani Press, 1982.

Adamson, I. *Ulster People: Ancient, Medieval and Modern*. Bangor: Pretani Press, 1991.

Akenson, D. H. *God's Peoples: Covenant and Land in South Africa, Israel and Ulster*. London: Cornell University Press, 1992.

Alibhai-Brown, Y. 'Muddled Leaders and the Future of the British National Identity'. *The Political Quarterly* 71, no. 1 (2000): 26–30.

An Phoblacht 'Remembering the Battle of St. Matthews', 30 July 2010.

Anderson, B. *Imagined Communities*. London: Verso, 1991.

Anderson, C. *The Billy Boy: The Life and Death of LVF Leader Billy Wright*. Edinburgh: Mainstream, 2004.

Anderson, J. 'Review of D. G. Pringle - One Island, Two Nations?: A Political-Geographical Analysis of the National Conflict in Ireland'. *Annals of the Association of American Geographers* 77, no. 3 (1987): 486–489.

Ankersmit, F. R. 'The Sublime Dissociation of the Past: Or How to Be(come) What One Is No Longer'. *History and Theory* 40, no. 3 (2001): 295–323.

Ankersmit, F. R. *Sublime Historical Experience*. Stanford, CA: Stanford University Press, 2005.

Armitage, D. 'Through the Archives', *News Letter*, 11 May 2009.

Arthur, P. *Government and Politics of Northern Ireland*. Harlow: Longman, 1987.

Assmann, A. 'From collective violence to a common future: four models for dealing with a traumatic past' (2011). Available: http://www.ysu.am/files/02A_Assmann.pdf; accessed 10 May 2013.

Assmann, A. 'To Remember or to Forget: Which Way Out of a Shared History of Violence?', in *Memory and Political Change*, edited by A. Assmann and L. Shortt. Basingstoke: Palgrave Macmillan, 2012: 53–71.

Assmann, J. and Czaplicka, J. 'Collective Memory and Cultural Identity'. *New German Critique* 65 (1995): 125–133.

Assmann, A. and Shortt, L. 'Memory and Political Change: Introduction', in *Memory and Political Change*, edited by A. Assmann and L. Shortt. Basingstoke: Palgrave Macmillan, 2012: 1–16.

Aughey, A. 'On Britishness'. *Irish Studies in International Affairs* 14 (2003): 45–56.

Aughey, A. 'Northern Ireland Narratives of British Democracy'. *Policy Studies* 33, no. 2 (2012): 145–158.

Bairner, A. 'The Cultural Politics of Remembrance: Sport, Place and Memory in Belfast and Berlin'. *International Journal of Cultural Policy* 14, no. 4 (2008): 417–430.

Ballymacarrett Research Group. *Lagan Enclave: A History of Conflict in the Short Strand, 1886-1997*. Belfast: Ballymacarrett Research Group, 1997.

Barker, C. *Making Sense of Cultural Studies: Central Problems and Critical Debates.*
    London: Sage, 2002.

Barker, C. *Cultural Studies: Theory and Practice.* London: Sage, 2003.

Barry, J. 'National Identities, historical Narratives and Patron States in Northern Ireland',
    in *Political Loyalty and the Nation-State*, edited by M. Waller and A. Linklater. London:
    Routledge, 2003: 173–198.

Bar-Tal, D. 'Collective Memory of Physical Violence: Its Contribution to the Culture of
    Violence', in *The Role of Memory in Ethnic Conflict*, edited by E. Cairns and M. D. Roe.
    Houndmills: Palgrave Macmillan, 2003: 77–93.

Bar-Tal, D. 'Sociopsychological Foundations of Intractable Conflicts'. *American
    Behavioural Scientist* 50, no. 11 (2007): 1430–1453.

Bar-Tal, D. *Intractable Conflicts: Socio-Psychological Foundations and Dynamics.*
    Cambridge: Cambridge University Press, 2013.

Bar-Tal, D. and Antebi, D. 'Siege Mentality in Israel'. *International Journal of Intercultural
    Relations* 16 (1992): 251–275.

Bar-Tal, D. and Hammack, P. L. 'Conflict, Delegitimization, and Violence', in *The Oxford
    Handbook of Intergroup Conflict*, edited by L. R. Tropp. Oxford: Oxford University
    Press, 2012: 29–52.

Bar-Tal, D. and Labin, D. 'The Effect of a Major Event on Stereotyping: Terrorist Attacks
    in Israel and Israeli Adolescents' Perceptions of Palestinians, Jordanians and Arabs'.
    European Journal of Social Psychology 31 (2001): 265–280.

Barnes, L. P. 'Religion, Education and Conflict in Northern Ireland'. *Journal of Beliefs and
    Values* 26, no. 2 (2005): 123–138.

Barnes, L. P. 'Was the Northern Ireland Conflict Religious?' *Journal of Contemporary
    Religion* 20, no. 1 (2005): 55–69.

Bartlett, T. *Ireland: A History.* Cambridge: Cambridge University Press, 2010.

Barton, K. and McCully, A. 'Teaching Controversial Issues… Where Controversial Issues
    Really Matter'. *Teaching History* 127 (2007): 13–19.

Batista, E. 'Mythical Re-Construction of the Past: War Commemoration and Formation of
    Northern Irish Britishness'. *Anthropological Notebooks* 15, no. 3 (2009): 5–25.

Bauder, H. *Immigration Dialectic: Imagining Community, Economy and Nation.* Toronto:
    University of Toronto Press, 2011.

Bauman, Z. *Culture as Praxis. Theory, Culture and Society.* London: Sage, 1999.

Bauman, Z. *Community.* London, Polity Press, 2001.

Bauman, Z. *Identity: Conversations with Benedetto Vecchi.* Cambridge: Polity Press, 2006.

Bauman, Z. *Liquid Fear,* Cambridge: Polity Press, 2006.

Baumann, M. M. 'The Trouble with the Peace Science's "Trouble Makers." ' *Peace Review*
    20 (2008): 455–461.

Baumann, M. M. 'Understanding the Other's "Understanding" of Violence'. *International
    Journal of Conflict and Violence* 3, no. 1 (2009): 107–123.

BBC News (2013) 'Jonathan Powell in appeal over loyalist communities', 21 April,
    available: http://www.bbc.co.uk/news/uk-northern-ireland-22237958; accessed
    12 June 2013.

BBC News (2013) 'Northern Ireland Orange Order leaders warn of cultural war', 12 July,
    available: http://www.bbc.co.uk/news/uk-northern-ireland-23267038; accessed
    12 November 2013.

Beach, S. W. 'Social Movement Radicalization: The Case of the People's Democracy in
    Northern Ireland'. *The Sociological Quarterly* 18, no. 3 (1977): 305–318.

Beck, U. *Risk Society: Towards A New Modernity*. London: Sage, 2000.

Becker, A. 'Memory Gaps, Maurice Halbwachs, Memory and the Great War'. *Journal of European Studies* 35 (2005): 102–113.

Beckett, J. C. *The Making of Modern Ireland, 1603–1923*. London: Faber and Faber, 2011.

Beiner, G. 'Between Trauma and Triumphalism: The Easter Rising, the Somme, and the Crux of Deep Memory in Modern Ireland'. *Journal of British Studies* 46 (2007): 366–389.

Belfast News Letter. 'Morning View: "Perfidious Albion" and the Insecurities Felt by Unionists', 22 November, 2001.

Belfast News Letter. 'UVF parade applauded for cultural significance', 30 September, 2013.

Belfast Telegraph. 'Loyalist band numbers at new high', 7 October, 2013.

Bell, C. and Newby, H. *Community Studies*, London: Unwin, 1971.

Bell, D. 'Acts of Union: Youth Sub-Culture and Ethnic Identity amongst Protestants in Northern Ireland'. *The British Journal of Sociology* 38, no. 2 (1987): 158–183.

Bell, D. *Acts of Union: Youth Culture and Sectarianism in Northern Ireland*. London: Macmillan, 1990.

Bell, D. 'Introduction: Memory, Trauma and World Politics', in *Memory, Trauma and World Politics*, edited by D. Bell. Basingstoke: Palgrave Macmillian, 2006: 1–30.

Bell, D. 'Agonistic Democracy and the Politics of Memory'. *Constellations: An International Journal of Critical and Democratic Theory* 15, no. 1 (2008): 148–166.

Bell, D. S. 'Mythscapes: Memory, Mythology, and National Identity'. *British Journal of Sociology* 54, no. 1 (2003): 63–81.

Bell, G. *The Protestants of Ulster*. London: Pluto Press, 1976.

Bell, J., Hansson, U., and McCaffery, N. 'The Troubles Aren't History Yet: Young People's Understanding of the Past'. Belfast: Community Relations Council, 2010.

Benson, J. *The Working Class in Britain, 1850–1939*. London: I. B. Tauris and Co. Ltd., 2003.

Bew, J. *The Glory of Being Britons: Civic Unionism in Nineteenth-Century Belfast*. Dublin: Irish Academic Press, 2008.

Bew, P. *Ireland: The Politics of Enmity 1789–2006*. Oxford: Oxford University Press, 2007.

Bew, P., Gibbon, P., and Patterson, H. *Northern Ireland, 1921–1996: Political Forces and Social Classes*. London: Serif, 1995.

Biggs-Davison, J. *The Hand Is Red*. London: Johnson Publications, 1973.

Billig, M. *Banal Nationalism*. London: Sage, 1995.

Blatz, C. W. and Ross, M. 'Historical Memories', in *Memory in Mind and Culture*, edited by P. Boyer and J. V. Wertsch. Cambridge: Cambridge University Press, 2009.

Bleakley, D. *Peace in Ulster*. Oxford: A. R. Mowbray, 1972.

Bloom, L. R. *Under the Sign of Hope: Feminist Methodology and Narrative Interpretation*. Albany: State University of New York, 1998.

Boal, F. W. 'Belfast: Walls Within', *Political Geography* 21 (2000): 687–694.

Borer, T. A., Darby, J., and McEvoy-Levy, S. *Peacebuilding after Peace Accords*. Notre Dame, IN: University of Notre Dame Press, 2006.

Borooah, V. 'Growth and Political Violence in Northern Ireland, 1920–1996', in *The Political Dimension of Economic Growth*, edited by S. Borner and M. Paldam. London: Macmillan, 1998.

Boulton, D. *The UVF 1966–1973: An Anatomy of Loyalist Rebellion*. Dublin: Torc Books, 1973.

Bowen, D. *History and the Shaping of Irish Protestantism*. New York and Washington, DC: Peter Lang, 1995.

Bowman, T. *Carson's Army: The Ulster Volunteer Force, 1910–1922*. Manchester: Manchester University Press, 2007.

Bowyer Bell, J. *Back to the Future: The Protestants and a United Ireland*. Dublin: Poolbeg Press, 1996.

Boyce, D. G. *The Irish Question and British Politics 1868–1986*. Basingstoke: MacMillan Education Ltd, 1988.

Boyce, D. G. 'Bigots in Bowler Hats? Unionism since the Downing Street Declaration 1993–1995', in *Political Violence in Northern Ireland: Conflict and Conflict Resolution*, edited by A. O'Day. Westport, CT: Praeger, 1997: 51–66.

Boyce, D. G. and O'Day, A. *Defenders of the Union: A Survey of British and Irish Unionism Since 1801*. London: Routledge, 2001.

Boyd, A. *Holy War in Belfast*. Tralee: Anvil Books, 1969.

Boyd, J. *Out of My Class*. Belfast: Blackstaff, 1985.

Boyd, J. *The Middle of My Journey*. Belfast: Blackstaff, 1990.

Boyer, P. and Wertsch, J. V. *Memory in Mind and Culture*. Cambridge: Cambridge University Press, 2009.

Brearton, F. 'Dancing unto Death: Perceptions of the Somme, the Titanic and Ulster Protestantism'. *The Irish Review* 20 (1997): 89–103.

Breuilly, J. *Nationalism and the State*. Manchester: Manchester University Press, 1982.

Brewer, J. 'Continuity and Change in Contemporary Ulster Protestantism'. *The Sociological Review* 52, no. 2 (2004): 265–283.

Brewer, J. 'Culture, Class and Protestantism in Urban Belfast'. Available: http://www.discoversociety.org/culture-class-and-protestantism-in-urban-belfast-2/; accessed 17 March 2014.

Brewer, J., Mitchell, D., and Leavey, G. *Ex-Combatants, Religion and Peace in Northern Ireland*. Basingstoke: Palgrave Macmillan, 2013.

Brewer, M. 'The Many Faces of Social Identity: Implications for Political Psychology'. *Political Psychology* 22, no. 1 (2001): 115–125.

British and Irish Communist Organisation. *Ireland - Two Nations*. Belfast: Athol Press, 1971.

British and Irish Communist Organisation. *On the Democratic Validity of the Northern Ireland State* – Policy Statement No. 2. Belfast: Athol Press, 1971.

British and Irish Communist Organisation. *The Home Rule Crisis*. Belfast: Athol Press, 1972.

British and Irish Communist Organisation. *The Economics of Partition*. Belfast: Athol Press, 1972.

British and Irish Communist Organisation. *The Birth of Ulster Unionism*. Belfast: Athol Press, 1984.

Brockmeier, J. 'Remembering and Forgetting: Narrative as Cultural Memory'. *Culture and Psychology* 8, no. 1 (2002): 15–43.

Brown, A., McCrone, D., and Paterson, L. *Politics and Society in Scotland*. Basingstoke: Palgrave Macmillan, 1996.

Brown, D. 'Ulster row over Powell's definition of Loyalism', *The Guardian*, 8 July, 1975.

Brown, D. 'Drumcree loyalists – but loyal to what exactly?', *The Guardian*, 5 July, 2000.

Brown, K. ' "Our Father Organization": The Cult of the Somme and the Unionist "Golden Age" in Modern Ulster Loyalist Commemoration'. *The Round Table – The Commonwealth Journal of International Affairs* 96, no. 393 (2007): 707–723.

Brown, T. 'The Whole Protestant Community: The Making of a Historical Myth', *A Field Day Pamphlet 7*, 1985.

Browne, B. 'Commemoration in conflict'. *Journal of Comparative Research in Anthropology and Sociology* 4, no. 2 (2013): 143–163.

Bruce, S. *The Red Hand: Protestant Paramilitaries in Northern Ireland*. Oxford: Oxford University Press, 1992.

Bruce, S. *The Edge of the Union: The Ulster Loyalist Political Vision*. Oxford: Oxford University Press, 1994.

Bruce, S. 'Fundamentalism and Political Violence: The Case of Paisley and Ulster Evangelicals'. *Religion* 31 (2001): 387–405.

Bruce, S. *Paisley: Religion and Politics in Northern Ireland*. Oxford: Oxford University Press, 2007.

Bruner, J. *Acts of Meaning*. Cambridge, MA: Harvard University Press, 1990.

Bryan, D. *Orange Parades: The Politics of Ritual. Tradition and Control*. London: Pluto, 2000.

Bryan, D., Fraser, T. G., and Dunn, S. *Political Rituals: Loyalist Parades in Portadown*. Coleraine: University of Ulster, 1995.

Bryan, D. and Stevenson, C. 'Flagging Peace: Struggles over Symbolic Landscape in the New Northern Ireland', in *Culture and Belonging in Divided Societies*, edited by M. H. Ross. Philadelphia: University of Philadelphia Press, 2009: 68–84.

Buchanan, R. H. 'The Planter and the Gael: Cultural Dimensions of the Northern Ireland Problem', in *Integration and Division – Geographical Perspectives on the Northern Ireland Problem*, edited by F. W. Boal and J. H. Douglas. London: Academic Press, 1982: 49–74.

Buckland, P. *Irish Unionism, 1885–1922*. London: Historical Association, 1973.

Buckland, P. *The Factory of Grievances: Devolved Government in Northern Ireland 1921–1939*. Dublin: Gill and Macmillan, 1979.

Buckland, P. *A History of Northern Ireland*. Dublin: Gill and Macmillan Ltd, 1989.

Burke, D. *A Sense Of Wonder: Van Morrison's Ireland*. London: Jawbone Press, 2013.

Burke, T. 'The 16th (Irish) and 36th (Ulster) Divisions at the Battle of Wijtschate-Messines Ridge, 7 June 1917: A Battlefield Tour Guide', Heuvelland, 2007.

Burke, T. 'Brotherhood among Irishmen? The Battle of Wijtschate-Messines Ridge, June 1917', *History Ireland*. Available: http://www.historyireland.com/20th-century-contemporary-history/brotherhood-among-irishmen-the-battle-of-wijtschate-messines-ridge-june-1917/; accessed 10 February 2014.

Burton, F. *The Politics of Legitimacy: Struggles in a Belfast Community*. London: Routledge and Kegan Paul, 1978.

Busteed, M., Neal, F., and Tonge, J. (eds.) *Irish Protestant Identities*. Manchester: Manchester University Press, 2008.

Byrne, E. 'The forgotten Irish soldiers who fought for Britain in the first world war'. Available: http://www.theguardian.com/world/2014/apr/05/irish-soldiers-who-fought-for-britain; accessed 16 April 2014.

Cadwallader, A. *Lethal Allies: British Collusion in Ireland*. Cork: Mercier Press, 2013.

CAIN [Conflict Archive on the Internet]. 'A background note on the protests and violence related to the Union Flag at Belfast City Hall, December 2012–January 2013'. Available: http://cain.ulst.ac.uk/issues/identity/flag-2012.htm; accessed 10 February 2014.

Bibliography

CAIN [Conflict Archive on the Internet]. 'A Chronology of the Conflict – 1970'. Available: http://cain.ulst.ac.uk/othelem/chron/ch70.htm#Jun; accessed 10 February 2014.

Cairns, D. 'The Object of Sectarianism: The Material Reality of Sectarianism in Ulster Loyalism', *Journal of the Royal Anthropological Institute* 6, no. 3 (2000): 437–452.

Cairns, D. and Richards, S. ' "Pissing in the Gale of History": Contemporary Protestant Culture and the "Ancient Curse." ' *Ideas and Production: A Journal in the History of Ideas* 8 (1988): 19–36.

Cairns, E. *Caught in Crossfire: Children and the Northern Ireland Conflict.* Belfast: Appletree Press, 1987.

Cairns, E. *Children and Political Violence.* Oxford: Blackwell, 1996.

Cairns, E., Lewis, A., Mumcu, O., and Waddell, N. 'Memories of Recent Ethnic Conflict and Their Relationship to Social Identity'. *Peace and Conflict: Journal of Peace Psychology* 4, no. 1 (1998): 13–22.

Cairns, E. and Roe, M. D. *The Role of Memory in Ethnic Conflict.* Houndmills: Palgrave Macmillan, 2002.

Cairns, E., Van Til, T., and Williamson, A. *Social Capital, Collectivism – Individualism and Community Background in Northern Ireland.* Report to the Office of the First Minister and Deputy First Minister, Coleraine: University of Ulster, 2003.

Cameron, D. and Jones, D. *Cameron on Cameron: Conversations with Dylan Jones.* London: Fourth Estate, 2008.

Campbell, J. 'Northern Ireland's poorest "still struggle after downturn" '. Available: http://www.bbc.co.uk/news/uk-northern-ireland-26721962; accessed 25 March 2014.

Canny, N. P. *Making Ireland British 1580–1650.* Oxford: Oxford University Press, 2001.

Cantle, T. *Community Cohesion: A Report of the Independent Review Team.* London: Home Office, 2001.

Cash, J. D. *Identity, Ideology and Conflict: The Structuration of Politics in Northern Ireland.* Cambridge: Cambridge University Press, 1996.

Cash, J. D. 'The dilemmas of political transformation in Northern Ireland', *Pacifica Review: Peace, Security and Global Change* 10, no. 3 (1998): 227–234.

Cassidy, K. J. 'Organic Intellectuals and the New Loyalism: Re-Inventing Protestant Working-Class Politics in Northern Ireland'. *Irish Political Studies* 23, no. 3 (2008): 411–430.

Cerulo, K. A. 'Identity Construction: New Issues, New Directions'. *Annual Review of Sociology* 23 (1997): 385–409.

Chaskin, R. 'Building Community Capacity: A Definitional Framework and Case Studies from a Comprehensive Community Initiative'. *Urban Affairs Review* 36, no. 3 (2001): 291–323.

Chrisafis, A. 'The death of Doris Day'. *The Guardian*, 12 October, 2005.

Clarke, J., Hall, S., Jefferson, T., and Roberts, B. 'Subcultures, Cultures and Class: A Theoretical Overview', in *Resistance through Rituals: Youth Subcultures in Post-War Britain*, edited by S. Hall and T. Jefferson. London: Hutchinson, 1976: 9–79.

Clarke, L. 'It takes two sides to tear apart a myth'. *Sunday Times*, 13 June, 2010.

Clarke, L. 'Middle class Protestants are least likely to vote: poll'. *Belfast Telegraph*, 7 March, 2012.

Clayton, P. *Enemies and Passing Friends.* London: Pluto, 1996.

Clayton, P. 'Religion, Ethnicity and Colonialism as Explanations of the Northern Ireland Conflict', in *Rethinking Northern Ireland: Culture, Ideology and Colonialism*, edited by D. Miller. London: Longman, 1998: 40–54.

Coakley, J. 'National Identity in Northern Ireland: Stability or Change?' *Nations and Nationalism* 13, no. 4 (2002): 573–597.

Cobb, S. 'Fostering Coexistence in Identity-Based Conflicts: Towards a Narrative Approach', in *Imagine Coexistence: Restoring Humanity after Violent Ethnic Conflict*, edited by A. Chayes and M. Minow. San Francisco, CA: Jossey-Bass, 2003.

Cochrane, F. *Unionist Politics and the Politics of Unionism since the Anglo-Irish Agreement*. Cork: Cork University Press, 1997.

Cohen, A. P. *The Symbolic Construction of the Community*. London: Routledge, 1985.

Coiste Chuimhneacháin Chath Naomh Máitiú. '40th Anniversary Commemorative Events'. Belfast: Battle of St. Matthews Commemorative Committee, 2010.

Combat 'Simply to remain British', November, 1990.

Commission for Racial Equality. *The Decline of Britishness: A Research Study*. London: CRE, 2005.

Community Convention and Development Company. *Protestant, Unionist, Loyalist Communities; Leading a Positive Transformation - Conference Report*. Belfast: CCDC, 2006.

Community Relations Council. *Community Development in Protestant Areas*. Belfast: Community Relations Information Centre, 1992.

Connell, J. and Gibson, C. *Sound Tracks: Popular Music Identity and Place*. London: Routledge, 2002.

Connerton, P. *How Societies Remember*. Cambridge: Cambridge University Press, 1989.

Coogan, T. P. *The Troubles: Ireland's Ordeal 1966–1996 and the Search for Peace*. Boulder, CO: Roberts Rinehart Publishers, 1997.

Cooper, B. *The 10th (Irish) Division in Gallipoli*. Dublin: Irish Academic Press, 2003 [1918].

Cooper, D. 'On the Twelfth of July in The Morning… or the Man Who Mistook His Sash for a Hat'. *Folk Music Journal* 8 (2001): 67–89.

Copeland, M. 'Primary Schools: East Belfast – Adjournment Debate'. *Northern Ireland Assembly*, 26 June 2012.

Corthorn, P. 'Enoch Powell, Ulster Unionism, and the British Nation'. *The Journal of British Studies* 51, no. 4 (2012): 967–997.

Coser, L. A. (ed.) *Maurice Halbwachs on Collective Memory*. Chicago: University of Chicago Press, 1992.

Coulter, C. The Character of Unionism, *Irish Political Studies* 9, no. 1 (1994): 1–24.

Coulter, C. *Contemporary Northern Irish Society: An Introduction*. London: Pluto 1999.

Craig, W. 'The Future of Northern Ireland', speech made at Ulster Vanguard's First Anniversary. Belfast: Vanguard, 1972.

Crawford, C. *Defenders or Criminals? Loyalist Prisoners and Criminalisation*. Belfast: Blackstaff, 1999.

Crawford, C. *Inside the UDA: Volunteers and Violence*. London: Pluto Press, 2003.

Crawford, R. G. *Loyal to King Billy: A Portrait of the Ulster Protestants*. Dublin: Gill and MacMillan, 1987.

Crownshaw, R., Kilby, J., and Rowland, A. (eds.) *The Future of Memory*. Oxford: Berghahn Books, 2010.

Crozier, M. (ed.) *Cultural Traditions in Northern Ireland: Varieties of Britishness*. Belfast: QUB, Institute of Irish Studies, 1990.

Cunningham, N. 'The Social Geography of Violence during the Belfast Troubles, 1920–1922', CRESC Working Paper No. 122, Manchester: University of Manchester, 2013.

Cunningham, N. 'The Doctrine of Vicarious Punishment: Space, Religion and the Belfast Troubles of 1920–1922'. *Journal of Historical Geography* 40 (2013): 52–66.

Cunningham, N. and Gregory, I. 'Hard to Miss, Easy to Blame? Peacelines, Interfaces and Political Deaths in Belfast during the Troubles'. *Political Geography* 40 (2014): 64–78.

Cusack, J. and McDonald, H. *UVF*. Dublin: Poolbeg, 1997.

D'ancona, M. (ed.) *Being British: The Search for the Values That Bind the Nation*. Edinburgh: Mainstream Publishing, 2009.

Da Fazio, G. 'Civil Rights Mobilization and Repression in Northern Ireland: A Comparison with the U.S. Deep South'. *Sixties: A Journal of History, Politics and Culture* 2, no. 2 (2009): 163–185.

Darby, J. *Intimidation in Housing, A Research Paper*. Belfast: The Northern Ireland Community Relations Commission, 1974.

Darby, J. *Intimidation and the Control of Conflict in Northern Ireland*. Dublin: Gill and Macmillan, 1986.

Darby, J. *Scorpions in a Bottle: Conflicting Cultures in Northern Ireland*. London: Minority Rights Publications, 1997.

Darby, J. *The Effects of Violence on Peace Processes*. Washington, DC: US Institute of Peace Press, 2001.

Darby, J. and MacGinty, R. *The Management of the Peace Process*. Basingstoke: Macmillan, 2000.

Darnton, J. 'Protestant and paranoid in Northern Ireland', *New York Times Magazine* 15 January 1995.

David, O. and Bar-Tal, D. 'A Socio-Psychological Conception of Collective Identity: The Case of National Identity'. *Personality and Social Psychology Review* 13 (2009): 354–379.

Davies, B. and Harre, R. 'Positioning: The Discursive of Selves'. *Journal for the Theory of Social Behaviour* 20, no. 1 (1990): 43–63.

Dawe, G. *The Rest is History*. Newry: Abbey Press, 1998.

Dawson, G. *Making Peace with the Past?: Memory, Trauma and the Irish Troubles*. Manchester: Manchester University Press, 2007.

Day, G. *Community and Everyday Life*. New York: Routledge, 2006.

De Cillia, R., Reisigl, M., and Wodak, R. 'The Discursive Construction of National Identities'. *Discourse and Society* 10, no. 2 (1999): 149–173.

De Paor, L. *Divided Ulster*. Hammondsworth: Penguin, 1970.

De Rosa, P. *Rebels: The Irish Rising of 1916*. New York: Fawcett Columbine, 1990.

Delanty, G. *Community*. London: Routledge, 2003.

Dempster, S. 'Peter Hain - unionism needs to shed its fears'. *Belfast News Letter*, 11 September, 2006.

Denman, T. *Ireland's Unknown Soldiers: The 16th (Irish) Division in the Great War*. Dublin: Irish Academic Press, 1992.

Devine-Wright, P. 'History and Identity in Northern Ireland – An Exploratory Investigation of the Role of Historical Commemorations in Contexts of Conflict'. *Peace and Conflict: Journal of Peace Psychology* 7, no. 4 (2001): 297–315.

Devine-Wright, P. 'Identity, Memory and the Social Status of Groups in Northern Ireland: Relating Processes of Social Remembering with Beliefs about the Structure of Society'. *Irish Journal of Psychology* 22, no. 2 (2001): 1–21.

Devine-Wright, P. 'A Theoretical Overview of Memory and Conflict', in *The Role of Memory in Ethnic Conflict*, edited by E. Cairns and M. Roe. Houndmills: Palgrave Macmillan, 2003: 9–33.

Devine-Wright, P. and Lyons, E. 'Remembering Pasts and Representing Places: The Construction of national Identities in Ireland'. *Journal of Environmental Psychology* 17 (1997): 33–45.

Devlin, P. *Yes We Have No Bananas: Outdoor Relief in Belfast 1920–1939*. Belfast: Blackstaff, 1981.

Dillon, M. *God and the Gun: The Church and Irish Terrorism*. London: Orion, 1997.

Dillon, M. *The Trigger Men*. Edinburgh: Mainstream, 2003.

Dixon, P. and O'Kane, E. *Northern Ireland since 1969*. Harlow: Pearson Education, 2011.

Doherty P. and Poole, M. A. 'Ethnic Residential Segregation in Belfast, 1971–1991', *Geographical Review* 87, no. 4 (1997): 520–536.

Donaldson, J. 'Loading the dice against state killing will not solve the legacy of the past'. Available: http://eamonnmallie.com/2014/06/loading-the-dice-against-state-killers-is-not-dealing-with-the-legacy-of-the-past-by-jeffrey-donaldson/; accessed 5 June 2014.

Dowling, M. W. 'Confusing Culture and Politics: Ulster Scots Culture and Music'. *New Hibernia Review* 11, no. 3 (2007): 51–80.

Doyle, M. *Fighting Like the Devil for the Sake of God: Protestants, Catholics and the Origins of Violence in Victorian Belfast*. Manchester: Manchester University Press, 2009.

Dungan, M. *They Shall Not Grow Old: Irish Soldiers in the Great War*. Dublin: Four Courts Press, 1997.

Dunn, S. and Morgan, V. *Protestant Alienation in Northern Ireland: A Preliminary Survey*. Coleraine: Centre for the Study of Conflict, University of Ulster, 1994.

East Belfast Historical and Cultural Society. *Murder In Ballymacarrett - The Untold Story*, Belfast: EBHCS, 2006.

East Belfast Partnership and the Department for Social Development. *East Belfast: Strategic Regeneration Framework*. Belfast: Paul Hogarth Company, 2008.

Edensor, T. *National Identity, Popular Culture and Everyday Life*. Oxford: Berg, 2002.

Edkins, J. *Trauma and the Memory of Politics*. Cambridge: Cambridge University Press, 2003.

Edwards, A. 'The Northern Ireland Labour Party and Protestant Working Class Identity' in *Irish Protestant Identities*, 347–359.

Edwards, A. *A History of the Northern Ireland Labour Party: Democratic Socialism and Sectarianism*. Manchester: Manchester University Press, 2009.

Edwards, A. 'Fearful of the Past or "Remembering the Future and Our Cause"? A Response to Cheryl Lawther'. *Irish Political Studies* 27, no. 3 (2012): 457–470.

Edwards, A. and Bloomer, S. (eds.) *Transforming the Peace Process in Northern Ireland: From Terrorism to Democratic Politics*. Dublin: Irish Academic Press, 2008.

Edy, J. A. *Troubled Pasts: News and the Collective Memory of Social Unrest*. Philadelphia, PA: Temple University Press, 2006.

Elcheroth, G. and Spini, D. 'Political Violence, Intergroup Conflict, and Ethnic Categories', in *Intergroup Conflicts and Their Resolution: A Social Psychological Perspective*, edited by D. Bar-Tal. New York: Psychology Press, 2011: 175–194.

Elliott, M. *When God Took Sides, Religion and Identity in Ireland - Unfinished History*. Oxford: Oxford University Press, 2009.

English, R. 'Coming to Terms with the Past: Northern Ireland: Richard English Argues That Historians Have a Practical and Constructive Role to Play in Today's Ulster'. *History Today* 54, no. 7 (July 2004): 24–26.

English, R. *Irish Freedom: The History of Nationalism in Ireland.* London: MacMillan, 2006.

English, R. and Walker, G. *Unionism in Modern Ireland.* Dublin: Gill and Macmillan, 1996.

Epstein, J. 'Remember to Forget: The Problem of Traumatic Cultural Memory', in *Shaping Losses: Cultural Memory and the Holocaust,* edited by J. Epstein and L. H. Lefkovitz. Chicago: University of Illinois Press, 2001: 186–204.

Ervine, D. 'Redefining Loyalism: A Political Perspective', in *Redefining Loyalism,* IBIS Working Paper No. 4. University College Dublin: Institute of British Irish Studies, 2001.

Eyerman, R. 'Music in Movement: Cultural Politics and Old and New Social Movements'. *Qualitative Sociology* 25, no. 3 (2002): 443–458.

Eyerman, R. 'The Past in the Present: Culture and the Transmission of Identity', in *The Collective Memories Reader,* edited by J. K. Olick, V. Vinitzky-Seroussi, and D. Levy. Oxford: Oxford University Press, 2011.

Eyerman R. and Jamison, A. E. *Social Movements: A Cognitive Approach.* University Park: Pennsylvania State University Press, 1991.

Falconer, A. and Liechty, J. *Reconciling Memories.* Dublin: Columba Press, 1998.

Falls, C. *The History of the 36th (Ulster) Division.* Aldershot Gale and Polden, (1922, reproduced 1996).

Farrell, M. *Northern Ireland: The Orange State.* London: Pluto, 1976.

Farrell, M. *Arming the Protestants: The Formation of the Ulster Special Constabulary and the Royal Ulster Constabulary, 1920–1927.* London: Pluto Press, 1983.

Farrell, S. *Rituals and Riots: Sectarian Violence and Political Culture in Ulster, 1784–1886.* Lexington: University Press of Kentucky, 2000.

Farren, S. and Mulvihill, R. F. *Paths to a Settlement.* London: Colin Smythe, 2000.

Farrington, C. *Ulster Unionism and the Peace Process in Northern Ireland.* Basingstoke: Palgrave Macmillan, 2006.

Farrington, C. 'Loyalists and Unionists: Explaining the Internal Dynamics of an Ethnic Group', in *Transforming the Peace Process in Northern Ireland: From Terrorism to Democratic Politics,* edited by A. Edwards and S. Bloomer. Dublin: Irish Academic Press, 2008: 28–43.

Farrington, C. and Walker, G. 'Ideological Content and Institutional Frameworks: Unionist Identities in Northern Ireland and Scotland'. *Irish Studies Review* 17, no. 2 (2009): 135–152.

Feeney, E. V. 'From Reform to Resistance: A History of the Civil Rights Movement in Northern Ireland', Unpublished PhD thesis, University of Washington, Seattle, Washington, 1974.

Ferguson, N. and Cairns, E. 'Political Violence and Moral Maturity in Northern Ireland'. *Political Psychology* 17, no. 4 (1996): 713–725.

Finlay, A. 'Defeatism and Northern Protestant "Identity"'. *Global Review of Ethnopolitics* 1, no. 2 (2001): 3–20.

Finlayson, A. 'Loyalist Political Identity after the Peace'. *Capital and Class* 23 (1999): 47–75.

Fisk, R. *The Point of No Return: The Strike Which Broke the British in Ulster.* London: Andre Deutsch, 1975.

Fitzduff, M. and Gormley, C. 'Northern Ireland: Changing Perceptions of the "other"'. *Development* 43, no. 3 (2000): 62–65.

Follis, B. A. *A State under Seige: The Establishment of Northern Ireland, 1920–1925.* Oxford: Oxford University Press, 1995.

Foster, J. W. *Colonial Consequences: Essays in Irish Literature and Culture.* Dublin: Lilliput Press, 1991.

Foster, J. W. 'Strains in Irish Intellectual Life', in *On Intellectuals and Intellectual Life in Ireland, International, Comparative and Historical Contexts*, edited by L. O'Dowd. Dublin: The Royal Irish Academy, 1996: 42–60.

Fraser, M. *Children in Conflict.* London: Seeker and Warburg, 1974.

Friel, L. 'Loyalist fascism exposes Brits', *An Phoblacht/Republican News*, 5 October, 1999.

Fulton, J. *The Tragedy of Belief: Division, Politics and Religion in Ireland.* Oxford: Clarendon Press, 1991.

Gallagher, M. 'Do Ulster Unionists Have a Right to Self-Determination'. *Irish Political Studies* 5 (1990): 11–30.

Gallagher, M. 'How Many Nations Are There in Ireland?' *Ethnic and Racial Studies* 18, no. 4 (1995): 715–739.

Ganiel, G. *Evangelicalism and Conflict in Northern Ireland.* Basingstoke: Palgrave MacMillan, 2008.

Ganiel, G. and Dixon, P. 'Religion, Pragmatic Fundamentalism and the Transformation of the Northern Ireland Conflict'. *Journal of Peace Research* 45, no. 3 (2008): 419–436.

Garbutt, N. 'Loyalist working class is a lost tribe'. *Newsletter*, 19 May 2011.

Gardner, L. *Resurgence of the Majority.* Belfast: Ulster Vanguard Publications, 1971.

Garland, R. *Gusty Spence.* Belfast: Blackstaff Press, 2001.

Gaskell, G. 'Attitudes, Social Representations and Beyond', in *Representations of the Social*, edited by K. Deaux and G. Philogène. Blackwell: Oxford (2001): 228–241.

Gedi, N. and Elam, Y. 'Collective Memory – What Is It?' *History and Memory* 8, no. 1 (1996): 30–50.

Geisler, M. *National Symbols, Fractured Identities: Contesting the National Narrative.* New York: Middlebury Press, 2005.

Giddens, A. *Consequences of Modernity.* Oxford: Blackwell, 1990.

Giddens, A. *Modernity and Self-Identity.* Oxford: Blackwell, 1991.

Gillis, J. R. (ed.) *Commemorations: The Politics of National Identity.* Princeton, NJ: Princeton University Press, 1994.

Gillis, J. R., 'Memory and Identity: The History of a Relationship', in *Commemorations: The Politics of National Identity*, edited by J. R. Gillis. Princeton, NJ: Princeton University Press, 1994: 3–26.

Goldthorpe J. H. and Lockwood D. 'Affluence and the British Class Structure', *Sociological Review* 11, no. 2 (1968): 133–163.

Goldthorpe, J. H., Lockwood, D., Bechhofer, F., and Platt, J. *The Affluent Worker: Political Attitudes and Behaviour.* Cambridge: Cambridge University Press, 1968.

Gordon, G. 'Captain Terence O'Neill: Visionary or failure?', BBC News Northern Ireland, Available: http://www.bbc.co.uk/news/uk-northern-ireland-21875466; accessed 7 June.

Graff-McRae, R. L. 'Popular Memory in Northern Ireland' in *War Memory and Popular Culture*, 41–56.

Graham, B. 'No Place of the Mind: Contested Protestant Representations of Ulster'. *Ecumene* 1, no. 3 (1994): 257–281.

Graham, B. (ed.) *In Search of Ireland: A Cultural Geography.* London: Routledge, 1997.

Graham, B. 'The Past in the Present: The Shaping of Identity in Loyalist Ulster'. *Terrorism and Political Violence* 16, no. 3 (2004): 483–500.

Graham, B. and Shirlow, P. 'The Battle of the Somme in Ulster Memory and Identity'. *Political Geography* 21, no. 7 (2002): 881–904.

Graham, B. and Whelan, Y. 'The Legacies of the Dead: Commemorating the Troubles in Northern Ireland'. *Environment and Planning, Society and Space* 25, no. 3 (2007): 476–495.

Grand Orange Lodge of Ireland. 'Grand Master leads Armistice Day tributes, 2013'. Available: http://www.grandorangelodge.co.uk/news.aspx?id=100413#.U-ic0yjmbfh; accessed 23 February 2014.

Grand Orange Lodge of Ireland. 'Speech Made by the Grand Master of the Grand Orange Lodge of Ireland, Edward Stevenson, at the Dungannon Demonstration, *GOLI Press Release*, 12 July, 2014.

Grayson, R. *Belfast Boys: How Unionists and Nationalists Fought and Died Together in the First World War*. London: Continuum, 2010.

Greenslade, R. 'Belfast's rioting loyalists feel abandoned by their politicians'. Available: http://www.theguardian.com/commentisfree/2013/jan/07/belfast-rioting-loyalists-politicians-union-flag; accessed 28 March 2014.

Gudgin, G. 'The Demonisation of the Protest Community; presentation to the Ulster Society on Thursday 26 September 1996'. Lurgan, Ulster Society, 1997.

The Guardian 'Census 2011: Northern Ireland', suggested twenty-nine percent held a Northern Irish identity, available: http://www.theguardian.com/news/datablog/2012/dec/11/2011-census-northern-ireland-religion-identity; accessed 18 September 2013.

The Guardian 'William Craig obituary: Stormont minister and founder of the Ulster Vanguard movement', 26 April 2011.

Gusfield, J. R. *The Community: A Critical Response*. New York: Harper Colophon, 1975.

Hackett C. and Rolston, B. 'The Burden of Memory: Victims, Storytelling and Resistance in Northern Ireland'. *Memory Studies* 2, no. 3 (2009): 355–376.

Hain, P. 'Unionism needs to shed its fears'. *News Letter*, 11 September, 2006.

Halbwachs, M. *The Collective Memory*, translated. F. J. Ditter, Jr. and V. Y. Ditter. New York: Harper Colophone Books, 1980.

Halbwachs, M. *On Collective Memory*, translated Lewis A Coser. Chicago: University of Chicago Press, 1992.

Hall, M. *Loyalism in Transition 1: Learning from Others in Conflict*. Belfast: Island Pamphlets, 2006.

Hall, M. *Loyalism in Transition 2: Learning from Others in Conflict*. Belfast: Island Pamphlets, 2007.

Hall, S. 'Cultural Identity and Diaspora', in *Identity: Community, Culture, Difference*, edited by J. Rutherford. London: Lawrence and Wishart, 1990: 222–237.

Hammack, P. L. 'Narrative and the Politics of Meaning'. *Narrative Inquiry* 21, no. 2 (2011): 311–318.

Hanley, B. 'Tragic period that transformed NI', 13 August, available: http://news.bbc.co.uk/1/hi/northern_ireland/8195962.stm; accessed 7 June 2013.

Harbinson, R. *No Surrender: An Ulster Childhood*. Belfast: Blackstaff Press, 1987 [1960].

Harris, L. 'Duck or Rabbit? The Value Systems of Loyalist Paramilitaries', in *Irish Protestant Identities*, 305–318.

Harris, L. '*Quis Separabit?* Loyalist Transformation and the Strategic Environment', in *Ulster Loyalism after the Good Friday Agreement*, edited by J. W. McAuley and G. Spencer. Basingstoke: Palgrave Macmillan, 2011: 87–104.

Hayes, B. C. and McAllister, I. 'Sowing Dragon's Teeth: Public Support for Political Violence and Paramilitarism in Northern Ireland'. *Political Studies* 40 (2001): 910–922.

Hayes B. C. and McAllister, I. *Conflict to Peace: Politics and Society in Northern Ireland over Half a Century*. Manchester: Manchester University Press, 2013.

Hayes, B. C., McAllister, I., and Dowds, L. 'The Erosion of Consent: Protestant Dissillusionment with the 1998 Northern Ireland Agreement'. *Journal of Elections, Public Opinion and Parties* 15, no. 2 (2005): 147–167.

HCNI Parliamentary Papers. 'Debate on the Cameron Report'. Volume 74, Columns 126–134, 1 October 1969.

Healing Through Remembering. *Making Peace with the Past: Options for Truth Recovery Regarding the Conflict in and about Northern Ireland* [written by Prof. Kerian McEvoy]. Belfast: Healing Through Remembering, 2006.

Heath, A., Rothon, C., and Andersen, R. 'Who Feels British', Working Paper No. 5. University of Oxford: Department of Sociology, 2005.

Hechter, M. *Internal Colonialism: The Celtic Fringe in British National Development*. New Brunswick: Transaction Publishers, 1999.

Heffer, S. *Like the Roman: The Life of Enoch Powell*. London: Weidenfeld and Nicolson, 1998.

Hennessey, T. *A History of Northern Ireland 1920–1996*. Dublin: Gill and Macmillan, 1997.

Hennessey, T. *Dividing Ireland, World War I and Partition, Ireland in 1914*. London: Routledge Press, 1998.

Hennessey, T. 'The Evolution of Ulster Protestant Identity in the Twentieth Century: Nations and Patriotism' in *Irish Protestant Identities*, 257–270.

Hepburn, A. C. 'The Belfast Riots of 1935'. *Social History* 15, no. 1 (1990): 75–96.

Heslinga, M. W. *The Irish Border as a Cultural Divide: A Contribution to the Study of Regionalism in the British Isles*. Assen: Van Gorcum, 1962, 1979, 2e.

Hewitt, C. 'Catholic Grievances, Catholic Nationalism and Violence in Northern Ireland during the Civil Rights Period: A Reconsideration'. *British Journal of Sociology* 32, no. 3 (1981): 362–380.

Hewitt, C. 'Discrimination in Northern Ireland: A Rejoinder'. *British Journal of Sociology* 34, no. 3 (1983): 446–451.

Hewitt, C. 'Catholic Grievances and Violence in Northern Ireland'. *British Journal of Sociology* 36, no. 1 (1985): 102–105.

Hewitt, C. 'Explaining Violence in Northern Ireland'. *British Journal of Sociology* 38, no. 1 (1987): 88–93.

Higgins, G. I. and Brewer, J. *Anti-Catholicism in Northern Ireland, 1600–1998: The Mote and the Beam*. Houndmills: Macmillan, 1998.

Hirsch, H. *Genocide and the Politics of Memory: Studying Death to Preserve Life*. Chapel Hill: University of North Carolina Press, 1995.

Hirst, C. *Religion, Politics, and Violence in Nineteenth-Century Belfast: The Pound and Sandy Row*. Dublin: Four Courts Press, 2002.

Hirst, W. and Manier, D. 'Towards a Psychology of Collective Memory'. *Memory* 16, no. 3 (2008): 183–200.

Hobsbawm, E. 'Introduction', in E. Hobsbawm and T. Ranger (eds.) *The Invention of Tradition*. Cambridge: CUP, 1984: 1–14.

Hobsbawn, E. and Ranger, T. (eds.) *The Invention of Tradition*. Cambridge: CUP, 1984.

Hopkins, S. 'History with a Divided and Complicated Heart? The Uses of Political Memoir, Biography and Autobiography in Contemporary Northern Ireland'. *The Global Review of Ethnopolitics* 1, no. 2 (2001): 74–81.

Hopkins, S. 'A Weapon in the Struggle? Loyalist Paramilitarism and the Politics of Auto/Biography in Contemporary Northern Ireland', in *Irish Protestant Identities*, 319–333.

Hopkins, S. *The Politics of Memoir in Northern Ireland*. Liverpool: Liverpool University Press, 2013.

Horgan, G. 'The State of Loyalism'. *Irish Marxist Review* 2, no. 5 (2013): 46–52.

Howard, J. A. 'Social Psychology of Identities'. *Annual Review of Sociology* 26 (2000): 367–393.

Howarth, C. 'Towards a Social Psychology of Community: A Social Representations Perspective'. *Journal for the Theory of Social Behaviour* 31, no. 2 (2001): 223–238.

Howe, S. (2005a) 'Mad Dogs and Ulstermen: The Crisis of Loyalism (part one)'. Available: http://www.opendemocracy.net/debates/article.jsp?id=6anddebateId=33andarticleId=2876; accessed 1 March 2012.

Howe, S. (2005b) 'Mad Dogs and Ulstermen: The Crisis of Loyalism (part two)'. Available: http://www.opendemocracy.net/democracy-protest/loyalism_2885.jsp; accessed 1 March 2012.

Hunt, N. and McHale, S. 'Memory and Meaning: Individual and Social Aspects of Memory Narratives'. *Journal of Loss and Trauma: International Perspectives on Stress and Coping* 13, no. 1 (2008): 42–58.

Hunter, J. A., Stringer, M., and Watson, R. P. 'Intergroup Violence and Intergroup Attributions'. *British Journal of Social Psychology* 30, no. 3 (1991): 261–266.

Hunter, J. A., Stringer, M., and Watson, R. P. 'Intergroup Attribution and Social Identity'. *The Journal of Social Psychology* 132, no. 6 (1992): 795–796.

Hutchinson, B. (2012) 'Why Loyalism Feels Cut Adrift'. Available: http://eamonnmallie.com/2012/10/why-loyalism-feel-cut-adrift-billy-hutchinson-explains/; accessed 14 June 2013.

Hutchinson, J. 'Ethnicity and Modern Nations'. *Ethnic and Racial Studies* 23, no. 4 (2000): 651–659.

Identity Exploration Limited and Trademark. *Community Identities and a Shared Future for Northern Ireland, Final Report*. Dunmurry: Identity Exploration Ltd., 2011.

Ignatieff, M. *Blood and Belonging: Journeys into the New Nationalism*. London: Vintage, 1993.

Inglehart, R. *Modernization and Postmodernization: Cultural, Economic, and Political Change in 43 Societies*. Princeton, NJ: Princeton University Press, 1997.

Inter Action Belfast. *The Role of Ex-Combatants on Interfaces*. Belfast: Inter-Action Belfast, 2006.

Intercomm and Byrne, J. Flags and Protests: Exploring the Views, Perceptions and Experiences of People Directly and Indirectly Affected by the Flag Protests. Belfast: Intercomm, 2013.

Ireland, P. R. 'Irish Protestant Migration and Politics in the USA, Canada, and Australia: A Debated Legacy'. *Irish Studies Review* 20, no. 3 (2012): 263–281.

Jackson, A. 'Unionist Myths 1912–1985'. *Past and Present* 136 (1992): 164–185.

Jackson, A. *Ireland 1798–1998: War, Peace and Beyond*. Oxford: John Wiley, 2010.

Jarman, N. *Material Conflicts: Parades and Visual Displays in Northern Ireland*. Oxford: Berg, 1997.

Jarman, N. 'For God and Ulster: Blood and Thunder Bands and Loyalists Political Culture', in *The Irish Parading Tradition*, edited by T. G. Frazer. Basingstoke: Macmillan, 2000: 158–172.

Jarman, N. 'Painting Landscapes: The Place of Murals in the Symbolic Construction of Urban Space', in *National Symbols, Fractured Identities: Contesting the National Narrative*, edited by M. Geisler. Lebanon, NH: University Press of New England, 2005: 172–194.

Jasonburkehistory. 'What does it mean to be a loyalist'. Available: http://www.jasonburkehistory.com/?cat=2; accessed 23 February 2014.

Jedlowski, P. 'Memory and Sociology: Themes and Issues'. *Time and Society* 10, no. 1 (2001): 29–44.

Jeffery, K. *Ireland and the Great War*. Cambridge: Cambridge University Press, 2000.

Jeffrey, K. 'Ireland and World War One'. Available: http://www.bbc.co.uk/history/british/britainwwone/irelandwwone01.shtml; accessed 1 March 2012.

Jeffrey, K. 'Ireland and the First World War: The Historical Context'. Available: http://www.qub.ac.uk/sites/irishhistorylive/IrishHistoryResources/ArticlesandLectures/IrelandandtheFirstWorldWar/; accessed 1 March 2012.

Jenkins, R. 'The Limits of Identity: Ethnicity, Conflict, and Politics'. Sheffield University: Sheffield Online Papers in Social Research, no date.

Jenkins, R. *Social Identity*. London: Routledge, 1996.

Johnson, N. C. *Ireland, the Great War and the Geography of Remembrance*. Cambridge: Cambridge University Press, 2003.

Johnstone, T. *Orange, Green and Khaki: the Story of the Irish Regiments in the Great War, 1914–1918*. Dublin: Gill and Macmillan, 1992.

Jordan, R. L. *The Second Coming of Paisley: Militant Fundamentalism and Ulster Politics*. New York: Syracuse University Press, 2013.

Jussim, L., Ashmore, R., and Wilder, D. 'Introduction: Social Identity and Intergroup Conflict', in *Social Identity, Intergroup Conflict, and Conflict Resolution*, edited by R. D. Ashmore, L. Jussim, and D. Wilder. Oxford: Oxford University Press, 2001: 3–14.

Kane, A. 'No voice for Loyalist working-class'. *Newsletter*, 4 July, 2011.

Kansteiner, W. 'Finding Meaning in Memory: A Methodological Critique of Collective Memory Studies'. *History and Theory* 41 (2002): 179–197.

Kaufmann, E. *The Orange Order: A Contemporary Northern Irish History*. Oxford: Oxford University Press, 2007.

Kay, S. 'Ontological Security and Peace-Building in Northern Ireland'. *Contemporary Security Policy* 33, no. 2 (2012): 236–263.

Kearney, H. 'The Importance of Being British'. *The Political Quarterly* 71, no. 1 (2000): 15–25.

Kearney, R. *Postnationalist Ireland*. London: Routledge, 1997.

Kelly, J. *Bonfires on the Hillside: An Eyewitness Account of Political Upheaval in Northern Ireland*. Belfast: Fountain Press, 1995.

Kennedy, D. *The Widening Gulf: Northern Attitudes to the Independent Irish State, 1919–1949*. Belfast: Blackstaff, 1988.

Kennedy M. *Division and Consensus: The Politics of Cross-Border Relations in Ireland, 1925–1969*. Dublin: Institute of Public Administration, 2000.

Kennedy-Pipe, C. *The Origins of the Present Troubles in Northern Ireland*. London: Longman, 1997.

Keren, M. and Herwig, H. H. (eds.) *War Memory and Popular Culture. Essays on Modes of Remembrance and Commemoration*. Jefferson, NC: McFarland and Company, 2009.

Kinnvall, C. 'Nationalism, Religion and the Search for Chosen Traumas: Comparing Sikh and Hindu Identity Constructions'. *Ethnicities* 2, no. 1 (2002): 79–106.

Kinnvall, C. 'Globalization and Religious Nationalism: Self, Identity, and the Search for Ontological Security'. *Political Psychology* 25, no. 5 (2004): 741–767.

Kinnvall, C. *Globalization and Religious Nationalism in India*. Abingdon: Routledge, 2006.

Kinnvall, C. 'European Trauma: Governance and the Psychological Moment'. *Alternatives: Global, Local, Political* 37, no. 3 (2012): 266–281.

Kissane, B. *The Politics of the Irish Civil War*. Oxford: Oxford University Press, 2005.

Klandennans, B. 'The Formation and Mobilization of Consensus', in *From Structure to Action: Comparing Social Movement Research across Cultures*, eds. B. Klandennans, H. Kriesi, and S. Tarrow (Greenwich: JAI Press, 1988), 173–196.

Koonz, C. 'Between Memory and Oblivion: Concentration Camps in German Memory', in *Commemorations: The Politics of National Identity*, edited by J. Gillis. Princeton, NJ: Princeton University Press, 1994: 258–280.

Koselleck, R. *Futures Past*, translated by Keith Tribe. Cambridge, MA: MIT Press, 1979.

Kray, K. 'Johnny Adair', in *Ultimate Hard Bastards*. London: John Blake, 2005: 9–26.

Kyle, J. 'On faith and loyalism'. Available: http://sluggerotoole.com/2012/01/23/john-kyle-on-faith-and-loyalism/; accessed 8 February 2012.

Kyle, J. 'Talking with Loyalists... is anybody listening?'. Available: http://blogs.qub.ac.uk/compromiseafterconflict/2013/11/02/talking-with-loyalists-is-anybody-listening/; accessed 17 March 2014.

Laing, R. D. *The Divided Self*. Harmondsworth: Penguin Books, 1973.

Lambert, A. J., Scherer, L. N., Rogers, C., and Jacoby, L. 'How Does Collective Memory Create a Sense of the Collective', in *Memory in Mind and Culture*, edited by P. Boyer and J. V. Wertsch. Cambridge: Cambridge University Press, 2009: 194–222.

Lawler, S. *Identity: Sociological Perspectives*. Cambridge: Polity, 2008.

Lawther, C. 'Unionism, Truth Recovery and the Fearful Past'. *Irish Political Studies* 26, no. 3 (2011): 361–382.

Lawther, C. 'Unionism, Truth and the Challenge of the Past: A Response to Aaron Edwards'. *Irish Political Studies* 27, no. 3 (2012): 471–478.

Lawther, C. 'Denial, Silence and the Politics of the Past: Unpicking the Opposition to Truth Recovery in Northern Ireland'. *The International Journal of Transitional Justice* 7 (2013): 157–177.

Leerssen, J. 'Monument and Trauma: Varieties of Remembrance' in *History and Memory in Modern Ireland*, edited by I. McBride. Cambridge: Cambridge University Press, 2001.

Lennon, B. *Peace Comes Dropping Slow*. Belfast: Community Dialogue, 2004.

Leonard, M. 'Parochial Geographies: Growing up in Divided Belfast'. *Childhood* 17 (2010): 329–342.

LeVine, R. A. and Cambell, D. T. *Ethnocentrism: Theories of Conflict, Ethnic Attitudes and Group Behaviour*. New York: Wiley, 1972.

Limavady District Loyal Orange Lodge. 'Limavady Orange Order Leadership calls for and end to attacks on local Orange Halls'. *Lodge No.6, Press Release*, 14 February 2011.

Lister D. and Jordan H. *Mad Dog: The Rise and Fall of Johnny Adair and 'C Company*. Edinburgh: Mainstream, 2003.

Little, A. *The Politics of Community: Theory and Practice*. Edinburgh: Edinburgh University Press, 2002.

Little, A. [with Scott, R.] *Give a Boy a Gun: From Killing to Peacemaking*. London: Darton, Longman and Todd, 2009.

Longkeshinsideout 'De-Bunking The Myth Of The Battle Of St. Matthews: 27/28 June 1970'. Available: http://www.longkeshinsideout.co.uk/?p=1993; accessed 26 June 2013.

Lorey, D. E. and Beezley, W. H. (eds.) *Genocide, Collective Violence, and Popular Memory: The Politics of Remembrance in the Twentieth Century*. Wilmington, DE: Scholarly Resources, 2002.

Loughlin, J. *Ulster Unionism and British National Identity since 1885*. London: Pinter, 1995.

Loughlin, J. 'Mobilising the Sacred Dead: Ulster Unionism, the Great War and the Politics of Remembrance', in *Ireland and the Great War: A War to Unite Us All?*, edited by A. Gregory and S. Paseta. Manchester, Manchester University Press, 2002: 136–145.

Loughlin, J. *The Ulster Question since 1945*. Basingstoke: Palgrave Macmillan, 2004.

Loughlin, J. 'Creating "a Social and Geographical Fact": Regional Identity and the Ulster Question 1880s–1920s'. *Past and Present* 195, no. 1 (2007): 159–196.

Loyalist Association of Workers (no date) 'The Long Awaited Loyalist Backlash Starts on Thursday', *LAW Newsheet*, 6: 1.

Loyalist Association of Workers (1974) 'Wilson's Anti-Ulster Speech', 1, 34: 1.

Loyalist Songbook. *Volume 1. All Gave Some. Some Gave All*. Belfast: no publisher, no date.

Loyalist Songbook. *Volume 2. The Ulster Volunteer Force*. Belfast: no publisher, no date.

Lynch, J. P. *An Unlikely Success Story: The Belfast Shipbuilding Industry 1880–1935*. Belfast: Belfast Society, 2001.

Lyons, F. S. L. *Ireland since the Famine*. London: Fontana, 1973.

MacDonald, D. *Blood and Thunder: Inside an Ulster Protestant Band*. Cork: Mercier Press, 2010.

MacDonald, M. *Children of Wrath: Political Violence in Northern Ireland*. Cambridge: Polity, 1986.

MacDougall, S. 'The Projection of Northern Ireland to Great Britain and Abroad, 1921–1939' in *The Northern Ireland Problem in British Politics*, edited by P. Catterall and S. MacDougall. Basingstoke: Macmillan, 1996: 29–46.

Macmillan, G. N. and Elam, Y. 'Collective Memory – What Is It?' *History and Memory* 8, no. 1 (1996): 30–50.

Mack, J. E. 'The Psychodynamics of Victimization among National Groups in Conflict', in *The Psychodynamics of International Relationships*, edited by A. Julius and J. V. Montville. Lexington, MA: D.C. Heath, 1990: 119–129.

Major, Sir J. 'Loyalists identity fears "phantom"'. Available: BBC News, http://www.bbc.co.uk/news/uk-northern-ireland-25357756; accessed 16 December 2013.

Maloney, E. *Voices from the Grave: Two Men's War in Ireland*. London: Faber and Faber, 2010.

Manktelow, R. 'The Needs of Victims of the Troubles in Northern Ireland: The Social Work Contribution'. *Journal of Social Work* 7, no. 1 (2007): 31–50.

Mastors, E and Drumhiller, N. 'What's in a Flag? The Protestant Community's Identity, Symbols, and Protests in Belfast'. *Peace and Change* 39, no. 4 (2014): 495–518.

(The) Mayo News. 'Interview: Poet Gerald Dawe looks back', 29 May 2012.

McAdams, D. *The Stories We Live By: Personal Myths and the Making of the Self*. New York: Guildford, 1993.

McAdam, D., Tarrow, S., and Tilly, C. *Dynamics of Contention*. Cambridge: Cambridge University Press, 2001.

McAlister, R. 'The struggle to belong when feeling disconnected: The experience of loyalist east Belfast', paper presented at the International RC21 conference, Amsterdam, 7–9 July 2011.

McAlister, R. J. 'Religious Identity and the Future in Northern Ireland'. *Policy Studies Journal* 28, no. 4 (2000): 843–857.

McAllister, I. 'The Devil, Miracles and the Afterlife: The Political Sociology of Religion in Northern Ireland'. *The British Journal of Sociology* 33, no. 3 (1982): 330–347.

McAllister, I. 'Class, Region, Denomination, and Protestant Politics in Ulster'. *Political Studies* 31, no. 2 (1983): 275–283.

McAllister, I, Hayes, B. C., and Dowds, L. 'The Erosion of Consent: Protestant Disillusionment with the Agreement'. *ARK, Research Update*, 32, January 2005.

McAtackney, L. *An Archaeology of the Troubles: The Dark Heritage of Long Kesh/Maze Prison*. Oxford: Oxford University Press, 2014.

McAuley, J. W. 'Cuchulainn and an RPG-7: The Ideology and Politics of the UDA', in *Culture and Politics in Northern Ireland*, edited by E. Hughes. Milton Keynes: Open University Press, 1991: 44–68.

McAuley, J. W. 'Not a Game of Cowboys and Indians' – The Ulster Defence Association in the 1990s', in *Terrorism's Laboratory The Case of Northern Ireland*, edited by A. O'Day. Dartmouth: Aldershot, 1995: 137–158.

McAuley, J. W. 'Mobilising Ulster Unionism: New Directions or Old?'. *Capital and Class* 70 (2000): 37–64.

McAuley, J. W. 'Redefining Loyalism – An Academic Perspective'. Dublin: Institute for British-Irish Studies, IBIS Working Paper no. 4, 2001.

McAuley, J. W. 'The Emergence of New Loyalism', in *Changing Shades of Orange and Green*, edited by J. Coakley. Dublin: University College Press, 2002: 106–122.

McAuley, J. W. 'Whither New Loyalism – Changing politics after the Belfast Agreement', *Journal of Irish Political Studies*, 20 no. 3, (2005) 323–340.

McAuley, J. W. *Ulster's Last Stand? (Re)Constructing Ulster Unionism After the Peace Process*, Dublin: Irish Academic Press, 2010.

McAuley, J. W. and Hislop, S. ' "Many Roads Forward": Politics and Ideology within the Progressive Unionist Party'. *Études Irlandaises* 25, no. 1 (2000): 173–192.

McAuley, J. W. and Spencer, G. (eds.) *Ulster Loyalism after the Good Friday Agreement*. Basingstoke: Palgrave Macmillan, 2011.

McAuley, J. W. and Tonge J. 'Faith, Crown and State: Contemporary Discourses within the Orange Order in Northern Ireland', K. Hayward and C. O'Donnell (eds) 'Political discourse as an instrument of conflict and peace: Lessons from Northern Ireland', *Peace and Conflict Studies*, Special Issue, 15, No 1, (2008) 156–176.

McAuley, J. W. and Tonge, J. ' "For God and for the Crown": Contemporary Political and Social Attitudes among Orange Order Members in Northern Ireland'. *Political Psychology* 28, no. 1 (2007): 33–54.

McAuley, J. W., Tonge, J. and Mycock, A. *Loyal to the Core?: Contemporary Orangeism and Politics in Northern Ireland* Dublin: Irish Academic Press, 2011.

McBride, I. *The Siege of Derry in Ulster Protestant Mythology*. Dublin: Four Courts Press, 1997.

McBride, I. (ed.) *History and Memory in Modern Ireland*. Cambridge: Cambridge University Press, 2001.

McBride, S. 'Heated meeting hears loyalist claims of abandonment over flag'. Available: http://www.newsletter.co.uk/news/politics/latest/heated-meeting-hears-loyalist-claims-of-abandonment-over-flag-1-5041902; accessed 28 March 2014.

McBride, S. 'DUP: No role for Sinn Fein in writing story of Troubles'. *Belfast News Letter*, 1 May 2014.

McCaffrey, B. 'Battle of Short Strand'. *The Irish News*, 25 June 2010.

McCaffrey, B. 'Flag report says loyalism feels abandoned by unionist parties', *The Detail*, Issue 227. Available: http://www.thedetail.tv/issues/297; downloaded15 December 2013.

McCall, C. 'Political Transformation and the Reinvention of the Ulster-Scots Identity and Culture'. *Identities* 9, no. 2 (2002): 197–218.

McCann, E. *War and an Irish Town.* London: Pluto Press, 1994: 3e.

McCann, E. 'Peace brings no dividend to the poorest in the North', *The Irish Times.* Available: http://www.irishtimes.com/news/politics/peace-brings-no-dividend-to-the-poorest-in-the-north-1.1739265?utm_source=dlvr.it&utm_medium=twitter; accessed 27 March 2014.

McCleery, M. J. 'The Creation of the "New City" of Craigavon: A Case Study of Politics, Planning and Modernisation in Northern Ireland in the Early 1960s'. *Irish Political Studies* 27, no. 1 (2012): 89–110.

McCracken, J. L. 'Northern Ireland, 1921–1966', *The Course of Irish History.* Dublin: Mercier Press, 1994: 313–323.

McDaid, S. Template for Peace: Northern Ireland, 1972–75, Manchester: Manchester University Press.

McDonald, H. 'Belfast union flag dispute is lightning rod for loyalist disaffection'. Available: http://www.theguardian.com/uk/2013/jan/06/belfast-union-flag-dispute-loyalist; accessed 28 March 2014.

McDonald, H. and Cusack, J. *UDA: Inside the Heart of Loyalist Terror.* London: Penguin, 2004.

McDowell, J. *Godfathers: Inside Northern Ireland's Drug Racket.* Dublin: Gill and Macmillan, 2008.

McEvoy, K. and Shirlow, P. 'Re-Imagining DDR: Ex-Combatants, Leadership and Moral Agency in Conflict Transformation'. *Theoretical Criminology* 13, no. 1 (2009): 31–59.

McGarry, F. *The Rising: Ireland Easter 1916.* Oxford: Oxford University Press, 2010.

McGaughey, J. G. V. *Ulster's Men: Protestant Unionist Masculinities and Militarization in the North of Ireland, 1912–1923.* Kingston, ON: McGill-Queen's University Press, 2012.

McGaughey, J. G. V. 'The Language of Sacrifice: Masculinities in Northern Ireland and the Consequences of the Great War'. *Patterns of Prejudice* 46 (2012): 2006: 299–317.

McGrattan, C. *Northern Ireland 1968–2008: The Politics of Entrenchment.* Basingstoke: Palgrave Macmillan, 2010.

McIntosh, G. *The Force of Culture: Unionist Identities in Twentieth-Century Ireland,* Cork: Cork University Press, 2003.

McIntosh, G. 'The Royal Visit to Belfast, June 1921', in *The Ulster Crisis, 1885–1921,* edited by D. G. Boyce and A. O'Day. Basingstoke: Macmillan, 2006: 259–278.

McKay, S. *Northern Protestants: An Unsettled People.* Belfast: Blackstaff, 2000.

McKearney, T. *The Provisional IRA: From Insurrection to Parliament.* London: Pluto Press, 2011.

McKittrick, D. 'These Belfast Riots Aren't Over the Flag – But the Creation of a Fairer Society', *The Independent,* [online] 9 January. Available: http://www.independent.co.uk/voices/comment/these-belfast-riots-arent-over-the-flag–but-the-creation-of-a-fairer-society-8444651.html; accessed 1 December 2013.

McKittrick, D., Kelters, S., Feeney, B., and Thornton, C. *Lost Lives: The Stories of the Men, Women and Children Who Died as a Result of the Northern Ireland Troubles.* Edinburgh: Mainstream Publishing, 1999.

McMillan, D. W. and Chavis, D. M. 'Sense of Community: A Definition and Theory'. *Journal of Community Psychology* 14 (1986): 6–23.

Meagher, K. 'Loyalism's one-sided love affair with the British state'. *Labour Uncut,* 11 December 2012.

Bibliography

Melucci, A. 'The New Social Movements: A Theoretical Approach'. *Social Science Information* 19 (1976): 199–226.

Melucci, A. *Challenging Codes: Collective Action in the Information Age*. Cambridge: Cambridge University Press, 1996.

Memmi, A. *Dependence: A Sketch for a Portrait of the Dependent*, [translated by Philip A. Facey]. Boston: Beacon Press, 1984.

Memmi, A. *The Colonizer and the Colonized*, [introduction by Jean-Paul Sartre; afterword by Susan Gilson Miller, translated by Howard Greenfeld]. Boston: Beacon Press, 1991.

Memmi, A. *Decolonization and the Decolonized*, [translated by Robert Bononno]. Minneapolis: University of Minnesota Press, 2006.

Meredith, F. 'How loyalism became a dirty word'. *Irish Times*, 8 December 2012.

Meredith, F. 'Loyalists feel sorry for themselves but the narrative of oppression doesn't hold up', *Irish Times*, 29 August 2013.

Miall, H., Ramsbotham, O., and Woodhouse, T. *Contemporary Conflict Resolution: The Prevention, Management, and Transformation of Deadly Conflicts*. Cambridge: Polity Press, 2000.

Middleton, D. and Edwards, D. (eds.) *Collective Remembering*. London: Sage, 1990.

Miles, A. and Savage, M. *The Remaking of the British Working Class, 1840–1940*. London: Routledge, 1994.

Miller, D. (ed.) *Rethinking Northern Ireland: Culture, Ideology and Colonialism*. London: Longman, 1998.

Miller, D. W. *Queen's Rebels: Ulster Loyalism in Historical Perspective*. Dublin: Gill and Macmillan, 1978.

Miller, D. W. *Queen's Rebels: Ulster Loyalism in Historical Perspective*, reprinted with a new introduction by John Bew. Dublin: University College Dublin Press, 2007.

Misztal, B. *Theories of Social Remembering*. Maidenhead: Open University Press, 2003.

Mitchel, P. *Evangelicalism and National Identity in Ulster 1921–1998*. Oxford: Oxford University Press, 2003.

Mitchell, B. 'Somme Commemoration Speech', Monkstown (copy in possession of the author), 25 June 2000.

Mitchell, B. *Principles of Loyalism: An Internal Discussion Paper*. Belfast: no publisher, 2002.

Mitchell, C. 'Behind the Ethnic Marker: Religion and Social Identification in Northern Ireland'. *Sociology of Religion* 66, no. 1 (2005): 3–21.

Mitchell, C. *Religion, Identity and Politics in Northern Ireland: Boundaries of Belonging and Belief*. Aldershot: Ashgate, 2006.

Mitchell, C. 'The Limits of Legitimacy: Former Loyalist Combatants and Peace-Building in Northern Ireland'. *Irish Political Studies* 23, no. 1 (2008): 1–19.

Mitchell, C. 'The Push and Pull between Religion and Ethnicity: The Case of Loyalists in Northern Ireland'. *Ethnopolitics: Formerly Global Review of Ethnopolitics* 9, no. 1 (2010): 53–69.

Mitchell, C. and Tilley, J. R. 'The Moral Minority: Evangelical Protestants in Northern Ireland and Their Political Behaviour'. *Political Studies* 52 (2004): 585–602.

Mitchell, S. 'The Permanent Crisis of 21st Century Ulster Unionism'. *Irish Marxist Review* 3, no. 9 (2014): 27–42.

Mitzen, J. 'Ontological Security in World Politics: State Identity and the Security Dilemma'. *European Journal of International Politics* 12 (2006): 341–370.

Moloney, E. *Voices from the Grave: Two Men's War in Ireland.* London: Faber and Faber, 2010.

Moody, T. W. 'Fenianism, Home Rule and the Land War', in *The Course of Irish History*, edited by T. W. Moody and F. X. Martin. Dublin: Mercier Press, 1994: 275–293.

Mooney, G. and Neal, S. 'Community: Themes and Debates', in *Community: Welfare, Crime and Society*, edited by G. Mooney and S. Neal. Maidenhead: Open University Press, 2009: 1–34.

Morag, N. 'The Emerald Isle: Ireland and the Clash of Irish and Ulster-British Nationalisms'. *National Identities* 10, no. 3 (2008): 263–280.

Morning View. '"Perfidious Albion" and the insecurities felt by unionists'. *Belfast News Letter*, 22 November 2001.

Morrissey, J. 'Ireland's Great War: Representation, Public Space and the Place of Dissonant Heritages'. *Journal of Galway Archaeological and Historical Society* 58 (2006): 98–113.

Morrow, D. 'Escaping the Bind in Northern Ireland – Teaching and Learning in the Ethnic Frontier', in *Meeting of Cultures and Clash of Cultures: Adult Education in Multi-Cultural Societies*, edited by K. Yarn and S. Boggler. Jerusalem: Magnus Press, 1994: 77–91.

Morrow, D. 'The weight of the past on the way to the future'. Community Relations Council Victims Conference, 29 October 2007.

Muldoon, O., Trew, K., Todd, J., Rougier, N., and McLaughlin, K. 'Religious and National Identity after the Belfast Good Friday Agreement'. *Political Psychology* 28, no. 1 (2007): 89–103.

Mulholland, M. *Northern Ireland: A Very Short Introduction.* Oxford: Oxford University Press, 2002.

Mulholland, M. 'Why Did Unionists Discriminate?', in *From the United Irishmen to Twentieth-Century Unionism: Essays in Honour of A.T.Q. Stewart*, edited by S. Wichert. Dublin: DCU, 2004: 187–206.

Müller, J. 'Introduction: The Power of Memory, Memory of Power and the Power over Memory', in *Memory and Power in Post-War Europe*, edited by J. Müller. Cambridge: Cambridge University Press, 2002: 1–10.

Mulvenna, G. 'The Protestant Working Class in Belfast: Education and Civic Erosion – An Alternative Analysis'. *Irish Studies Review* 20, no. 4 (2012): 427–446.

Munck, R. 'Class Conflict and Sectarianism in Belfast: From Its Origins to the 1930s'. *Contemporary Crises* 9 (1985): 156–157.

Munck, R. 'Class and Religion in Belfast – A Historical Perspective'. *Journal of Contemporary History* 20, no. 2 (1985): 241–259.

Munck, R. and Rolston, B. 'Oral History and Social Conflict'. *Oral History Review* 13 (1985): 1–21.

Murray, D. (ed.) *Protestant Perceptions of the Peace Process in Northern Ireland.* Limerick: University of Limerick, Centre for Peace and Development Studies, 2000.

Murray, G. R. and Mulvaney, M. K. 'Parenting Styles, Socialization, and the Transmission of Political Ideology and Partisanship'. *Politics and Policy* 40, no. 6 (2012): 1106–1130.

Murphy, D. *Irish Regiments in the World Wars.* Oxford: Osprey Publishing, 2007.

Murshed, S. M. 'On the Salience of Identity in Civilizational and Sectarian Conflict'. *Peace Economics, Peace Science and Public Policy* 16, no. 2 (2010): 1–20.

Nairn, T. *The Break-Up of Britain.* London: New Left Books, 1977.

Nelson, S. *Ulster's Uncertain Defender: Loyalists and the Northern Ireland Conflict*. Belfast: Appletree Press, 1984.

Nets-Zehngut, R. 'Major Events and the Collective Memory of Conflicts'. *International Journal of Conflict Management* 24, no. 3 (2013): 209–230.

New Ulster Political Research Group. *Beyond the Religious Divide*. Belfast: NUPRG, 1979.

Nic Craith, M. *Plural Identities - Singular Narratives: The Case of Northern Ireland*. Oxford: Berghahn, 2002.

Niens, U., Cairns, E., and Hewstone, M. 'Contact and Conflict in Northern Ireland', in *Researching the Troubles: Social Science Perspectives on the Northern Ireland Conflict*, edited by O. Hargie and D. Dickson. Edinburgh: Mainstream Publishing, 2003: 85–106.

Nolan, P. *Northern Ireland Peace Monitoring*, Number 3. Belfast: Community Relations Council, 2014.

Nora, P. 'Between Memory and History: Les Lieux de Memoire'. *Representations* 26 (1989): 7–25.

Northern Ireland 2011 Census. Available: http://www.nisra.gov.uk/Census/2011_results_detailed_characteristics.html; accessed 12 October 2013.

Northern Ireland Life and Times 2012 Survey. Available: www.nilt.ac.uk; accessed 8 October 2013.

Northern Ireland Youth Forum. *Sons of Ulster: Exploring Loyalist Band Members Attitudes towards Culture, Identity and Heritage*. Belfast: NIYF, 2013.

Northrup, T. A. 'The Dynamic of Identity in Personal and Social Conflict', in *Intractable Conflicts and Their Transformation*, edited by L. Kriesberg, T. A. Northrup, and S. J. Thorson. New York: Syracuse University Press, 1989: 55–82.

Novick, P. *The Holocaust and Collective Memory*. London: Bloomsbury, 2001.

Novosel, T. *Northern Ireland's Lost Opportunity: The Frustated Politics of Political Loyalism*. London: Pluto Press, 2013.

O'Callaghan, M. and O'Donnell, C. 'The Northern Ireland Government, the "Paisleyite Movement" and Ulster Unionism in 1966'. *Irish Political Studies* 21, no. 2 (2006): 203–222.

O'Connor, F. *In Search of a State: Catholics in Northern Ireland*. Belfast: Blackstaff, 1994.

O'Connor, F. 'Where to now for loyalism?'. *Irish Times*, 29 July 2005.

O'Donnell, R. (ed.) *The Impact of the 1916 Rising: Among the Nations*. Dublin: Irish Academic Press, 2008.

O'Dowd, L. 'New Introduction', in A. Memmi, *The Colonizer and the Colonized*. London: Earthscan, 1990: 29–66.

O'Dowd, L., Rolson, B., and Tomlinson, M. *Northern Ireland: Between Civil Rights and Civil War*. London: CSE Books, 1980.

O'Hearn, D. 'Catholic Grievances, Catholic Nationalism: A Comment'. *British Journal of Sociology* 34, no. 3 (1983): 438–445.

O'Hearn, D. 'Again on Discrimination in Northern Ireland: A Reply to the Rejoinder'. *British Journal of Sociology* 36, no. 1 (1985): 94–101.

O'Neill, T. 'Television Broadcast by Captain Terence O'Neill, Prime Minister of Northern Ireland on BBC (Northern Ireland) and Ulster Television', Monday, December 9, 1968, at 6.00 PM, *Ulster Office Press Notice*, London.

Ó Broin, A. *Beyond the Black Pig's Dyke: A Short History of Ulster*. Cork: Mercier Press, 1995.

Officer, D. ' "For God and for Ulster": The Ulsterman on the Somme', in *History and Memory in Modern Ireland*, 160–183.

Officer, D. and Walker, G. 'Protestant Ulster: Ethno-History, Memory and Contemporary Prospects'. *National Identities* 2, no. 3 (2000): 293–307.

Olick, J. K. 'Collective Memory: The Two Cultures'. *Sociological Theory* 17, no. 3 (1999): 333–348.

Olick, J. K. (ed.) *States of Memory: Continuities, Conflicts and Transformations in National Retrospection*. Durham and London: Duke University Press, 2003.

Olick, J. K. *The Politics of Regret - On Collective Memory and Historical Responsibility*. London: Routledge, 2007.

Olick, J. K. '"Collective Memory": A Memoir and Prospect'. *Memory Studies* 1 (2008): 23–29.

Olick, J. K. and Robbins, J. 'Social Memory Studies: From "Collective Memory" to the Hsociology of Mnemonic Practices'. *Annual Review of Sociology* 24 (1998): 105–140.

Olick, J. K., Vinitzky-Seroussi, V., and Levy, D. (eds.) *The Collective Memories Reader*. Oxford: Oxford University Press, 2011.

Ollerenshaw, P. 'Businessmen and the Development of Ulster Unionism, 1886–1921'. *The Journal of Imperial and Commonwealth History* 28, no. 1 (2000): 35–64.

Orange Cross Committee. *Orange Cross Book of Songs, Poems and Verse*. Belfast: Orange Cross Committee, no date.

Orange Standard. 'Eroding of British Identity'. July, 2007.

Orr, P. *The Road to the Somme: Men of the Ulster Division Tell Their Story*. Belfast: Blackstaff Press, 1987.

Orr, P. *New Loyalties: Christian Faith and the Protestant Working Class*. Belfast: Centre for Contemporary Christianity in Ireland, 2008.

Osborne, R. D. 'Voting Behaviour in Northern Ireland 1921–1977' in *Integration and Division*, 137–166.

Páez, D., Basabe, N., and González, J. L. 'Social Processes and Collective Memory: A Cross-Cultural Approach to Remembering Political Events', in *Collective Memory of Political Events: Social Psychological Perspectives*, edited by J. W. Pennebaker, D. Páez, and B. Rimé. Hillsdale: Lawrence Erlabaum, 1997: 147–174.

Páez, D., Bellelli, G., and Rimé, B. 'Flashbulb Memories, Culture and Collective Memories: Psychological Processes Related to Rituals, Emotions and Memories', in *Flashbulb Memories: New Issues and New Perspectives*, edited by O. Luminet and A. Curci. Hove: Phycology Press, 2009: 227–246.

Páez, D. and Liu, J. 'Collective Memory of Conflicts', in *Intergroup Conflict and Their Resolution: Social Psychological Perspectives*, edited by D. Bar-Tal. Hove: Psychology Press, 2011: 105–124.

Paisley, I. 'Leader's Speech', DUP 25th Anniversary conference, Broughshane. *DUP Press Release*, 1996.

Parekh, B. *Report of the Commission on the Future of Multi-Ethnic Britain*. London: Profile Books, 2000.

Parekh, B. 'Defining British National Identity'. *The Political Quarterly* 71, no. 1 (2000): 4–14.

Parkinson, A. F. *Ulster Loyalism and the British Media*. Dublin: Four Courts Press, 1998.

Patterson, H. *Ireland's Violent Frontier: The Border and Anglo-Irish Relations during the Troubles*. Basingstoke: Palgrave Macmillan, 2013.

Pehrson, S., Gheorghiu, M. A., and Ireland, T. 'Cultural Threat and Anti-Immigrant Prejudice: The Case of Protestants in Northern Ireland'. *Journal of Community & Applied Social Psychology* 22, no. 2 (2012): 111–124.

Pennebaker, J. W. and Banasik, B. L. 'On the Creation and Maintenance of Collective Memories: History as Social Psychology', in *Collective Memory of Political Events: Social Psychological Perspectives*, edited by J. W. Pennebaker, D. Paez, and B. Rimel. Mahwah, NJ: Lawrence Erlbaum, 1997: 3–19.

Pennebaker, J. W., Páez, D., and Rimé (eds.) *Collective Memory of Political Events: Social Psychological Perspectives*. Hillsdale: Lawrence Erlabaum, 1997.

Perkins, H. C. and Thorns, D. C. *Place, Identity and Everyday Life in a Globalizing World*. Houndmills: Palgrave Macmillan, 2012.

Phibbs, S. 'Four Dimensions of Narrativity: Towards a Narrative Analysis of Gender Identity That Is Simultaneously Personal, Local and Global'. *New Zealand Sociology* 23, no. 2 (2008): 47–60.

Pichardo, N. A. 'New Social Movements: A Critical Review'. *Annual Review of Sociology* 23 (1997): 411–430.

Pinkerton, P. 'Resisting Memory: The Politics of Memorialisation in Post-Conflict Northern Ireland'. *The British Journal of Politics and International Relations* 14, no. 1 (2012): 131–152.

Polletta, F. and Jasper, J. M. 'Collective Identity and Social Movements'. *Annual Review of Sociology* 27 (2001): 283–305.

Porter, N. *Rethinking Unionism: An Alternative Vision for Northern Ireland*. Belfast: Blackstaff, 1996.

Prager, J. *Presenting the Past: Sociology and the Psychoanalysis of Misrememberin*. Cambridge, MA: Harvard University Press, 1998.

Pringle, D. G. *One Island, Two Nations?: A Political-Geographical Analysis of the National Conflict in Ireland*. Letchworth: Research Studies Press/ John Wiley and Sons, 1985.

Probert, B. *Beyond Orange and Green: The Political Economy of the Northern Ireland Crisis*. London: Academy Press, 1978.

Public Records Office of Northern Ireland. (CAB/3A/68 A-B) 'Ministry of Public Security report on air raids including photographs, news cuttings and a map with raid areas indicated'.

Public Records Office of Northern Ireland. (CAB/3A/3) 'Detailed report on the damage inflicted on Harland and Wolff Ltd. and to Short and Harland Ltd. during the air raids of 1941'.

Public Records Office of Northern Ireland. (D1896) 'Aerial photographs of German air raid targets – Harland and Wolff Ltd and Belfast Corporation Electrical Works'.

Public Records Office of Northern Ireland. (D3038/3/12) 'Bombs on Belfast 1941' – booklet of photographs by the *Belfast Telegraph* showing the bomb damage inflicted on Belfast'.

Public Records Office of Northern Ireland. (HA/32/1/761) 'Ministry of Home Affairs, National Defence file – After Blitz action to be taken'.

Public Records Office of Northern Ireland. (FIN/30/AA/99) 'Ministry of Public Service file – Intelligence summaries of air raids on Belfast in April and May 1941'.

Public Records Office of Northern Ireland. (HA/32/1/764) 'Ministry of Home Affairs, National Defence file – Reports as to damage caused by air raids', 1941.

Purdie, B. *Politics in the Streets: The Origins of the Civil Rights Movement in Northern Ireland*. Belfast: Blackstaff Press, 1990.

Purvis, D., Shirlow, P., and Langhamner, M. *A Call to Action?* Belfast: Dawn Purvis MLA Office, 2012.

Putnam, R. D. *Bowling Alone: The Collapse and Revival of American Community*. New York: Simon and Schuster, 2000.

Radford, K. 'Creating an Ulster Scots Revival'. *Peace Review* 13, no. 1 (2001): 51–57.

Radford, K. 'Red, White, Blue and Orange: An Exploration of Historically Bound Allegiances through Loyalist Song'. *The World of Music* 46, no. 1 (2004): 71–89.

Radstone, S. and Hodgkin, K. (eds.) *Regimes of Memory*. London: Routledge, 2003.

Ramsey, G. *Music, Emotion and Identity in Ulster Marching Bands: Flutes, Drums and Loyal Sons*. Oxford: Peter Lang, 2011.

Ramsey, G. 'Practice: Class, Taste and Identity in Ulster Loyalist Flute Bands'. *Ethnomusicology* 1 (2011): 1–20.

Ranger, T. 'The Invention of Tradition Revisited: The Case of Colonial Africa', in *The Collective Memory Reader*, edited by J. Olik, V. Vinitzky-Seroussi, and D. Levy. Oxford: Oxford University Press, 2011: 275–278.

Redpath, J. 'Left Behind and Locked Out', 15 August. Available: http://greatershankillpartnership.org/news-blogs/shankill-inside-out/171-blog-left-behind-and-locked-out.html; accessed 23 April 2013.

Reed, R. 'Blood, Thunder and Rosettes: The Multiple Personalities of Paramilitary Loyalism between 1971 and 1988'. *Irish Political Studies* 26, no. 1 (2011): 45–72.

Reicher, S. and Hopkins, N. *Self and Nation*. London: Sage, 2001.

Reid, C. 'Protestant Challenges to the "Protestant State": Ulster Unionism and Independent Unionism in Northern Ireland, 1921–1939'. *Twentieth Century British History* 19, no. 4 (2008): 419–445.

Reid, G. 'Author's Note' in *Love Billy*, programme. Belfast: Lyric Theatre, 2013.

Ricoeur, P. *Time and Narrative*, translated by K. McGlaughlin and David Pellauer. Chicago: University of Chicago Press, 1984.

Ricoeur, P. *Memory, History, Forgetting*, translated by K. Blamey and D. Pellauer. Chicago: University of Chicago Press, 2004.

Robinson, H. 'Remembering War in the Midst of Conflict: First World War Commemorations in the Northern Irish Troubles'. *20th Century British History* 21, no. 1 (2010): 80–101.

Robinson, H. 'Defenders of the Faith: Twelfth of July Rhetoric in the Later Brookeborough Era, 1954–1962'. *Irish Political Studies* 27, no. 3 (2012): 377–393.

Robinson, P. 'Plantation and Colonisation: The Historical Background', in *Integration and Division – Geographical Perspectives on the Northern Ireland Problem*, edited by F. W. Boal and J. H. Douglas. London: Academic Press, 1982: 19–48.

Robinson, P. 'Speech to DUP Annual Conference 1998'. Available: http://www.dup.org; accessed 21 September 1999.

Rodriguez, J. and Fortier, T. *Cultural Memory: Resistance, Faith and Identity*. Austin: University of Texas Press, 2007.

Rolston, B. *Unfinished Business: State Killings and the Quest for Truth*. Belfast: Beyond the Pale, 2000.

Rolston, B. 'Dealing with the Past: Pro-State Paramilitaries, Truth and Transition in Northern Ireland'. *Human Rights Quarterly* 28, no. 3 (2006): 652–675.

Rose, R. *Governing without Consensus: An Irish Perspective*. Boston, MA: Beacon Press, 1971.

Rosenbaum, S. (ed.) *Against Home Rule The Case for the Union*. London: Frederick Warne and Co, 1912.

Rosland, S. 'Victimhood, Identity, and Agency in the Early Phase of the Troubles in Northern Ireland'. *Identities: Global Studies in Culture and Power* 16, no. 3 (2009): 294–320.

Ross, M. H. (ed.) *Culture and Belonging in Divided Societies: Contestation and Symbolic Landscapes*. Philadelphia: University of Pennsylvania Press, 2009.

Rowthorn, B. and Wayne, N. *Northern Ireland: The Political Economy of Conflict*. Cambridge: Polity Press, 1998.

Ruane, J. and Todd, J. *The Dynamics of Conflict in Northern Ireland: Power, Conflict and Emancipation*. Cambridge: Cambridge University Press, 1996.

Rumelili, B. 'Identity and Descecuritisation: The Pitfalls of Conflating Ontological and Physical Identity'. *Journal of International Relations and Development* 1 (2013): 1–23.

Russell, N. 'Collective Memory before and after Halbwachs'. *The French Review* 79, no. 4 (2006): 792–804.

Said, E. *Orientalism*. Hammondworth: Penguin, 1978.

Samuel, R. 'Four Nations History', in *Island Stories: Unravelling Britain, Theatres of Memory, Volume II*, edited by A. Light, S. Alexander, and G. S. Jones. London: Verso, 1998: 21–40.

Samuel, R. *Theatres of Memory: Past and Present in Contemporary Culture*. London: Verso, 2012.

Savage, M. 'Working Class Identity in the 1960: Revisiting the Affluent Workers Study'. *Sociology* 39, no. 5 (2005): 929–946.

Schmid, K., Hewstone, M., Hughes, J., Jenkins, R., and Cairns, E. 'Residential Segregation and Intergroup Contact: Consequences for Intergroup Relations, Social Capital and Social Identity', in *Theorizing Identities and Social Action*, edited by M. Wetherell. Basingstoke: Palgrave Macmillan, 2009: 177–197.

Schudson, M. 'The Present in the Past versus the Past in the Present'. *Communication* 11 (1989): 105–113.

Schudson, M. 'Dynamics of Distortion in Collective Memory', in *Memory Distortion: How Minds, Brains and Societies Reconstruct the Past*, edited by D. Schacter. Cambridge, MA: Harvard University Press, 1997: 346–364.

Schuman, H. and Scott, J. 'Generations and Collective Memories'. *American Sociological Review* 54 (1989): 359–381.

Schwartz, B. 'The Social Context of Commemoration: A Study in Collective Memory'. *Social Forces* 61 (1982): 375–402.

Schwartz, B. 'Social Change and Collective Memory: The Democratization of George Washington'. *American Sociological Review* 56 (1991): 221–236.

Schwartz, B. *Abraham Lincoln and the Forge of National Memory*. Chicago: Chicago University Press, 2000.

Sengupta, K. 'The Loyalist view', *The Independent*, 29 July 2000.

Shankill Think Tank. *A New Beginning*. Island Pamphlets 13, Newtownabbey: Island Publications, 2005.

Shirlow, P. *The End of Loyalism?* Manchester: Manchester University Press, 2012.

Shirlow, P., Graham, B., McEvoy, K., O'hAdhmaill, F., and Purvis, D. *Politically Motivated Former Prisoner Groups: Community Activism and Conflict Transformation*. Belfast: Report to the Northern Ireland Community Relations Council, 2005.

Shirlow, P. and McEvoy, K. *Beyond the Wire: Former Prisoners and Conflict Transformation in Northern Ireland*. London: Pluto, 2008.

Shirlow, P. and McGovern, M. (eds.) *Who Are 'The People'? Unionism, Protestantism and Loyalism in Northern Ireland.* London: Pluto, 1997.

Shirlow, P., Tonge, J., McAuley, J. W., and McGlynn, C. *Abandoning Historical Conflict? Former Paramilitary Prisoners and Political Reconciliation in Northern Ireland.* Manchester: Manchester University Press, 2010.

Siemienska, R. 'Intergenerational Differences in Political Values and Attitudes in Stable and New Democracies'. *International Journal of Comparative Sociology* 43, nos. 3–5 (2002): 368–390.

Simms, J. Y. *Farewell to the Hammer: A Shankill Boyhood.* Belfast: White Row Press, 1992.

Simon, B. and Klandennans, B. 'Politicized Collective Identity'. *American Psychologist* 56 (2001): 319–331.

Simpson, K. *Unionist Voices and the Politics of Remembering the Past in Northern Ireland.* Basingstoke: Palgrave Macmillan, 2009.

Simpson, K. *Truth Recovery in Northern Ireland: Critically Interpreting the Past.* Manchester: Manchester University Press, 2009.

Simpson, K. 'Political Strategies of Engagement: Unionists and Dealing with the Past in Northern Ireland'. *British Politics* 8, no. 1 (2013): 2–27.

Sinnerton, H. *David Ervine: Uncharted Waters.* Dingle: Brandon, 2002.

Smith, A. D. *Nationalism and Modernism.* London: Routledge, 1998.

Smith, A. D. *Myths and Memories of the Nation.* Oxford: Oxford University Press, 1999.

Smith, M. L. R. *Fighting for Ireland? The Military Strategy of the Irish Republican Movement.* London: Routledge, 1997.

Smithey, L. A. 'Conflict Transformation, Cultural Innovation, and Loyalist Identity in Northern Ireland', in *Culture and Belonging in Divided Societies*, edited by M. H. Ross. Philadelphia: Pennsylvania University Press, 2009: 85–106.

Smithey, L. A. *Unionists, Loyalists, and Conflict Transformation in Northern Ireland.* Oxford: Oxford University Press, 2011.

Smyth, C. *Ian Paisley: Voice of Protestant Ulster.* Edinburgh: Scottish Academic Press, 1987.

Smyth, M. and Fay, M. T. (eds.) *Personal Accounts from Northern Ireland's Troubles: Public Conflict, Private Loss.* London: Pluto Press, 2000.

Smyth M. and Thomson, K. *Working with Children and Young People in Violently Divided Societies.* Belfast: CCIC and the University of Ulster, 2001.

Somers, M. R. 'Narrativity, Narrative Identity, and Social Action: Rethinking English Working-Class Formation'. *Social Science History* 16, no. 4 (1992): 591–630.

Somers, M. and Gibson, G. 'Reclaiming the Epistemological "other": Narrative and the Social Construction of Identity', in *Social Theory: The Politics of Identity*, edited by C. Calhoun. Oxford: Blackwell, 1994: 705–709.

Southern, N. 'Protestant Alienation in Northern Ireland: A Political, Cultural and Geographical Examination'. *Journal of Ethnic and Migration Studies* 33, no. 1 (2007): 159–180.

Spencer, G. 'Constructing Loyalism: Politics, Communications and Peace in Northern Ireland'. *Contemporary Politics* 10, no. 1 (2004): 37–55.

Spencer, G. 'The Decline of Ulster Unionism: The Problem of Identity, Image and Change'. *Contemporary Politics* 12, no. 1 (2006): 45–63.

Spencer, G. *The State of Loyalism in Northern Ireland.* Houndmills: Palgrave Macmillan, 2008.

Stanbridge, K. 'Nationalism, International Factors and the "Irish question" in the Era of the First World War'. *Nations and Nationalism* 11, no. 1 (2005): 21–42.

Stapleton, K. and Wilson, J. 'A Discursive Approach to Cultural Identity: The Case of Ulster Scots', *Belfast Working Papers in Language and Linguistics*, 16, Belfast: University of Ulster, 2003: 57–71.

Stapleton, K. and Wilson, J. 'Ulster Scots Identity and Culture: The Missing Voices'. *Identities: Global Studies in Culture and Power* 11 (2004): 563–591.

Staub, E. *The Roots of Evil: The Origins of Genocide and Other Group Violence*. New York: Cambridge University Press, 1989.

Staub, E. *The Psychology of Good and Evil: Why Children, Adults and Groups Help and Harm Others*. Cambridge: Cambridge University Press, 2003.

Steele, B. J. *Ontological Security in International Relations*. Abington: Routledge, 2008.

Steenkamp, C. *Violence and Post-War Reconstruction: Managing Insecurity in the Aftermath of Peace Accords*. London: I. B. Tauris, 2009.

Stets, J. E. and Burke, P. J. 'Identity Theory and Social Identity Theory'. *Social Psychology Quarterly* 63, no. 3 (2000): 224–237.

Stone, M. *None Shall Divide Us*. London: John Blake, 2004.

Storey, J. *Cultural Theory and Popular Culture: An Introduction*. Abington: Routledge, 2013.

Street, J. *Politics and Popular Culture*. Cambridge: Polity Press, 1997.

Sumartojo, S. and Wellings, B. (eds.) *Nation, Memory and Great War Commemoration: Mobilizing the Past in Europe, Australia and New Zealand*, Oxford: Peter Lang, 2014.

Switzer, C. *Unionists and Great War Commemoration in the North of Ireland 1914–1939*. Dublin: Irish Academic Press, 2007.

Switzer, C. *Ulster, Ireland and the Somme: War Memorials and Battlefield Pilgrimages*. Dublin: The History Press Ireland, 2013.

Stone, M. *None Shall Divide Us*. London: John Blake, 2003.

Tajfel, H. 'Social Categorization'. English Manuscript of 'La catégorisation sociale', in *Introduction à la Psychologie Sociale*, edited by S. Moscovici. Paris: Larousse (1972): 272–302.

Tajfel, H. *Differentiation between Social Groups: Studies in the Social Psychology of Intergroup Behaviour*. London: Academic Press, 1978.

Tajfel, H. 'Individuals and Groups in Social Psychology'. *British Journal of Clinical Psychology* 18, no. 2 (1979): 180–190.

Tajfel, H. *Human Groups and Social Categories*. Cambridge: Cambridge University Press, 1981.

Tajfel, H. 'Social Psychology of Intergroup Relations'. *Annual Review of Psychology* 33 (1982): 1–39.

Tajfel, H. and Turner, J. C. 'An Integrative Theory of Intergroup Conflict', in *The Social Psychology of Intergroup Relations*, edited by W. G. Austin and S. Worchel. Monterey, CA: Brooks/Cole, 1979: 33–47.

Tajfel, H. and Turner, J. C. 'The Social Identity Theory of Intergroup Behavior', in *Psychology of Intergroup Relations*, edited by S. Worchel and W. G. Austin. Chicago: Nelson-Hall, 1986: 7–24.

Taylor, P. *Loyalists*. London: Bloomsbury, 2000.

Terra, L. 'New Histories for a New State: A Study of History Textbook Content in Northern Ireland'. *Journal of Curriculum Studies* 46, no. 2 (2014): 225–248.

Todd, J. 'Two Traditions in Unionist Political Culture'. *Irish Political Studies* 2 (1987): 1–26.

Todd, J. 'Unionist Political Thought and the Limits of Britishness'. *The Irish Review* 5 (1989): 11–16.

Todd, J. 'Loyalism and Secularisation', in *La Sécularisation en Irlande*, edited by P. Brennan. Caen: Presses Universitaires de Caen, 1998: 195–206.

Todd, J 'Introduction: National Identity in Transition? Moving Out of Conflict in (Northern) Ireland'. *Nations and Nationalism* 13, no. 4 (2007): 565–571.

Todd, J., O'Keefe, T., Rougier N., and Cañás Bottos, L. 'Fluid or Frozen: Choice and Change in Ethno-National Identification in Contemporary Northern Ireland'. *Nationalism and Ethnic Politics* 12, nos. 3–4 (2006): 323–347.

Todman, D. 'The Ninetieth Anniversary of the Battle of the Somme', in *War Memory and Popular Culture*, edited by M. Keren and H. H. Herwig. Jefferson, NC: McFarland and Co., 2009: 23–40.

Tonge, J. *Comparative Peace Processes*. Cambridge: Polity Press, 2014.

Tonge, J. and McAuley, J. W. 'The contemporary Orange Order in Northern Ireland' in *Irish Protestant Identities*, 289–302.

Tonge, J., Braniff, M., Hennessey, T., McAuley, J. W., and Whiting, S. *The Democratic Unionist Party: From Protest to Power*. Oxford: Oxford University Press, 2014.

Townshend, C. *Easter 1916: The Irish Rebellion*. Hammondsworth: Penguin, 2006.

Trew, J. D. 'Negotiating Identity and Belonging: Migration Narratives of Protestants from Northern Ireland'. *Immigrants & Minorities: Historical Studies in Ethnicity, Migration and Diaspora* 25, no. 1 (2007): 22–48.

Trew, K., Muldoon, O., McKeown, G., and McLaughlin, K. 'The Media and Memories of Conflict in Northern Ireland'. *Journal of Children and Media* 3, no. 2 (2009): 185–203.

Turner, J. C. 'Social Categorization, Social Identity and Social Comparisons', in *Differentiation between Social Groups: Studies in the Social Psychology of Intergroup Relations*, edited by H. Tajfel. London: Academic Press, 1978: 61–76.

Turner, J. C. *Rediscovering the Social Group: A Self-Categorization Theory*. Oxford: Blackwell, 1987.

Turner, J. C. 'Some Current Issues in Research on Social Identity and Self-Categorization Theories', in *Social Identity: Context, Commitment, Content*, edited by N. Ellemers, R. Spears, and B. Doosje. Oxford: Blackwell, 1999: 6–34.

Turner, J. C., Brown, R. J., and Tajfel, H. 'Social Comparison and Group Interest in Ingroup Favouritism'. *European Journal of Social Psychology* 9 (1979): 187–204.

Turner, J. C., Hogg, M. A., Oakes, P. J., Reicher, S. D., and Wetherell, M. S. *Rediscovering the Social Group: A Self-Categorization Theory*. Oxford: Blackwell, 1987.

Ulster Political Research Group. *Common Sense*. Belfast: UPRG, 1987.

Ulster-Scots Community Network. *Understanding the Ulster Covenant*. Belfast: Ulster-Scots Agency, 2012.

Ulster Unionist Party. *Declaration of Principle and Statement of Policy for the General Election, Ulster at the Crossroads*. Belfast: UUP, 1969.

Ulster Vanguard. *Ulster – A Nation*. Belfast: Ulster Vanguard, 1972.

UTV News. 'Thousands recreate signing of Covenant'. Available: http://www.u.tv/news/Thousands-recreate-signing-of-Covenant/86ccf333-f15f-4bb1-a307-2620f719407a; Accessed: 30 September 2012.

UTV News. 'SF "fighting cultural war" – Hutchinson'. Available: http://www.u.tv/News/SF-fighting-cultural-war-Hutchinson/891157d6-1378-408f-9a6f-508541cd17f9; Accessed 28 March 2014.

UTV News. 'Hate attack on Orange war memorial'. Available: http://www.u.tv/News/Hate-attack-on-Orange-war-memorial/ba9ab99f-7c8a-4f58-88ad-5a43c848456a; accessed 28 March 2014.

Vadher, K. and Barrett, M. 'Boundaries of Britishness'. *Journal Community Applied Social Psychology* 19 (2009): 442–458.

Villiers, T. 'Loyalists who attack police "grotesque"'. Available: http://www.bbc.co.uk/news/uk-northern-ireland-24359712; accessed 11 October 2013.

Wagner-Pacifici, R. and Schwartz, B. 'The Vietnam Veterans Memorial: Commemorating a Difficult Past', *The American Journal of Sociology* 97, no. 2 (1991): 376–420.

Walker, B. *Dancing to History's Tune: History, Myth and Politics in Ireland*. Belfast: Queen's University of Belfast, 1996.

Walker, B. *Past and Present: History, Identity and Politics in Ireland*. Belfast: Queen's University of Belfast, 2000.

Walker, B. 'Remembering the siege of Derry: The Rise of Popular Religious and Political Tradition, 1689–1989', in *The Sieges of Derry*, edited by W. Kelly. Dublin: Four Courts Press, 2001: 123–141.

Walker, B. 'Northern Ireland Troubles: Battle of the Bogside'. *Belfast Telegraph*, 11 August 2009.

Walker, B. M. *A Political History of the Two Irelands: From Partition to Peace*. Houndmills: Palgrave Macmillan, 2012.

Walker, G. 'The Northern Ireland Labour Party in the 1920s'. *Saothar* 14 (1984): 19–30.

Walker, G. *A History of the Ulster Unionist Party: Protest, Pragmatism and Pessimism*, Manchester: Manchester University Press, 2004.

Walker, R. and English, G. (eds.) *Unionism in Modern Ireland*, Dublin: Gill and Macmillan, 1996.

Wallace, M. *Drums and Guns: Revolution in Ulster*. London: Geoffrey Chapman, 1970.

Wallis, R., Bruce, S., and Taylor, D. *"No Surrender!" Paisleyism and the Politics of Ethnic Conflict in Northern Ireland*. Belfast: Department of Social Studies, The Queens University of Belfast, 1986.

Ware, V. *Who Cares about Britishness?: A Global View of the National Identity Debate*. London: Arcadia Books, 2007.

Watson, G. ' "Meticulously Crafted Ambiguities": The Confused Political Vision of Ulster Vanguard'. *Irish Political Studies* 28, no. 4 (2013): 536–562.

Wertsch, J. *Voices of Collective Remembering*. Cambridge: Cambridge University Press, 2002.

Wertsch, J. 'Collective Memory', in *Memory in Mind and Culture*, 117–137.

White, B. 'The day Catholic and Protestant workers marched – and fought – side by side against the common enemy of poverty and destitution'. *Belfast Telegraph*, 8 October, 1982: 10–11.

White, R. 'Social and Role Identities and Political Violence: Identity as a Window on Violence in Northern Ireland', in *Social Identity, Intergroup Conflict, and Conflict Resolution*, edited by R. D. Ashmore, L. Jussim, and D. Wilder. New York: Oxford University Press, 2001: 159–183.

White, R. W. *Provisional Irish republicans: An Oral and Interpretive History'*. Westport, CT: Greenwood Publishing Group, 1993.

Whitehead, A. *Memory*. Abingdon, Oxon: Routledge, 2009.

Wilson, D. 'Ulster Loyalism and Country Music, 1969–1985', in *Country Music Goes to War*, edited by C. K. Wolfe and J. E. Akenson. Lexington: University Press of Kentucky, 2005: 192–207.

Wilson, H. 'On UWC Strike'. Available: http://www.totalpolitics.com/speeches/labour/labour-politics-general/34883/uwc-strike.thtml; accessed 1 March 2012.

Winter, J. *Sites of Memory, Sites of Mourning*. Cambridge: Cambridge University Press, 2014.

Witherow, J. 'Band Development in Northern Ireland: Ethnographic Researcher to Policy Consultant'. *Anthropology in Action* 13, nos. 1–2 (2006): 44–54.

Wodak, R. and Richardson, J. E. 'On the Politics of Remembering (or not)'. *Critical Discourse Studies* 6, no. 4 (2009): 231–235.

Wood, I. S. *Crimes of Loyalty: A History of the UDA*. Edinburgh: Edinburgh University Press, 2006.

Wright, F. 'Protestant Ideology and Politics in Ulster'. *European Journal of Sociology* 14, no. 1 (1973): 213–280.

Wright, F. *Northern Ireland: A Comparative Analysis*. Dublin: Gill and Macmillan, 1987.

Young, J. *The Exclusive Society: Social Exclusion, Crime and Difference in Late Modernity*. London: Sage, 1999.

Young, J. *The Vertigo of Late Modernity*. London: Sage, 2007.

Young, J. E. 'Memory and Monument after 9/11', in *The Future of Memory*, edited by R. Crownshaw, J. Kilby, and A. Rowland. Oxford: Berghahn Books, 2010.

Young, M. and Willmott, P. *Family and Kinship in East London*. Harmondsworth: Penguin, 1957.

Zarakol, A. 'Ontological (In)security and State Denial of Historical Crimes: Turkey and Japan'. *International Relations* 24, no. 1 (2010): 3–23.

Zarakol, A. 'What Made the Modern World Hang Together: Socialisation or Stigmatisation?' *International Theory* 6, no. 2 (2014): 311–332.

Zelizer, B. 'Reading the Past Against the Grain: The Shape of Memory Studies'. *Critical Studies in Mass Communication* 12 (1995): 214–239.

Zerubavel, E. 'Social Memories: Steps to a Sociology of the Past'. *Qualitative Sociology* 19, no. 3 (1996): 283–299.

Leabharlanna Poibli Chathair Bhaile Átha Cliath

Dublin City Public Libraries

Index